Peaceful Death, Joyful Rebirth

Peaceful Death,

Joyful Rebirth

A Tibetan Buddhist Guidebook

Tulku Thondup

Edited by Harold Talbott

SHAMBHALA
Boston & London
2005

SHAMBHALA PUBLICATIONS, INC.
Horticultural Hall
300 Massachusetts Avenue
Boston, Massachusetts 02115
www.shambhala.com

©2005 by Tulku Thondup Rinpoche

The Buddhayana Foundation Series X

All rights reserved. No part of this book may be
reproduced in any form or by any means, electronic
or mechanical, including photocopying, recording,
or by any information storage and retrieval system,
without permission in writing from the publisher.

9 8 7 6 5 4 3 2 1

First Edition
Printed in the United States of America

♾ This edition is printed on acid-free paper that
meets the American National Standards Institute
z39.48 Standard.

Distributed in the United States by Random House, Inc.,
and in Canada by Random House of Canada Ltd

Library of Congress Cataloging-in-Publication Data
Thondup, Tulku.
Peaceful death, joyful rebirth: a Tibetan Buddhist guidebook /
Tulku Thondup; edited by Harold Talbott.
p.   cm.
Includes bibliographical references and index.
ISBN 1-59030-182-x (hardcover: alk. paper)
1. Death—Religious aspects—Buddhism. 2. Funeral rites and
ceremonies, Buddhist—China—Tibet. 3. Intermediate state—Buddhism.
I. Talbott, Harold. II. Title.
BQ4487.T56 2005
294.3'423—dc22
2004017594

The true nature of life and death is peaceful and joyful.
The true world of peace and joy is the Blissful Pure Land.
The true source of bliss and blessing is the Infinite Light.
The true heart of you and me is the blessing light.

Contents

Acknowledgments

I OFFER MY GRATITUDE to Kyabje Dodrupchen Rinpoche and Kyala Khenpo Rinpoche for their profound teachings of Buddhism that made my life meaningful and their meticulous instructions and practices on death rituals, which gave birth to this book, and to my kind parents, foreparents, and loving friends, to whom I am indebted for my life and sanity.

I am very thankful to Harold Talbott for editing *Peaceful Death, Joyful Rebirth* with patience, dedication, and wisdom. I am especially thankful to Kendra Crossen Burroughs for her mastery in the art of editing and knowledge of the subject that gave birth to this book in its final form. I am grateful to Ian Baldwin for navigating through the publishing world and for his great editorial advice; to Zenkar Rinpoche for providing many rare delog texts; to Gene Smith and the Tibetan Buddhist Resource Center for being an invaluable research resource; to Larry Mermelstein for translating the Sanskrit mantras (unfortunately, we could not use the diacritical marks that he provided); to Mahasiddha Nyingmapa Center, the late Chagdud Rinpoche, Gyalse Putrug Rinpoche, Gyatul Rinpoche, Sherab Raldhi Lama, Lama Migmar Tseten, Ani Lodro Palmo, and Madeline Nold for sharing their valuable libraries; to Jonathan Miller, Byron Brumbaugh, and Philip Richman for reading the manuscript and giving valuable suggestions; to David Dvore for his computer skills; to Michael Krigsman for promoting our works at www.tulkuthondup.com; and to Victor and Ruby Lam for a peaceful place to work.

I am deeply indebted to Michael Baldwin for single-handedly providing for all the human needs that have kept our research and writing projects productive and to all the patrons of The Buddhayana Foundation (3 Barnabas Road, Marion, MA 02738) for their most generous support over the past twenty-five years.

I am highly grateful to Acharya Samuel Bercholz for trusting in my work and to Peter Turner, Jonathan Green, Lenny Jacobs, Hazel Bercholz, and the staff of Shambhala Publications for giving great care to this book. Thanks also go to L. S. Summer for preparing the index.

Finally, I am thankful to Lydia Segal for her constant inspiration during the writing of this book and for lending her literary skills to the project with love and knowledge.

I dedicate all the merits associated with this book with heartfelt prayers to all the friends who shared their most precious transitional moments with me in different ways and to all who will be enjoying the teachings shared in this book. May they fully realize and always be one with the blessings of the Buddha of Infinite Light and all the blessed ones.

About This Book

THIS BOOK DISTILLS thousands of years of profound wisdom from the Tibetan Buddhist tradition, conveyed in simple words that are easy for anyone to comprehend. My main goal is to present teachings that not only heal our pain and confusion about death and dying but also help us realize the enlightened goal of ultimate peace and joy, not only for this life, but also for death and beyond.

The Buddha taught various ways for us to prepare ourselves for the unknown situations of death and make the best of them. Numerous enlightened masters of truth have written treatises on this very subject. Tibetan Buddhism has produced some of the most elaborately detailed teachings in the field of death and afterdeath—the famous *Bardo Thodrol* (popularly known in English as *The Tibetan Book of the Dead*) being only one of them. In fact, all Buddhist teachings are about recognizing and improving the situations of life, death, and the next life. My sources for this book thus include a great variety of texts,* as well as the direct teachings I received from my spiritual masters and my firsthand experiences in dealing with the deaths of great spiritual masters, close friends, and strangers.

TIBETAN WISDOM TEACHINGS

Tibetan Buddhist teachings divide our journey of our cyclical existence into four periods:

---

* The texts on which I drew are cited in abbreviated form in the notes at the back of the book; the "References" section provides the key to these abbreviations and the full facts of publications about these sources.

1. the period of life;
2. the period of dying;
3. the period of glimpsing the ultimate nature of the mind and its luminous visions; and
4. the bardo, or transitional passage, between the afterdeath state and the next rebirth.

Chapters 1 through 4 summarize these four periods. To illustrate the experiences of death and the bardo, I draw extensively from the historical records of *delogs*, Tibetan "returners from death," whose accounts are often remarkably similar to the contemporary Western literature of near-death experiences. Because the lengthiest accounts that I cite concern the bardo itself, I have devoted an entire chapter—chapter 5, "Tales of the Bardo"—to these stories of unusual journeys in hellish or blissful realms beyond death.

Why, where, and how do we take rebirth in various realms at the end of the bardo? Chapter 6, "Rebirth," focuses on these questions and provides a roadmap to help us avoid taking rebirth in the wrong places and know how to choose the right ones, such as the joyful paradises known as pure lands.

The pure lands are the abodes of the celestial buddhas, who are embodiments of wisdom and compassion. Tibetan rituals for the dead and dying typically involve devotional meditation on these buddhas and their pure lands, which are a source of blessing and power. In this book we focus on one of the most popular of these spiritual representations, the Buddha of Infinite Light. Remembering and praying to the Buddha of Infinite Light will enable the deceased to take rebirth in his Blissful Pure Land, a realm of great peace and joy. Chapter 7, "The Buddha of Infinite Light and His Blissful Pure Land," presents a vivid picture of this source of blessing, based on the descriptions given in the sutras.

Survivors have a very important role to play in helping the dying and deceased in their journey to death and beyond. Chapter 8, "How to Help the Dying and the Dead," gives some practical guidelines for family members and other survivors, helpers, and caretakers, whether they are Buddhists or non-Buddhists.

For those interested in going more deeply into the Tibetan tradition, chapter 9, "Ritual Services for the Dying and the Dead," describes traditional rituals practiced by lamas for the dying and the dead in the communities of Eastern Tibet, where I grew up and was trained in the

Nyingma tradition of Tibetan Buddhism. I close with a brief tenth chapter of some concluding thoughts.

I have placed further Buddhist material into two appendixes because it is a little more technical. Here you will find some very simple but essential death rituals that can be performed by a lama or the helper for a dying or dead person. Appendix A, "Meditations on the Four Causes of Taking Rebirth in the Blissful Pure Land," presents common Buddhist meditations, with Tibetan text and explanation. Appendix B, "Eight Esoteric Buddhist Rituals for the Dying and the Dead," presents eight important liturgical services, with Tibetan texts and explanations. Also in appendix B, and of interest to many readers, is the description of *phowa*, a unique meditation for transferring the consciousness of the dying person (yourself or someone whom you are helping) to an enlightened pure land.

SOME PERSONAL CONSIDERATIONS

This book is, in a sense, my cherished child, for the teachings that I have gathered here are precious. To some people, it may not seem like a traditional work of Tibetan scholarship, which is usually filled with technical terms and deep philosophical presuppositions. For others, it may appear lacking in the kind of scientific findings that Western scholars consider indispensable. But my concern is not to try to answer such objections. My aim and hope is to make this information as accessible as possible to all readers, both Buddhist and non-Buddhist, while preserving the authentic essence of the original teachings.

I became interested in writing the book for several reasons. A quarter century ago, when I came to the United States, many of my Western friends were struggling to finish their degrees, secure a job, and find a life partner; but now a number of them are dealing with sickness and the prospect of death—and so am I. Personal reasons for writing the book were thus part of my motivation.

As a Buddhist, I was taught to study and work to improve the quality of both life and death, for both myself and others. Two of my previous books, *The Healing Power of Mind* and *Boundless Healing*, are primarily concerned with healing the ills of this life. Life is important and precious, and we must take care of it; but since death is the entrance to the gateway to our countless future lives, doesn't it call for special attention too? And so *Peaceful Death, Joyful Rebirth* is designed to guide us in facing death with confidence and securing a joyful rebirth—and in helping others to do the same. This, too, is a form of healing work.

From early childhood I grew up at the famed Dodrupchen Monastery in Eastern Tibet, studying Buddhism under the loving tutelage of the great master Kyala Khenpo and other wise teachers. They taught and trained me in their centuries-old tradition of scholarly and meditative attainments, in which they themselves were engaged day in and day out. While leading their lives to the fullest, they were always preparing for their deaths, knowing that life is short, death is certain, and what happens after death is of crucial importance for the future. They were always eagerly involved in helping others to improve their lives and prepare for death.

One of the world's most isolated inhabited settlement clusters, our monastery was situated in a deep valley surrounded by high, majestic mountains. With the mind of a child, I was totally convinced that our monastery was a sanctuary of everlasting peace and joy. No force could ever touch its sacred existence, I believed. But I was mistaken, for the forces of political turmoil changed our lives forever. The centuries-old vibrant tradition of religious life at the monastery came to a sudden end, and we were compelled to flee. Under the guidance of one of the sublime masters of the monastery, Kyabje Dodrupchen Rinpoche, who was endowed with a special gift of natural wisdom, a few of us escaped to India as refugees, after traveling across the Land of Snow (the ancient name for Tibet), a distance of more than one thousand miles.

It would be tempting to blame others for the sufferings, both mental and physical, that people endure as a result of political, military, and social conflicts and violence all over the world. Although blaming may bring a feeling of satisfaction or vindication, Buddhism insists that all the miseries of our life are the consequences of our own past deeds, so that merely blaming others will not help to make things right. This is not a self-blaming game, a neurotic turning of anger against oneself instead of directing it toward the real cause. Instead, it is how we take responsibility for our lives into our own hands. Only when we accept this responsibility can we take our place in the driver's seat and begin to give real direction to the course of our karmic journey.

In India, like many other refugees, I enjoyed firsthand the experience of being treated kindly by people who shared whatever they had. Such a welcome was a great marvel to be remembered even today, after four decades. The freedom to pray had a special meaning that comforted those with wounded hearts.

After years of effort I adjusted to the sophisticated culture and values of the new world. It is easier for the minds of young people to heal—like their physical injuries—if they are allowed to. So I survived without any long-lasting damage.

I am thankful for and greatly value the good fortune of twenty-two years of life in India as a refugee and then as a university professor. They have been followed by more than twenty-four years in the United States, which have enabled me to work on the nectar-like teachings of Buddhism in great comfort. All the opportunities, great and small, in the free world not only enriched my everyday life but also extended the depth and scope of my spiritual journey.

Nevertheless, modern temptations are too numerous and too powerful to resist. The days ran so swiftly, like the speed of lightning. They were gone before I was able even to realize what was happening or take the opportunity to enjoy it. A great many golden opportunities of this precious life passed by forever, never to be encountered again. But every step of life was an important challenge, and every precious moment was a source of true blessings. I was also able to secure the survival of many precious fruits of my hard labor and dedication for the days to come, solely because of the kind help of so many teachers and friends.

In these pages, I draw on the teachings of profound wisdom that I received in Tibet and also what I learned through the painful events that I experienced there. But without the life that I experienced in the world outside Tibet—with its material richness and diversified knowledge as well as its struggles with temptations—this book would never have been conceived. It will, I hope, become a guiding light for my own journey to the unknown as well as for many others who will use it.

Peaceful Death, Joyful Rebirth

Introduction
Death Is Not the End

THE DAY OF DEATH is the most crucial time for every person, universally. Whether you are from the East or the West, whether you are a Buddhist or a follower of some other teaching, a believer or a non-believer—it makes no difference. The moment when consciousness departs from your most cherished body will be a momentous turning point of your life, for death will launch you on a journey into an unknown world.

When the last hour is at hand, you will stand at a crossroad. If you have prepared in advance, you will be ready to move on with great ease and confidence, like an eagle soaring into the sky. If not, according to Buddhist teachings, you will journey again and again through the passages of life, death, and rebirth.

Most people do not like to be reminded of their inevitable death, which may arrive at any moment. They are scared even to think about it, let alone discuss it. To some, the notion of contemplating death never even arises, absorbed as they are in the affairs of daily living. Although people of faith express confidence in an afterlife, many others insist that there is nothing at all after death.

Today, we are in the golden age of science and technology. But the scope of our amazing knowledge about life ends where our breathing stops. Science and technology cannot offer the slightest clue to whether there is any continuity of our consciousness after our last breath. Researchers who study the question seriously are dismissed by the medical and scientific mainstream. In these skeptical times, people are often reluctant to believe in an afterlife, for fear of being labeled irrational, unsophisticated, or naive.

Dramatic images of death greet us whenever we turn on the television—whether they are fictional deaths in a movie or news clips of people around the world succumbing to disease or violence. Yet real, natural images of ordinary individuals who are dying or deceased are seldom visible. We are more likely to witness rosy eulogies and bodies all made up in flowery caskets. If only we dared to gaze at the realities of life and death with open eyes, we would receive a powerful demonstration of the ever-changing cycles of existence that all beings must endure, from life to death and back to life again.

What Happens at Death?

The world's major religions agree that death is not the end, that "something" survives, although they differ in details and interpretation. Mind, consciousness, soul, spirit—whatever we call it—will continue to exist in one form or another. Buddhism identifies "mind" (Tib. *sem, Sems;* Skt. *chitta*)* as the fundamental nature that survives the death of the physical body. Though our bodies will dissolve back into the elements of which they are formed, we will continue as mind and consciousness, which will transmigrate into another existence.

As long as we are alive, the mind cohabits together with the body, which provides an earthy structure that gives us a sense of identity. Thus, we feel more or less like the same person throughout our life span. Environmental influences and cultural habits also impart a continuity of experience. We have a sense of solidity about our bodies and the phenomenal appearances of the material world around us; all the things and happenings that arise within our awareness, perceived by our senses, seem totally real, external, and separate from our minds.

But at the moment of death, all these appearances will vanish. The mind will separate from the physical body, which will begin to decay. As soon as consciousness departs from the body, the things that we saw and the feelings that we had in life will change utterly. What we experience

---

* In the text and glossary, I have indicated some Tibetan (Tib.) and/or Sanskrit (Skt.) terms that may be of importance or interest to some readers. For Tibetan, I give first a phonetic rendering and then a scholarly system of transliteration, in which I capitalize all the main letters or Ming gZhi syllables.

after death will depend solely on our mind, on the habitual mental tendencies and thoughts that we created and fostered while we were alive.

If our mind is peaceful and joyful, then whatever we do physically will be an expression of peace and joy. Whatever we say vocally will be words of peace and joy. Then all our activities will become virtuous, and we will be a source of peace and joy to everyone we come into contact with. At the time of death—when we are released from the constraints of the physical body, cultural restrictions, and environmental influences—we will be free to enjoy peace and joy, the true dispositions of our own mind. Similarly, if we train our minds in the proper way during life, then, at the time of death, all the phenomena before us will arise as a world of peace, joy, and enlightenment.

But if our mind is immersed in negative emotions such as hatred, then whatever we think will be afflicted by thoughts and feelings of burning anger. Whatever we say or do will be an explosive expression of hatred and anger. Then the day of peace may never have a chance to dawn in our hearts. Our pain will become a source of hatred and pain for those close to us. At the time of death, we may encounter a world burning in the flames of hell—the manifestation of our own anger and hatred.

KARMA, THE NATURAL LAW OF CAUSALITY

The world's great religions agree that a kind and helpful life will lead to a happy and peaceful existence after death, whereas a hateful and harmful one will bring harsh consequences. Christianity, for example, extols good works and acts of charity, and Judaism urges the performance of good deeds commanded by the Torah. Buddhists speak of merits, which we accumulate by cultivating positive thoughts and deeds. These and other traditions accept that a natural law of causation operates in our universe. *Karma* is the word that Buddhists use for this law, which governs every event. Every mental and physical action initiated by mental volition becomes a cause that precipitates an individual effect as the result; Buddhism, in particular, teaches in great detail what exact consequences will follow from what specific acts. Generally speaking, the patterns of positive thoughts, emotions, words, and deeds cause happiness, while negative mental and physical actions cause suffering—the events of life's cycle.

All our destructive emotions, as well as our habitual mental concepts and patterns of thought, are rooted in what Buddhism calls grasping at "self" and the dualistic notion of subject and object. As stated by Nagarjuna, one of the great philosophers of Buddhism: "All beings have come from grasping at 'self.'"[1] That is, the mind's tendency to grasp at and become attached to objects of thought and perception is the very cause of our coming into existence in the world of duality.

Grasping at self is the mind's way of perceiving mental objects by apprehending them as truly existing entities. Mental objects include all the phenomena that arise in our awareness, such as "myself," "you," "he," "she," "money," or "table," as well as ideas, feelings, and sensations such as "pain." As soon as we have grasped a mental object and held on to it as real and solid, we have formed a subject-object duality. Then comes the concept of liking or disliking the mental object, and that tightens the mental grip of grasping. In the end there is the feeling of excitement or pain, full of stress and pressure.

In the Buddhist view, "self" includes "me" and "mine," but it also encompasses all phenomena arising in our consciousness. However, according to the highest understanding of Buddhism, there is no "self" that truly exists as a solid, fixed, unchanging entity. Our grasping attitude is thus based on delusion. However, because we are in the grip of karma, our delusory thinking and behavior result in pain and suffering that are all too real to us.

That cycle of grasping goes on repeating itself continuously as the causal order, the karmic law of life. It produces and enflames the afflicting emotions (Skt. *klesha*) of confusion, hatred, miserliness, greed, jealousy, arrogance, and fear. These afflicting emotions rooted in grasping at self are the causes of rebirth, while positive states of mind are the means of liberation.

The changing theaters of life, death, and afterdeath take place neither by choice nor by chance. No one else has created them for us. They are reflections and reactions of our own thoughts, words, and deeds. Therefore, we must train our minds and practice steadily to secure a happy and peaceful death and rebirth.

The Cycle of Life, Death, and Afterdeath

The endless delusory cycle of life, death, and afterdeath is known as *samsara* in Sanskrit. It is sometimes pictured as a ceaselessly turning wheel, as in the illustration on page 172. Cyclic existence has been divided into four periods or passages representing different stages of experiences: [2]

1. The passage of this life starts at conception and ends with the "fatal sickness," or whatever is the cause of death. Each moment of existence is also considered a "passage of life" that arises and then dissolves in an endless chain of changing events moving between birth and death, waking and sleeping, happiness and suffering.
2. The passage of dying begins with the fatal sickness and goes through the gross and subtle dissolution, when physical, mental, and emotional components disintegrate. This phase ends at the cessation of breathing.[3]
3. The passage of ultimate nature starts at the moment when the "luminosity of the basis"—the true nature of the mind, as it is—arises. This period is characterized by the spontaneous arising of "luminous visions"—the appearance not just of light but also of sounds and images. It ends when these visions dissolve. However, ordinary people will not recognize the luminous visions as expressions of their own nature. Instead, they will perceive them all as objects of fear or attachment. For them, the experience will last only a moment, because they will fall into unconsciousness.
4. The transitional passage, or bardo, starts either when the spontaneously arisen visions dissolve or when we regain consciousness. It ends with the conception of our next life.

In Tibetan Buddhist texts, each of the four major periods or passages described above is considered a bardo—an intermediate or transitional passage—because each comes between two other periods. Thus, even life is called a bardo, strange as that may sound, for it is simply the transition between birth and death. Nevertheless, many people use the word *bardo* exclusively for the interval between death and the next birth—a momentous time, rich with many vivid experiences and offering crucial opportunities for determining one's future existence. Therefore, in this book I also use the term *bardo* to mean the fourth passage, the interval between the glimpses of ultimate nature and the next rebirth.

To illumine what it is like to cross the threshold of death and what we may meet on the other side, I have translated and retold some of the amazing stories in Tibetan Buddhist literature about meditators who leave their physical bodies for days at a time to travel through the invisible world. These meditators, known as *delogs*, or those who "return from death," would then come back to their bodies and record their extraordinary journeys, which could span the lowest rungs of hell and the sublime pure lands.

Pure lands are ineffably joyful and peaceful paradises that the buddhas, the enlightened ones, manifested through their compassion so that devotees might take rebirth there without needing to be highly realized. Being reborn in a pure land is not the same as attaining enlightenment. But once there, we will make continuous progress toward enlightenment.

Some delogs tell of visits to pure lands, where they receive teachings from the buddhas. Other delogs spend more time describing the bardo, with its court of judgment and the various realms where ordinary beings may be reborn, such as realms of hungry ghosts or gods.

Delogs' accounts are deeply moving. Most delogs are profoundly religious people and were sent back to our world by enlightened beings to tell us about what lies ahead and how to prepare for it. Each tale is a gift, for by opening a window into the vastness of our futures beyond this current life, delogs broaden our perspective and inspire us to improve our lives.

Through delogs' eyes we become privy to the sorts of things that will matter in determining where we will be reborn. We witness the power of spiritual practices to cleanse negative deeds and thoughts. We realize the power of prayer to help the dead secure better rebirths. We observe how devotion—which is in reality a skillful way to open up our minds—allows the lamas and blessed ones to intercede on behalf of beings in the bardo and lead them to pure lands.

Most delogs bring back messages from departed loved ones to friends and relatives. These personal pleas reinforce the basic message to change our lives while we are alive in human form and have the chance.

In the West, people who were revived from clinical death sometimes had "near-death experiences" (NDEs). Although NDEs share many similarities with delog experiences,[4] they may last only a few minutes or so, whereas delog experiences usually last many days. Delogs also seem to penetrate much further into the afterdeath realm.

Many delog texts came into my hands. However, due to space limitations, I could include only small parts of them in the book. The accounts you will read in chapters 2, 3, and 5 generally date from the nineteenth to the mid-twentieth century (dating was not available for all the texts). Delogs are not a modern phenomenon, however. Nor are they exclusively Tibetan. They are discussed in the teachings of the Buddha.[5]

As you read the accounts, some of you might wonder why the tales are tinted by Tibetan and Tibetan Buddhist culture and iconography. How come the delogs keep meeting Tibetan acquaintances? Why do the judges resemble those in Buddhist iconography?

The main answer is that the terrain that unfolds before us in the bardo is a reflection of our habits and emotions. Whatever we see and experience after death accords with the way our culture and belief system have shaped our thinking. All of us—whether child or adult, pious or atheist, communist or capitalist—are immersed in acquired habits of perceiving. Since the delogs were all Tibetan Buddhists, or familiar with Buddhism, they perceived things from that perspective.

However, while the details of our habits differ across cultures, we all share—regardless where we're from—a mentality of seeing the world in terms of rewards and penalties for right and wrong. We constantly bounce between hope and fear under the all-seeing eyes of some imagined higher authority or judge. Our perceptions are soaked in this judgmental mentality. That is why, when we have been unvirtuous, we fear being judged, and after death we will perceive a judge handing us a harsh sentence.

In reality, there is no external judge. There is no sentence. Our afterdeath experiences are simply the dividends we earn from our own mental and emotional investments. That is why the great Indian master Shantideva said about the hell realms:

> Who constructed all those burning iron grounds [of hell]?
> Where did those flames come from?
> "All of them are [mere reflections of] your unvirtuous mind,"
> The Buddha has said.[6]

All of us might well see some higher power in the bardo. Its form will correspond with our habits. Tibetan texts describe a courthouse presided over by the Dharma King and his assistants, the Lords of the Dead. Other cultures and religions envision the judgment seat of a divine being, a book in which virtues and sins are recorded by an angel, or the weighing of deeds on a scale. Western near-death experiencers often describe "life reviews" in which they are encouraged to judge their own lives. Common to all, however, is the universal law that positive habits and deeds result in joy, while negative ones lead to suffering.

TAKING REBIRTH

After we emerge from the bardo, we will take rebirth with a different body and identity. Just as our experience in the bardo depends upon our karmic deeds, mental and emotional tendencies, and spiritual attainments, these same factors will be the determining force behind our next rebirth.

It is possible to recognize our true nature—our intrinsic awareness as it is—in the bardo, or indeed in any of the four passages of life. If we can maintain that realization, then we will be fully enlightened, free forever from rebirth in the cycle of delusion. However, enlightenment takes many years of total dedication; it is not achieved by attending weekend workshops or doing a few minutes of meditation for several years. Fully accomplished adepts—advanced masters of spiritual practice—may attain enlightenment and then take rebirth by choice rather than because of past karma. Their habitual chain of karma would have ceased or been transcended. For them, phenomenal existents (that is, all the things that appear to exist in the phenomenal world) are nothing but projections of the qualities of their own minds.

If we keep aspiring to enlightenment, and if we stay on the meritorious path, one day we too will reach this goal. But for now, the path taken by fully accomplished adepts is not feasible for ordinary people like ourselves, who are without great spiritual attainment. According to previous karmic causation, ordinary people are bound to take rebirth in one of the six realms of samsaric existence (described in chapter 6, "Rebirth").

People who have trained spiritually and possess an abundance of merits will enjoy healthy future lives in happy world systems. If we have been peaceful, kind, caring, helpful, and wise, and if we have put our meritorious attitudes into practice by word and deed, we will enjoy rebirths in the worlds of peaceful, joyful, and helpful existence. If in this life we have practiced seeing, thinking, feeling, and believing in the presence of a pure land, we will take birth in a pure land, because of the mental habits that we have cultivated. Such a pure land will not be the ultimate pure land of the enlightened state, but a manifested pure land of great peace and joy. Not only will we enjoy the qualities of a joyful world, but we will also radiate blessings of the pure land infinitely to all who are open to receiving them. We will still be under the control of karmic law, but it will be a karmic cycle of happiness. Following such a path of life is practical and attainable for many people, and we must make it our main priority.

What about ordinary people whose lives have been filled with negative emotions? If our mind has indulged in anger, greed, or ignorance, we are bound to face a very hellish existence as the consequence. As we travel through the four transitional passages, the severe consequences of our negative mind will be just like wearing tinted glasses that darken everything we see. Instead of the familiar surroundings we knew when we were alive, all around us will be images, sounds, and experiences of fear and misery. Such will be the phenomenal appearances that arise in our awareness as a result of the prevailing mental state that we nourished in life.

Many of us, whether we acknowledge it or not, are engaged in and cherishing such a mindset—day in and day out. Often it is an unconscious process. Although externally we may not think of ourselves as such "bad" people, we may be secretly bathed in the toxic emotions, selfishness, and craving that modern culture encourages. We must stop fooling ourselves and start to change our ways this very day, while we are still lucky enough to be in a human body and have a degree of choice. Once we are dead, we will not be able to make changes, because our karmic tendencies will take over. They will drive us to be born again—possibly in nonhuman realms, where spiritual progress cannot be made. We will wander through an unending cycle of birth, death, and rebirth, full of suffering and excitement.

Transforming Our Future

It is important to reiterate that the hellish realms or pure lands in which we may travel after death or take birth are not external world systems situated somewhere else. The experiences of enjoyment or suffering in different world systems after death are merely reflections of our own karmic tendencies. It is like a dream journey, fabricated by our own habitual mental impressions. Let us bear this point in mind whenever we read about karmic consequences. The mind generates its own experiences of happiness and suffering after death as a result of tendencies gathered and reinforced through successive lifetimes. Produced by the mind, these experiences also take place in the mind, nowhere else.

It is equally important to know that as long as we are alive, it is possible to change and improve our future. Of course, we will always be subject to unavoidable limitations imposed by physical and environmental laws. But when we die, our minds will be less restricted by external forces, so we will be driven by the ingrained mental tendencies that we fostered in the past. This is precisely the reason why the best way to improve the quality of our life, death, and afterlife is to work on changing our conceptual and emotional habits from negative to positive.

So there are three choices open to us while we still have some time:

- We could continue to endure the pain and suffering of this life as we ordinarily do, without taking the opportunity to make any progress. The karma of mental confusion, afflicting emotions, and external situations will control our future destination. Then there will be no chance for true happiness to arise.

- We could try to secure the happiest and healthiest state that an ordinary cyclic existence in samsara can provide. If we maintain a peaceful, joyful, helpful, loving life, then a happier and healthier future will be ensured as the result, at least for a while.

- Or we could go beyond this momentary cyclic existence, the samsara of our life, and secure the everlasting state of ultimate peace and joy, called nirvana. Such an attainment can only come about through realization of the absolute truth, reached through meditation and supported by the right ways of thinking, feeling, and serving others.

If we let our minds face the right direction, then whatever steps we take will lead us closer to our intended goal.

The meditations and practices described in this book are mainly based on the liturgies of the Buddha of Infinite Light (in Sanskrit, Amitabha) and his Blissful Pure Land (Sukhavati). But there are other buddhas and pure lands whose liturgies may be used, and even the prayers of non-Buddhist belief systems with similar qualities will be effective. The important thing is to prepare in advance by meditating regularly on a liturgy associated with a source of blessings.

In this book, the term *source of blessings* refers to any object of prayer, reverence, and refuge that is a source of protection and blessing. The source of blessings could be any higher, inner, or true source such as a buddha, bodhisattva, saint, sage, or adept master. Any mental object will be a powerful source of blessings if it has positive qualities and is appreciated by the mind as positive. The dying and dead as well as their helpers must rely on sources of blessings as the support for their prayers, meditations, and rites. The ultimate source of blessings is in ourselves, as we all possess the enlightened nature. However, until we have realized our own potential, we must rely on an external source of blessings to awaken our own blessed nature and qualities.

In Tibetan Buddhism, repeating the prayers of a source of blessing, such as the name-prayer of the Buddha of Infinite Light, is one of the popular ways to reach and receive blessings from the Buddha. The Buddha of Infinite Light vowed to liberate beings who invoke his name with devotion, just as a mother flies to her child's side as soon as she hears him cry, "Mommy!"

A colleague of mine once asked Yukhog Chatralwa, a great meditation master, to give him some instructions on Dzogchen (the primary teaching and practice of the Nyingma school of Tibetan Buddhism). Without saying a word about Dzogchen, Chatralwa replied:

> You should first try to say the name-prayer of the Buddha of Infinite Light one hundred times a day with strong devotion. Then try to increase it to two hundred, three hundred, and so forth. If you could keep doing more and more, one day, a time might come for you that whatever you are doing, you will always be with the name of the Buddha in your breath and the feeling of his presence in your mind. If that happens, then when you die, you will die with the name of the Buddha and the feelings of his presence. If that happens, as soon as you die, because of the merits, the blessings of the Buddha and your devotional habits, all your perceptions will arise as the Blissful Pure Land of the Buddha of Infinite Light. Your future will be in peace and happiness. You will become a source of benefits for many others. Isn't it wonderful!

Though I didn't realize it at the time, years later I started to understand how profound and meaningful his words were.

If we have trained in the mindfulness of seeing all as a buddha and his pure land, then even if we encounter negative images, sounds, or feelings in the bardo, they will be powerless to hurt us, and everything will turn into positive phenomena. It is like having a nightmare: if we are able to recognize it as a dream and an illusion, we can immediately render it impotent, causing the attackers to vanish like mist in the sunlight. In the same way, if we can recognize any frightening experience of the bardo as an illusion or as a pure land, it will become ineffective or will turn positive. The frightening Lords of the Dead will turn into enlightened angels of wisdom and love, as we will see later.

But we must begin to train now, before death arrives. If we practice every day or many times every day, we will not be at a loss when the crucial hour arrives.

CEREMONIES FOR THE DEAD AND DYING

We have seen that we can do something to help ourselves in negotiating the momentous transition of death. But what about the deaths of others, including those who have not had an opportunity to practice any teachings in advance? Can we, the living, help them?

Every religion has rituals and liturgies or sacred texts intended to assist the dying and dead, which are also a comfort to the survivors. In traditional Judaism, for example, the dying are supposed to recite a prayer of confession and repentance, and others will help them to do so if they are incapacitated. After a death, the survivors periodically recite the Kaddish, a Hebrew prayer in praise of God's name. In Islam, people gather to offer their collective prayers for divine forgiveness of the deceased. In Catholicism there is the priestly sacrament of anointing a person on the point of death, prayers for the souls of the dead, and the funeral mass. Tibetan Buddhism, too, has a rich ceremonial tradition associated with death.

During the journey of my long and turbulent life, I have had many firsthand experiences of dealing with the deaths of great spiritual masters, close friends, and unknown strangers. Some were respected or powerful, and many mourned their deaths. Others were poor, uncared for, and unknown.

From the age of five, I lived and grew up in Dodrupchen Monastery, a famous learning and meditation institution in Eastern Tibet. Along with my fellow monks and novices, I oriented my entire life toward learning Buddhism, prayer, and meditation. After the completion of the preliminary training, we studied and meditated on the advanced teachings and began to serve the community. We were taught to help the dead and those who survived them through devotional prayers, ceremonial rites, traditional teachings, and meditations, according to the meticulous Tibetan Buddhist death service manuals.

Trying to take care of a dead person by performing death ceremonies can be the saddest yet most serene and honest time of our lives. We have no appetite to aspire to anything else as we summon from the depths of our being all the support that we can for this person's crucial journey into the unknown world. At the side of a dying or a dead person, prayers come from the heart, uttered with our whole mind and body. The truth of life, its fragility, is naked before us. For the departed, all the structures of dignity, career, and earnings have unexpectedly collapsed. Even their most cherished body is humbled, lying cold, stiff, and motionless, with no breath—dead.

Ceremonies for the dying and the dead were among the most important community services we offered. I usually assisted the senior lamas in performing them, but sometimes I led a group of lamas. On a couple of occasions, I led elaborate services lasting weeks (as outlined in chapter 9). Most of the time, we would spend an hour or two offering brief services (as provided in appendix B).

Death ceremonies are performed sitting right by the dying person or near the body of the deceased. All ceremonies follow the same basic pattern: we start by trying to open up our own hearts in devotion to the source of blessings, such as the Buddha of Infinite Light. Then we direct our minds to the dying or dead person with strong compassion and unconditioned love from the depth of the heart. With this devotional and compassionate attitude, we begin the main ceremony: saying prayers, meditating, and receiving blessings from the source of blessings for ourselves and the deceased. Finally, we see, feel, and contemplate all as one with great peace. We conclude by offering all the merits we have created to the deceased and to all mother-beings (all sentient beings, who in previous existences have been our mothers) and by making aspirations that the deceased be reborn in the Blissful Pure Land or as a joyous human being.

I wouldn't dare give readers even a hint of the impression that I have any power to change the destiny of others or that I have any special insight into where the dying or dead person will go. But because of my trust in Buddhist teachings, after performing these ceremonies with strong devotion and love, I myself, at least, would often feel great peace. I would feel grateful, too: "How fortunate I am to have the opportunity to be with this person at their most important hour of need, to try to offer the best helping hand that I can." At the same time, I have always been careful not to push myself beyond my own mental, physical, and spiritual limits.

Many death ceremonies were occasions of great joy, with an almost celebratory atmosphere as people recalled all the peace and joy that the deceased had brought to themselves and others during their lives. But there were also many great somber moments of sadness and hopelessness, when the barrier between the dead and the living was so great that no one could reach the deceased, even if we could touch them physically. Their mind was sinking into a deep darkness, an unknown and lonely world. Sitting beside a deathbed, staring into the face of life's fragility, leaves us no secure corner to hide. It is always a powerful wake-up call.

The Death of a Great Teacher

My first direct encounter with death was a source of great joy and celebration. There was a great Lama called Sonam Tragpa in the Wangrol tribe, my mother's tribal community of Golok province, Eastern Tibet. He was known as Pushul Lama to the native tribespeople. He lived and taught in a small monastic hermitage at a distance of two days' travel by horse from our monastery. He was a great teacher and scholar, the author of volumes of treatises, and a master of tantric meditation and Dzogchen, but his main prayers and meditations were on the Blissful Pure Land of the Buddha of Infinite Light.

Pushul Lama died at around age sixty. I was in my early teens. As messengers arrived at our monastery bearing the news, I, along with my teacher, Kyala Khenpo, and others, rushed to him on galloping horses. We reached his hermitage late that evening and were met by his weeping monks, nuns, and lay devotees.

I had a special relationship to Pushul Lama. He was one of the masters who recognized me shortly after my birth as the reincarnation, or *tulku*, of his principal teacher. He was also the most important lama of my mother's tribal group. So I had a special obligation to look after his funeral services.

As instructed by Kyala Khenpo, I went alone into the lama's room. His body was lying on his bed in the sleeping lion posture, a meditation position. I was young, so I didn't think much about it, but I felt that the whole area and the room were in absolute peace. I touched his heart area and felt a little warmth, though he had died more than forty-eight hours earlier. That was a sign that his mind was still in meditative absorption within his body. I informed Khenpo, who said, "No one must enter his room or make any noise around the house, until his meditation is finished." All kinds of prayers and ceremonies were going on, but in tents far away from the lama's temple residence. Traditionally, even the announcement of the death of a great lama would have been kept secret for days, but in this case that wasn't possible. The sad news had already spread through the tribal lands like wildfire.

When I checked on Pushul Lama the next morning, I found no warmth at his heart area, so four chosen monks were called in. They washed his body with blessed saffron water, dried it with new white cloths, and completed all the usual preparations needed to preserve a body for days. Then they seated his body on a small throne in the lotus meditation posture, dressed in his monastic robes with a ceremonial crown over his head. His hands were crossed at his heart, holding a *vajra* (a ritual scepter) and a bell. Flowers, lamps, food, and other offerings were arranged on a couple of low tables in front of him. I am quite sure that the lama would have preferred the simplest funeral, but it turned into an elaborate ceremony because the community wished it so.

Although only about thirty monks lived in the hermitage, streams of people from all walks of life kept coming and going from far-distant nomadic camps, day and night, crying and praying.

Meanwhile, we found a small sheet of paper with the lama's handwriting on it. It said: "As soon as I die, I will take rebirth in the Blissful Pure Land. I have recited the texts on the Perfection of Wisdom [the *Prajnaparamita* in fifteen volumes] one hundred and eight times and meditated on their profound meaning in this lifetime. Therefore, my name will be Bodhisattva Sherab Nyingpo [Wisdom Heart]. Whoever prays to me with devotion, I will protect from any danger they might face while they are alive. I will lead them to the Blissful Pure Land when they die."

He concluded the piece with the following five-line prayer to himself to be chanted by his devotees:

> In the Blissful Pure Land you are Sherab Nyingpo.
> In the Snow Land [Tibet] you were Sonam Tragpa.
> In the future you will be known as the Buddha of Infinite Life.*
> My root lama—to you I pray.
> Please bless us/me to take rebirth in the Blissful Pure Land.

This letter was amazing, as Pushul Lama was known for his utmost humility and honesty. He never said anything he did not mean. The surprising thing was not *what* he wrote, as we all had the highest esteem for him, but *that* he wrote it.

On the dawn of the eighth day, his body was cremated in a freshly built half-stupa structure. Monks and nuns busily performed the cremation rites. A crowd of laypeople covered the whole hillside, trying to circumambulate the cremation area as an exercise of devotion, chanting prayers for rebirth in the Blissful Pure Land. The whole atmosphere was transformed into a total devotional celebration, echoing with the sounds of prayers and musical instruments. Never have I felt so much energy of profound sorrow and so many sounds of heartfelt devotion from so many hearts merged into one huge celebration.

Pushul Lama's death demonstrates great attainment. In his teens, he had been so disturbed that his family had to literally tie him up to stop him from hurting himself and others. But through prayer and meditation, he transformed himself and attained a fearless confidence of being reborn in the Blissful Pure Land and leading all devotees there. To this day, I know of no one more learned, cheerful, and kind.

By following his example, we too can transform. We too can attain joy and fearless confidence in life and at death.

Dr. Elisabeth Kübler-Ross, the late psychiatrist who revolutionized attitudes toward death and the care of the dying in the United States, reflected a similar view when she said: "The only incontrovertible fact of my work is the importance of life. I always say that death can be one of the greatest experiences ever. If you live each day of your life right, then you have nothing to fear."[7]

---

* The Buddha of Infinite Light and the Buddha of Infinite Life are facets of the same buddha, though they have different names, forms, and functions. See the glossary.

1

Human Life
Our Precious Days

Human life is precious, with great potential.
But it is impermanent and full of dissatisfaction.
So we must take full advantage of it by spiritual
training now.

T HE PASSAGE of our human life—the interval between conception and death—is often rich with enjoyments and attainments, the source of great benefits. Yet it is also subject to innumerable forms of unavoidable suffering, mental and physical. Even a miserable lifetime seems to pass too swiftly, while a happy one may nonetheless end with a sense of incompleteness. Life is thus fleeting and ultimately unsatisfying as it swings between positive and negative experiences over which we seem to have no control.

Life begins at conception and ends with a "fatal sickness," or whatever is the cause of death. The body and mind coexist in harmony as long as we are breathing and our body retains heat. When breathing stops and the heat is lost, the mind and body separate, and the person is dead.*

---

* In the West, death used to be defined as the moment when the heartbeat and breathing stopped. With the advent of medical technologies capable of restarting both heartbeat and respiration, thinking shifted to the concept of "brain death," and people were considered dead when the electrical activity in the brain stopped. This cessation of brain activity was regarded as the end of consciousness. Even though the body might continue to function in some cases, modern medicine regards brain death as "clinical death."

According Buddhism, however, the cessation of "inner breathing" is death. The stopping of the pulse and the loss of heat at the heart are used as signs of dying and death. Even if a person's pulse has stopped, they may not have died. If one feels warmth when touching the dying person's heart level, they are not yet dead; they could be in meditative absorption.

What Is Our Real Nature?

The body is not the real identity of a person. It is merely a guesthouse where our mind is residing for a while. Upon the separation of mind and body, the body blends with the natural elements and soon disappears forever. But our mind will not end. It will continue by taking rebirth with a different body and identity according to the chain of our past habitual tendencies, the law of karma. Our future fate—whether we will be happy or unhappy—depends on our habitual tendencies, mental concepts, and ingrained emotions, as well as the ways in which we have expressed these habits in words and deeds.

Mind, in its true nature, is open and pure. Its innate quality is peaceful, joyful, omniscient, and benevolent. This quality is called the enlightened nature or buddha-nature. In Sanskrit, *buddha* means "awake" or "awakened one." Every being, each one of us, possesses this enlightened nature. It is a wisdom that is free from the self-limiting conditions of dualistic thinking, which divides experience into subject and object, "self" and "other." The true nature of mind is omniscient and sees all simultaneously and nondually, as oneness without limit. In our ultimate universal nature, not only is our mind omniscient, but space is boundless and time is timeless.*

So how is it that most of us have no clue to the splendors buried within our minds? The reason is that the authentic inner qualities of our mind have been covered over by our habitual dualistic conceptions, a discriminating mentality that constantly emphasizes dualities and opposites, afflicting emotions, and sensations of craving. In this way, our real nature has become unconscious and foreign to us. Nevertheless, no matter what negative emotions of attachment or revulsion we nurture, our innate wisdom remains unstained and unafflicted.

In order to uncover the true nature of our mind, we must embark on vigorous meditation with total dedication. We must recognize and meditate on the right ways of viewing, thinking, feeling, believing, and being. But even if we could just entertain the notion that we possess a pure and

---

* In esoteric Buddhism there are four times: past, present, future, and timeless time. The first three are the time of relative or conventional truth; they are always changing. Timeless (Tib. *tu-me*, *Dus med*) time is the ultimate time in ultimate or absolute truth, which is beyond the changing quality of relative time.

positive nature within—that alone will help us build confidence, enhance our spiritual practice, and propel us toward the right goal.

Some of us might think that the character of our mind is simply too fixed and solid to be trained in a new spiritual direction. We might believe that we have become too mired in our negative habits to adopt new ways of thinking, viewing, and feeling. In reality, however, every moment is a chance to start, restart, or change the direction and quality of our life.

Contrary to what it seems, our mind is not one single, solid stream. It is not one piece, like an iron rod. It is a chain of separate moments that change every instant, the way rosary beads under our fingers change from moment to moment. Every event is a flowing series of births and deaths, an experience preceded by the death of another event and followed by the birth of the next. The impression that our life span is one solid, unbroken continuum is just an illusion—like the illusion of a solid ring of light produced by children twirling a flashlight or firebrand in the dark.

If we become discouraged or feel we're in a rut, it is often because we don't truly understand the momentary character of life, as it is. We grasp at events as mental objects and conceptualize them as truly existing entities. Actually, events have already changed before we can even think about them. The events we ponder over are shadows, the reflections of what has already happened.

Every event, every moment, is new and fresh, like childbirth. We are malleable and can educate and train ourselves as we would a newborn baby. Through meditation we can improve at every juncture of every moment and thus uncover our enlightened nature.

Why Meditate?

Some people question this emphasis on meditation. They see it as self-indulgent, even selfish, asking: If you just sit and enjoy peace and joy in your own mind, what are you doing for society? How can you claim to care about others?

It's too bad that some people misunderstand meditation in this way. But maybe it shouldn't be surprising, for the benefits of meditation are not readily perceptible to most of us.

In reality, everything we think and feel generates a corresponding positive or negative imprint in our consciousness. Selfless, peaceful, and joyful thoughts sow seeds that will give birth to the most beautiful forms, sounds, and feelings; negative thoughts, to monsters and terrifying sounds. But it is only when we leave our gross bodies and cross into the bardo that many of these will become visible and audible to us, as we will read later on.

Meditation is a powerful tool to create sublime forms, sounds, and feelings that can help us and countless others who are open to them. Beings in the bardo, in particular, are very receptive to meditation and prayers, as they live in a world of thought. Without a physical body to anchor them, if they think "New York," then New York is where they are; if immediately afterward they think "London," London is where they will instantly be, karma permitting. Blown around in this way, they often feel exhausted, scared, and alone.

The peace, joy, and compassion that we generate through meditation provide a safe harbor where bardo beings can rest and gain confidence, peace, and joy. Meditation is a more powerful way to help these beings than our usual discursive thoughts and feelings because it comes from a deeper, more peaceful level in our mind. Like a magnet, a grounded mind draws floating consciousnesses and stabilizes them. The longer we remain in contemplation, the longer we can comfort these beings and the greater the chance to improve their futures.

Meditation lets us contribute greatly to the living, too. As long as our minds are filled with negative emotions, if we try to help others even at a physical level, we might accidentally infect them with our ills.

Meditation is a way to purify our impurities, strengthen our virtuous qualities, and awaken our true nature. It may be an experience of virtuous qualities, such as devotion, peace, love, and strength generated by heartfelt thoughts and feelings. This is conceptual meditation. Or it may be an experience of the awakened state of the mind. That is nonconceptual meditation. Both are an experience, an attainment, that cleanses and fills us with the inexhaustible treasures of love, peace, joy, and devotion, thus enhancing our life and, in turn, our ability to serve others. When our mind is filled with these qualities, whatever we say and do will spontaneously express and reflect these qualities. We become a source of love, peace, and joy for all associated with us. Our mere presence brings solace to others. So, just as we cannot neglect the roots of a tree if we want to share in its fruits and flowers, so too we cannot neglect our mind if we want to benefit others.

Many of us know, at least at the intellectual level, the importance of meditation; yet we put it off or don't do it wholeheartedly. The reason is usually that we haven't brought our intellectual understanding to the level of feeling. If we could involve our feelings, nothing would be able to stop us from practicing. So how do we get there?

There are two basic sources of motivation to practice: one is inspiration; the other, shock or fear. Life is a rich source of both. Meeting an amazing teacher, for instance, can be a pivotal event to inspire us. Or perhaps it will take an event like our own illness, the sudden passing of a loved one, or a large-scale tragedy, such as the tsunami disaster in South and Southeast Asia, to awaken us from the slumber of our daily lives.

Buddhism urges us to think deeply about five aspects of life that serve both to inspire and to shock or scare us:

' Having a virtuous life is very rare and precious.
' Life is impermanent and changeable.
' All life's happenings are the consequences of karmic causes.
' Life is full of misery.
' Life has the potential to reach the highest goals.

These points are not artificially fabricated for the purpose of getting us to practice. They are the naked truth about our lives. It is just that our attention needs to be deliberately drawn to them because we otherwise take them for granted, or feel too uncomfortable to even think about them. In my monastery in Tibet, every morning we would start our mediation by contemplating these five points. However, it is not necessary to sit in one-pointed concentration to ponder them. We can think about them anywhere, anytime. As we do, we will see how they teach us what life really is, set us on the right spiritual path, and spark in us the enthusiasm and commitment to follow it through.

Precious Human Life Is Rare

Our precious human life provides us with the foundation to enhance not just this life, but also all our lives hereafter. It offers us the chance to attain enlightenment, realize true peace and joy, and radiate those qualities effortlessly to benefit countless beings. If we realize our enlightened nature, the universe will become a source of peace and joy for us, and we will become a source of peace and joy for the universe.

If we recognize how precious this opportunity is and understand the value of our own existence, we will immediately feel a sense of great appreciation and thankfulness for the blessings of life that we enjoy. That gratitude will turn into a strong determination never to waste a moment of this life, and to dedicate it entirely in the best way that we possibly can.

Let us consider how many beings in the world have this extraordinary opportunity, as doing so can help us realize just how fortunate we are. Looking around, we can see that there are countless beings in the world. If we turn over a single rock, hundreds of insects could be crawling. If we had a microscope, trillions more creatures would become visible. Billions of bacteria, I am told, live in our intestines alone. According to Buddhism, every one of them has a mind and seeks happiness.

The beings we can see, moreover, are just the tip of the iceberg. Like the cultures around the world that traditionally believe in invisible beings such as angels, gods, demons, and ghosts, Buddhists also believe in numerous classes of invisible beings. Many of these beings exist in our midst, in the very place where we now sit and breathe. The only reason we don't see one another and don't interfere in one another's lives is that we lack the common causal (karmic) connections that would produce mutual perception.

Yet among this vast and wondrous array of visible and invisible life, human beings possess the greatest potential for realizing enlightenment, as we have the intellectual capacity, incentive, and stamina to seek a spiritual path and stick with it. Consider animals and hell-beings, to take two examples. These beings endure such fear, pain, and dullness that they lack the strength to gather even a trace of the qualities of enlightenment. Now take beings like the long-lived gods, who might seem to be luckier than we are, what with their beautiful light-bodies and access to all sorts of delights. The truth, however, is that the gods—unlike human beings, who taste both happiness and suffering and therefore have the incentive and the ability to seek enlightenment—are too rapt in their sensual pleasures and lack any experience of pain that might spur them to do spiritual work.

Yet even among human beings, if we look closely, we see that there are actually very few who have the disposition and are likely to seize the opportunity to work toward enlightenment. Many people today don't believe in the spiritual. Many have no inkling of their mind's potential. This is so even among some educated people. An intellectual once told me, "Mind is just a fungus on the brain."

Some people are too submerged in the struggle against poverty or illness or too caught up in addiction to indulgences and excitements to give time to spiritual development. Others pour every ounce of their energy into achieving material success and fame. And still other people, who might have some spiritual inclination, never get on track because they fall in with the wrong crowd and pick up the wrong values. So when we boil it all down, only a tiny percentage of human beings have a realistic chance of taking advantage of the opportunity for spiritual growth.

Buddhist teachings lay out the ideal conditions for spiritual progress. They are known as the eight freedoms and ten endowments. The eight freedoms are the freedom from being born in the realms of (1) hell, (2) hungry ghosts, (3) animals, or (4) the long-lived gods, for none of these realms offers beings as good a chance to make spiritual progress as the human realm does. (See chapter 6, "Rebirth," for more details on the various realms.) One must also be free from having (5) a perverted viewpoint, (6) barbarous behavior, (7) a nihilistic view, or (8) being born in a place where no enlightened teacher has appeared.

The ten endowments include having (1) a human life with (2) sense faculties intact and (3) a wholesome occupation, or right livelihood. One must have been born in a land where (4) Dharma teachings are available, (5) an enlightened teacher appeared, (6) the teacher taught the nectar-like Dharma (enlightened teachings of Buddhism), and (7) the Dharma teaching still flourishes. Finally, one must (8) have faith in the teaching, (9) follow the teachings, and (10) have the guidance of an authentic living teacher.

As you can see, it is extremely rare to have all eighteen of these ideal conditions. Those who do have them possess what Buddhists call a precious human life. Regardless how many of these ideal conditions we possess, we should rejoice over whichever ones we do have, recognize that they are blessings, and take full advantage of them. We should also work to obtain the conditions we are lacking. If we realize what precious blessings we have, we will never dare waste this golden chance, and, sooner or later we will realize the meaning of precious life—true peace, joy, and openness.

If we don't take the opportunity to give our life meaning and turn it into a precious human life, there is no guarantee that we will get another chance in the future. After all, while human beings have the sharpest intellect among all beings, we also have the strongest emotions. It is all too easy for us to be swept up by passions and make tragic blunders that may consign us to rebirth in worse realms. As Shantideva says:

> It is exceedingly difficult to obtain human life endowed with
>   freedom and endowments.
> Today we have the chance to fulfill the goal of life;
> But if we do not take advantage of it,
> How can we get such an opportunity again?[1]

Life Is Impermanent

Death has a way of focusing the mind as practically nothing else does. When we contemplate our mortality and the impermanence of life, it is hard not to feel a sense of urgency to make the most of our precious human life. Understanding the principle of impermanence makes us realistic about life's true characteristics and inspires us to improve without wasting a moment.

We all know that our zero hour will arrive, but we don't know when or how it will come. We simply take it for granted that our life will last a long time. In fact, we stay alive only as long as the mind resides in the body. Many things could very easily separate that fragile union. Not only could sickness and accidents be fatal, but even medicine, food, houses, recreation, and friends could turn deadly.

Although life seems to possess a continuing existence, it is a chain of events fluctuating from moment to moment. The phases of birth and death alternate back and forth continuously, like the turning faces and bodies of dancers. One after another, moment after moment, changes in life come endlessly, like the beads on a rosary as our fingers move from bead to bead.

Not only life, but everything else—nature, friendships, possessions, and positions—is ever-changing. The Buddha said:

> The three worlds* are impermanent like the clouds of autumn.
> The turns of births and deaths of beings are like watching a dance.
> The speed of human lives is like lightning in the sky.
> Life passes swiftly like a stream down a steep mountain.[2]

---

* The world of desire, the world of form, and the formless world.

Gungthang Tenpe Dronme tells a poignant parable. A man is taking a pleasant walk one day when he accidentally falls off a steep cliff. Halfway down the rocky slope, he breaks his fall by grabbing on to a tuft of grass. He hangs on to the grass with all his might to keep from tumbling down the rocky slope to his death. But soon a white mouse comes along and starts to nibble on a bit of the grass. Then a dark mouse arrives and eats a bit more of the grass. The two mice take turns nibbling away until finally, one mouse gnaws through the last blade of grass, and the man slips off the rock and plummets to his death.

In this parable, the white mouse represents day and the dark mouse, night. Little by little, the passing of each day and each night brings us closer and closer to the end of life. Fortunately, we are alive for a while, but all along we have been heading for death. The Buddha said:

> Whatever is accumulated will end up exhausted.
> Whatever has arisen will end by falling down.
> Whoever meets will end up separating.
> Whoever lives will end up in death.
> Since life ends in death,
> All sentient beings will die.[3]

Many of us know this, at least at an intellectual level. We also know that the end often arrives without warning. Still, we feel cozier burying our heads in the sand, pretending that life will remain as it is forever. So we fail to prepare for death. When the time comes, we will regret it. But by then it will be too late.

So we must realize the impermanent nature of life and feel its changing character from the depth of our heart. This realization will force us to travel the path of peace and joy to the goal of peace and joy, without daring to waste any more time.

Using Impermanence to Dissolve Negative Emotions

The benefits to be gained from understanding impermanence from the depth of our heart are vast. In addition to motivating us to practice, contemplating impermanence can dissolve negative emotions and lead to higher realization.

The impermanence of anger and hatred. A real understanding of impermanence makes us more tolerant. Suppose we feel like exploding in anger at someone who harms us. If we see the impermanent nature of enmity, we will realize that this person who appears as our enemy today might have been our child in a past life. Tomorrow, they might be our best friend. That thought will let the air of hatred out of our chest. We might also feel the pointlessness and emptiness of fighting with anyone, as beings are constantly changing faces. We could even feel compassionate toward this so-called enemy of ours, for, in the course of time, their efforts to harm us will end up hurting them as they face the consequences.

The impermanence of craving. When we become obsessed with attachment to someone or something, we must think of their impermanent qualities. Young, attractive people become old and ugly before our very eyes. Things that bring pleasure today turn into sources of sorrow tomorrow through loss or change. Material wealth and social status only enslave us. To embrace them is like strangling our neck with our own hands.

We fool ourselves if we pursue the fleeting appearances of life. By thinking again and again about the impermanence of the mental objects that intrigue us, we will realize their unreliable, momentary nature and will gradually lose our appetite for them. As the tightness of our craving loosens, we may be able to bring feelings of true contentment and joy to whatever we are and whatever we have. To be free from craving, which tightens the grip of the mind's grasping at mental objects, is the greatest source of joy. The Buddha said:

> All the sensual pleasures of the world and
> All the joys of the god realm
> Cannot compare to even one-sixteenth
> Of the joy of freedom from craving.[4]

The impermanence of depression. When our mind is cast down with the burden of losing something close to our heart, we should think about and feel the impermanence of that sadness and its source. This feeling could lift our sorrow by uprooting its cause, which is our grasping at something unreal and unreliable as if it were real and reliable. Perhaps we are sad because we must deal with things that we don't want. The feeling of the impermanence of these things disarms and dissipates the power of sadness.

The impermanence of excitements. Thinking about impermanence can also help us avoid becoming overly excited. Say we receive news about some great stroke of good luck. Instead of letting our hearts swell up with ego, we should remember that the situation is temporary. Studies conducted in the United States over the past few decades to follow up on lottery winners are very revealing. It turns out that winning a multimillion-dollar lottery often doesn't make the winners happier. In fact, it may bring them more suffering owing to family conflicts, lawsuits, and unwise spending. One study found that "instant millionaires are no happier than recent accident victims."[5]

When we die, the only things that we will take with us are the spiritual realizations that we attained and our karma, the habits that we sowed in our mental stream, while we were alive. Whether we enjoyed wealth, fame, beauty, long life, and sensual pleasure or endured poverty, obscurity, ugliness, premature death, and pain will be irrelevant. Shantideva writes:

> One person wakes up after joyful dreams lasting a hundred
> years.
> Another wakes up after joyful dreams lasting but a moment.
> Yet when both wake up, their joyful experiences will be gone.
> The same will be the case at the time of death, whether one has
> had a long life or a short one.[6]

The road to higher realization. If we are experienced meditators, contemplating impermanence could lead to the state of deepest awakening, which is the universal truth, the enlightened nature. Milarepa tells what happened to him:

> Frightened by death
> I ran to the mountains.
> Meditating on the uncertainties of death,
> I realized the deathless state, the innate nature.
> Now I have lost all fear of death.[7]

If we realize the certainty of death and the impermanent nature of mental objects, all our unhealthy mental habits related to them will be eased. Our mind will become more open instead of grasping, relaxed instead of tight, calm instead of restless, peaceful and harmonious instead of conflicted and chaotic, aware instead of ignorant, and wise instead of confused. Our whole life, which functions through the habits of our past deeds, will change from an unhealthy and unwholesome cycle to a healthy and wholesome one. Master Putowa advises:

Let us think about the uncertainty of the time of death.
A feeling of the certainty of death will arise in us.
Then we will have no difficulty staying away from evil deeds
And committing ourselves to virtuous deeds.[8]

If we understand impermanence and feel it in our hearts, no goal will be too high for us. All our spiritual efforts will be strong and will lead us to the real spiritual goal. Our negative emotions will depart. And our love and wisdom, the pure qualities of our true nature, will shine forth and illuminate everything.

We must therefore be thankful for impermanence! Thanks to its grace, life's miseries will end if we make the right effort, and blessings will have a chance to transform our existence into a precious human life.

LIFE IS CREATED BY KARMIC CAUSALITY

One of the strongest spurs to spiritual practice is knowing that we will reap the fruits of whatever we do and think. This is the principle of karma.[9]

Karma has become a widespread concept in the West, but many people seem to think that it refers to fate or some sort of punishment that they just have to accept. "Oh well, it must be my karma," people sometimes sigh when they face misfortune.

This is a misconception. First, karma isn't just bad. It refers to *all* intentional actions, both positive and negative, causing happiness as well as suffering.

Second, karma isn't fate. Nor is it a punishment imposed on us by some external agent. We create our own karma. Karma is the result of the choices that we make every moment of every day. As Walpola Rahula writes, "The theory of karma is the theory of cause and effect, of action and reaction; it is natural law, which has nothing to do with the idea of justice or reward and punishment. Every volitional action produces its effects or results."[10] Karmic consequences are the results of what we have implanted in our mindstream with our own actions and reactions.

The notion that we have to just sit and wait for the impact of our past deeds to hit us is a misunderstanding. By doing good things now—whether in thought, word, or act—we create positive karmas and can erase our past negative karmas and reshape our future. On the other hand, if we indulge in unvirtuous acts, we could destroy or minimize our past good deeds. How exciting to know that we are in the driver's seat!

When we cross the gates of death, our karma is all we take with us. Everything else that we enjoyed in this life we leave behind. As the Buddha says:

> If, when his time comes, even a king should die,
> His wealth and his friends and relatives will not follow him.
> Wherever people go, wherever they remain,
> Karma like a shadow will follow them.[11]

Our karma is the only thing that will count in determining our rebirth, for our next life is nothing but the effects of our karmic tendencies that materialize in our perception. The Buddha says:

> Because of one's virtuous deeds, one experiences happiness.
> Because of one's unvirtuous deeds, one experiences miseries.
> So these experiences are the karmic fruits
> Of one's virtuous and unvirtuous deeds.[12]

If we understand and believe in karma, we will want to seize the present moment in order to improve our many lives to come. Since our intentions precipitate our actions and words, we will want to work on our mental attitudes to ensure that they are peaceful and joyful. We will want to stop any negative thoughts before they roam too far. For if we really believe in karma, we will never dare indulge in anything negative, as we won't want to deliberately hurt ourselves. If we do engage in counterproductive activities, it is only because we do not understand and believe in karmic consequences.

Improving our own karma also gives us a chance to improve the world with which we are interlinked. We might think that our karma concerns us alone. In reality, however, there is collective karma as well as individual karma. Individual karma is responsible for our individual bodies and personal experiences. Collective karma is the karma we share with those with whom we are connected. The closer we are to others, the more karma we share with them. Collective karma is the reason many beings share similar experiences and perceptions. So by generating positive deeds, we can help elevate our shared karma. The more powerful we are as meditators, the more helpful we can be in this regard.

It is thus essential, for our own and others' sake, to understand how karma works in detail.

The Root of Karma Is Grasping at "Self"

Karma is volitional action that arises from mental intention. The mind therefore has the prominent role in karma and has the power to produce results (Skt. *phala*, "fruit") or maturation (Skt. *vipaka*).

Until we are able to perceive with a mind of enlightened omniscience, karma is a fact of life. We generate it the moment we perceive mental objects as truly existing entities. Perceiving an object as a real, truly existing entity separate from our minds is called seeing it with "self." As we discussed earlier, this way of perceiving is called grasping at "self." We grasp first at the "self" of our own body and mind as "I," and then at the "self" of other people or things as "this," "that," "table," "friend," and so on.

When we apprehend the *aggregates*, or illusory elements of the personality,* and identify them as "I," this is called grasping at the "self of personhood." Apprehending objects—the body, feelings, senses, and phenomena—as real or solid is called grasping at the "self of phenomena."[13] Grasping at "self" is the root of karma.

Everything that appears in life results from karmas created by the way the mind perceives and interacts with mental objects—concepts, feelings, sensations, and all phenomena that appear in our mental awareness. Material objects that we perceive are not necessarily *created* by our individual karma. But it is due to our karma that these objects become the source of effects in our lives, such as happiness or suffering.

How Does Karma Form?

Karma develops when our grasping mentality ignites a craving (Skt. *trishna*, "thirst") for the grasped object. *Craving* refers not only to a desire for or attraction to an object but also to the flip side of desire—dislike or aversion. Both liking and disliking further tighten the grip of our

---

* These elements are known in Sanskrit as the *skandhas*, literally "aggregates" or "heaps": (1) form (matter or corporeality), (2) feeling (sensation), (3) perception, (4) mental formations (including forces such as volitional impulses), and (5) consciousness. The presence of these five together produces the illusion of "self."

mental grasping, which, in turn, triggers confusion (or ignorance), greed, and aggression (or hatred), known as the three afflicting emotions or three poisons. We then form karmas through our three "doors," our mind, speech, and body.[14] They are likened to doors because we express everything we do through them—physically, verbally, and mentally. This progression of events originating from our own mental perception is responsible for all our physical, mental, and social ills. As Gampopa says, "The root of all faults and suffering is the [grasping at] 'self.'"[15] The *Abhidharmakosha* says:

> Intention is the karma of the mind.
> Physical and vocal [deeds] are the karmas created by that
>   intention.[16]

Although we cannot help generating karma, we can choose between happiness and suffering because we can choose whether to engage in positive or negative deeds, which give rise to good or bad karmas. Buddhist texts lay out the ten virtuous and ten unvirtuous deeds, or karmas, that we create with our body, speech, and mind.

The three physical unvirtuous deeds are (1) killing, (2) stealing, and (3) sexual misconduct. The four vocal unvirtuous deeds are (4) lying, (5) divisive speech, (6) harsh speech, and (7) senseless chattering. The three mental unvirtuous deeds are (8) covetousness, (9) harmful intent, and (10) wrong views.

The ten virtuous deeds involve abandoning the ten unvirtuous ones. They include the physical acts of (1) protecting others' lives, (2) offering charity, and (3) pursuing pure moral conduct; the vocal acts of (4) speaking the truth, (5) causing others to reconcile, (6) saying soothing words, and (7) pleasing others with meaningful words; and the mental deeds of training in (8) generosity, (9) loving-kindness, (10) and right views.[17]

The single most important factor in determining whether our karma is virtuous or not, however, is our motivation or intention. Je Tsongkhapa says, "Just as a magnet spontaneously causes a piece of iron to move, so too intention, a mental event, inspires and causes the mind to be attracted to virtuous, unvirtuous, or neutral thoughts."[18]

If our intentions are under the grip of the three poisons of hatred, greed, and confusion, then no matter what we do, say, or think, we will generate unvirtuous karma and reap unfortunate consequences. Nagarjuna says:

The karmas created by greed, hatred, and ignorance are
   unvirtuous. . . .
Unvirtuous karmas generate all the miseries
As well as births in the inferior realms.[19]

On the other hand, if we are motivated by loving-kindness, selfless generosity, and wisdom—the opposites of the three poisons—then whatever we do, say, or think, we will create virtuous karma and secure fortunate results. Nagarjuna says:

Karmas generated without greed, hatred, or ignorance
   are virtues. . . .
Virtuous karmas produce the births of the happy realms
And all the happiness of successive births.[20]

If our intentions are mixed, our karma will be too. And if our intentions are neutral, we form neutral karmas, which produce neither happy nor unhappy results and cause births in neither superior nor inferior realms.[21]

Some might wonder why we sometimes see good people suffering and bad people prospering. The answer has to do with when different karmas ripen. Each of us has produced infinite karmas during our countless lifetimes. Every deed that we put into expression leaves its imprint in the universal ground of our mindstream.[22] The universal ground (Skt. *alayavijnana;* Tib. *kunzhi, Kun gZhi*) is a neutral, inactive, unconscious state of the mind, the basis for samsaric experience. The various karmic patterns imprinted in our mind's universal ground become an infallible motivating force that will bear fruit in our future lives. These fruits—whether they are positive, negative, or neutral experiences—are the maturation of the karmic seeds that we have sown in the universal ground, in the natural course of actions and their consequences. The Buddha says:

The universal ground is like the ocean, and
The characteristics of karma are like the waves.[23]

Thus the unvirtuous person who now enjoys success is reaping the fruits of some good past deed, while the good person happens to be culling the fruits of some past negative deed. But when these particular karmas run their course, the imprints of other karmas stored in the universal ground of their minds will come to the fore.

In what order do karmas mature? The general rule is that the most serious, intense, powerful karmas will ripen first. They are followed by the karmas we created at the crucial time of death. Third to ripen are the karmas with which we have spent the longest time and are most familiar. After that, karmas will be experienced in chronological order, starting with the ones we created first.[24] So we will experience some karmic results in this lifetime, some in the next life, and others in any life thereafter.

Even though we have infinite karmas, we do not feel their presence, because most of them are latent or unripe. But when the time comes for a particular karma to mature, it will become active and we will experience the effects in our lives. Buddhist texts give the analogy of a person being bitten by a certain type of poisonous rat.[25] If the bite is received during the winter, the poison will not take effect. But in the spring, when the person hears the sound of thunder (which heralds the change of season), the poison will be activated—barring the application of an antidote. Thus, the results of our karmas will certainly mature when the time comes, if we do nothing to counteract them. Then, as the Buddha says:

Karmas [committed] by embodied beings
Will never be dissipated even for a hundred eons.
When the circumstances and the time have come,
Their fruit will certainly ripen.[26]

If we counteract and purify our negative karmas, however, we can alter, reduce, or completely wipe them out. One very strong positive karma may erase many negative ones. The more intense and pure our motivation, the more potent our positive karma. We should never underestimate the fruits that pure intentions produce. The Buddha says:

The performance of even a tiny meritorious action
Will, in the next world, bring great joy
And accomplish great purposes,
Like seeds producing an abundant harvest.[27]

The reverse is also true, however. One powerful bad deed can dilute or wipe out many good ones.

Although motivation is most crucial, the potency of a particular karma also depends on whether it is complete, that is, whether it has gone through the following four stages. Consider the act of charity. First we need something to give. That's known as the *object* (or *basis*) of that karma. Next we need the all-important motivation. Third comes the actual giving, known as the *execution*. When the gift is accepted, that's the *completion*. Any action that includes these four stages is a fully constituted karma, which will bear fruit with full consequences.

The chain of karmic causation fans out endlessly and limitlessly. A single karma can cause many results. A single result can also be the product of numerous karmic causes and conditions. While experiencing the result of one karma, we will be fertilizing many new karmic causations. Every aspect and every moment of our life is produced and maintained by a web of *dependent origination*, which means that all things in existence are interlinked, arising and functioning through depending on one another.

Going Beyond Karmic Causality

Right now, karma is a fact of life. The ultimate goal, however, is to transcend karma. This happens when we awaken to the fully enlightened state and no longer grasp at "self." When we liberate ourselves from karmic causation, we become free to help countless beings in countless ways, for we have the omniscience to know exactly what every individual being needs and the power to manifest in whatever forms and sounds are most helpful.

The way to transcend karma is through the path of positive karmas. The more good karmas we generate, the more peace and joy we reap. And the more peace and joy we have, the more we generate even greater peace and joy. This progressively loosens the tightness of grasping at "self." Eventually, we glimpse the true luminous nature of our mind. If we perfect this realization, we uproot the grasping at "self" and become fully awakened. In this way, the path of good karmas leads us, not to some state "out there," but right back to the ultimate peace and joy present in all of us, all the time.

Is Life an Illusion?

Some teachings say that life is an illusion; others, that it is created by karma. For realized masters who are beyond the control of karmic law, the world appears like a mirage, not as solid or real. For them, what is there to cause hatred or attachment, since everything appears to them as an illusion?

For most of us, however, life appears and functions as solid and real. As long as we function through karmic causation, we must follow its strict laws precisely. Phenomena seem to exist and continue because of our own karmic tendencies. It is like a dream: because we're asleep, we believe it to be real.

Buddhist teachings say that the world is the creation of the mind. But how, we may ask, can our mind create a solid mountain in front of us? No one is saying that the mind created the mountain. It is the *concept* of the mountain that the mind created. If there is no mind, then—whether the mountain is there or not—the idea, name, or thought of the mountain's existence or nonexistence would not even come up. So the idea and designation of "mountain" is a fabrication of the mind. The Buddha says in the *Karmashataka Sutra*:

> Various karmas
> Have created various worlds.[28]

The Buddha says in the *Mahakarunapundarika Sutra*:

> The world is produced and manifested by karma.
> Beings are created by karma.
> They are caused by karma.
> They are individualized by karma.[29]

The *Abhidharmakosha* says:

> The variety of the world is born from karma.[30]

Some might wonder: If life is like an illusion, what is the point of trying to improve our situation? After all, our lives are based on our reactions and the reflections of our mental habits, which in truth have no reality. Nevertheless we must try to improve our illusory life. Otherwise we will keep getting bruised by illusory events. Since we don't realize they're illusions, we suffer just as if they were real.

The Importance of Understanding Karma

When we truly understand karma, we will not willingly indulge in even the most trivial unwholesome deed. And instead of waiting for the impurities that we are carrying in our mindstream to surface and make a mess of our lives, we will start cleaning up now.

In my monastery in Tibet, before my time, there lived a great master known as Khenpo Damcho. As a child, he had had enormous difficulties remembering his lessons. One day, his teacher sat right in front of him and asked him to repeat a single sentence after him one hundred times, with the teacher and novice alternately saying it. When they finished, the teacher asked the novice to repeat the sentence all by himself—but he could not remember it. So the teacher had the child recite a short mantra of the Buddha of Purification one hundred thousand times. As soon as the child finished, his memory completely changed and his lessons started going very well. He grew up to become one of the most brilliant scholars of his time. Why? The recitation of the mantra created positive karmas that cleared the negative karmas that had been obstructing his memory.

We too can change our karma with the right effort. The key is to train our minds to go from bad karma to good karma to perfection, which is liberation from the karmic web of illusions altogether. Once we begin to taste the fruits of our efforts, our trust in karma and in our meditation will grow and become firmly established in the core of our mind.

Life Is Full of Miseries

All of us yearn for happiness. But as long as we are preoccupied primarily with samsara, the activities of the mundane world, we will never find it, for this world is ultimately dissatisfying and filled with pain. To truly understand this is to receive a jolt or inspiration that sets us going in the right direction, like a rocket launching toward its destination.

People sometimes accuse Buddhism of being pessimistic for saying that life is suffering. But as the world-renowned scholar Dr. Walpola Rahula points out, "Buddhism is neither pessimistic nor optimistic. If anything at all, it is realistic. It looks at things objectively."[31]

When we truly see the pointlessness of trying to extract happiness from a world that is unreal, we will stop blaming ourselves for failing to attain that idyllic life we pine for, and instead follow the path to nirvana, the cessation of suffering. This is the wisdom of the path and the goal.

It is important to face the pain of our mundane world for another reason, too. If we want to reach the goal, we need to start from where we are, not from where we imagine we should be. That is why the Buddha's very first sermon was on the "truth of suffering," the first of the four noble truths at the heart of his teachings.* And that is why we too should ex-

---

* The four noble truths are the truth of suffering, the truth of the cause of suffering, the truth of the cessation of suffering, and the truth of the path of cessation.

amine our own lives objectively. If our life has been mostly immersed in confusion and unhappiness, we should acknowledge that and know that that's our launching pad, the place from which we set out for the path.

Suffering: The First Noble Truth

Let us further consider the nature of the suffering we endure. We are all familiar with the suffering we see all around us, such as depression, heartbreak, grief, and illness. This universally recognized pain is known in Buddhism as the "suffering of suffering."

If we look more closely, we will see another suffering that tinges all our joy and satisfaction: the worry that all good things must end or change, as they inevitably must. Our children will grow up and leave; our loved ones will die; we will lose our looks and vigor. Not only do all good things end, but they may also revert into their opposites and become sources of pain. So our financial investments may wind up giving us ulcers; our cigarettes, lung cancer. This is called the "suffering produced by change."

At an even deeper level is "all-pervasive suffering." This suffering is inherent in the five aggregates (the components of human individual existence: form, feeling, perception, mental formations, and consciousness), in which nothing is truly satisfying. "All compounded things are subject to change and decay," according to a well-known saying of the Buddha. "Compounded things" are those that arise from causes and conditions. They are created by the causes of suffering, the unhealthy karmas of dualistic concepts and afflicting emotions, and are conditioned and hardwired to suffering.

In a way, all-pervasive suffering so thoroughly impregnates our world that we have become numb to it. Part of the reason that we do not realize it is that we have no awareness of any other spectrum of life and so have nothing with which to compare our own.

So let us consider our situation from the perspective of the gods. In my book *Enlightened Journey*,[32] I offer this simple illustration: Imagine that we have a rainbow-like "light-body" like those possessed by beings in the realm of the gods. It is a nonphysical body of light that enables us to fly through space whenever we move or travel. There is no darkness around us and no need for the light of sun or moon, as our own body-light illuminates the area around us. There is no physical pain and pressure, as our body is immaterial, intangible, and indestructible. We enjoy it for years.

Then one day this light-body suddenly changes into a body of flesh, bone, and blood wrapped in a bag of skin and filled with all kinds of filth. We cannot move except by measuring the ground with the two bone-poles of the legs, step by step. We cannot see anything if there is no light from other sources. We could easily be crushed, smashed flat, pierced through, broken into parts, or cut into pieces, never to heal or walk again, if we do not carefully watch, avoid, and negotiate everything all the time. This would be an intolerable form of suffering.

Of course, the gods' happiness cannot compare to the joy of the ultimate state. Since they too exist in samsara, the gods must inevitably suffer. When their good karmas have run their course, they die in terrible anguish because they sense the painful future that awaits them in their next incarnation in one of the lower realms.

We must remember that Buddhism teaches that all beings in their true nature possess buddha-nature. That enlightened nature is the goal to be realized through various kinds of training such as meditation. But for most of us, that buddha-nature has been covered by karmic turbulence rooted in grasping at "self" and aggravated by the afflicting emotions. As a result, we have fallen into the delusory nightmares of confusion and suffering, and we are stuck wandering endlessly in the six realms, like a potter's wheel spinning on and on. The Buddha says:

> Due to ignorance, craving, and becoming
> In the worlds of humans, gods, and the three inferior spheres* —
> The five realms†—beings revolve foolishly,
> Like the swirling of a potter's wheel. [33]

Like a bee buzzing around a closed room, we will keep taking rebirth in various realms depending on the predominant character of our habitual karma up until that point.

1. If our mind was soaked in *anger* and *hate* and we harmed others, then at death our perceptions will arise in the form of a *hellish* rebirth.

---

* The three inferior spheres are the realms of hell-beings, hungry ghosts, and animals.
† Some texts speak of five realms instead of six because they count the gods and demigods as one realm.

Burning and freezing, pain and sorrow, oppression and aggression—the characteristics of the hell realms—will become our life.

2. If we gave way to *miserliness*, then after death we will perceive ourselves to be born in impoverished surroundings, tormented by hunger, thirst, and destitution day and night—the characteristics of the realm of *hungry ghosts*.

3. If our mind and actions were permeated with *ignorance* and *foolishness*, we will perceive that we are born as animals and insects. We will suffer from confusion, torture, servitude, and being slaughtered—the experiences of the *animal* realm.

4. If we were ridden by *jealousy*, we will perceive our rebirth to be in the world of warring spirits, or *demigods*, where, propelled by fear and envy, we will be embroiled in relentless fighting and intrigue.

5. If *arrogance* marked our thoughts and deeds, then at death our perceptions will arise as those of *gods* in celestial realms, where we will waste time in pleasurable diversions until we die and plunge to inferior realms.

6. If our mind and actions were characterized by *desire* and *attachment*, we will be reborn as *human beings*.

Although the human realm offers the best chance for spiritual progress, even if we are reborn as humans, we must still face the big risk that we might veer off course and possibly fall into lower realms. There is no telling whether we might be overwhelmed by such jealousy or hatred that we do something terrible in response to the bumps and bruises of human life. Also, the human incarnation is filled with so much struggle that there is no guarantee that we will have the energy to do spiritual work.

Consider the struggles we face from birth to death. First we must go through birth and infancy. Then, if we're lucky, we spend our next twenty years or so in school. After that, we devote our prime to building a family and spend most of our waking hours earning a living. Before we know it, retirement strikes and old age pounces. Before long, it may become hard for us to walk, sleep, or take care of ourselves. All kinds of ailments fill our days and nights with worry, pain, and craving. We may exhaust all of what we earned and saved during our prime.

Finally, death will be waiting at our door, and our life will end. Our body will disappear from this earth forever as its elements merge with those of the earth. Eventually, even our name will disappear from this world's memory. Only our mind migrates—and round the realms we go, unless we attain liberation or are reborn in a pure land, where we can never regress spiritually and will one day attain liberation.

On top of all these struggles, human beings also endure four predicaments throughout their lives: the fear of having to accept what we don't want and losing what we love, and the misery of not getting what we want and encountering what we hate.

The only sane alternative is to free ourselves from this misery by going through the following three stages:

' Recognizing our negative attitudes, emotions, and behaviors
' Moving from negative to positive
' Transforming positive to perfection

Ambition can be a wonderful quality. The West in particular is blessed with an amazing "can do" mentality. We must harness it wisely to our advantage. If we are running a marathon and want to get to the goal so badly that we try to jump directly to the finish line without beginning from the starting block or running the entire course, we won't win the prize. So, while keeping our eye on the ultimate prize, buddhahood, we need to start with first things first: knowing where we are. We must recognize that our lives are mostly negative and painful. We must then generate the urge to free ourselves from the imprisonment of our own creation. We need to move from negative to positive by training in the path of peace, joy, love, and positive view. Finally, we must attain perfection and liberate ourselves from our bondage to the fear of suffering and craving for happiness, by awakening the enlightened nature of our mind.

Buddhism offers a way to free ourselves from the root of suffering through a step-by-step training that leads us right to the finish line, the fully enlightened state. Buddhism thus maintains an openness, a revolutionary view that avoids the extreme of either pessimism or optimism. Nagarjuna says:

> For whom openness* is possible,
> All is possible.[34]

---

* Openness, or emptiness (Skt. shunyata), is the absence of existence in all phenomena in their true nature.

The Great Potential of Life

Many people are by nature peaceful, joyful, and wise. Their mere presence can bring peace and happiness to those around them. There is no one among us who cannot awaken such qualities from our hearts, if only we could open up to this possibility and make an effort. Every one of us possesses an enlightened nature. Our true qualities are peaceful, joyful, and wise. Our negative emotions and unhealthy expressions are just afflictions—a kind of pollution—not our true nature.

That is why Buddhism teaches us that human life is amazingly precious, that we can use impermanence to improve our lives, that we can use the laws of karma to ensure a peaceful death and a joyful rebirth, and that all of us can become fully enlightened, as this is just realizing our own inherent nature. We can earn peace, joy, and enlightenment, not only for this life but also for lives to come; and not only for ourselves but also for countless others.

The choice is up to us. If we cultivate the awareness of peace and joy, have positive perception, and strengthen these good habits in our mindstream, this awareness will transform our life and mental character. Unhappy situations will have little effect on us, and the strength of peace and joy will prevail. But if we don't take advantage of our life right now, in the future we could fall into the misery of confusion, fear, and pain.

To attain the goal, we must pursue a spiritual path. It can be any path that generates awareness of peace and joy, loosens the grip of our mental grasping, purifies emotional afflictions, and refines our words and deeds. This is the only way to change our negative habits into meritorious karmas and realize inner wisdom.

Our path might entail any or all of the following practices:

- ' The meditation of watching our breath and remaining in awareness of our breathing from moment to moment, in order to bring tranquility to the mind and awaken the wisdom of insight
- ' Cultivating thoughts and feelings of love and compassion for others and putting the compassionate mind into practice by serving the needs of others without any selfish intention
- ' Devotion to a divine presence that opens our mind and heart boundlessly, breaking down all our mental sadness and emotional limitations
- ' The pure perception of seeing and transforming all mental objects into positive sources of benefit

- Contemplating with a mind of openness the awareness of subjective and objective oneness
- Trying to see and feel what is happening in life as unreal, like a dream fabricated and strengthened by our mental tendencies

The last item above is one of the distinctive aspects of the Tibetan tradition, used in dream yoga and other meditations. Training the mind to see life as a dream helps loosen the grip of grasping and craving for this life. Then, when death and afterdeath experiences come upon us, we will see them as insubstantial, like dreams, and will be able to handle them with greater ease.

People who are asleep sometimes experience a spontaneous awareness that they are dreaming and that what is happening is just a dream. There are ways to train ourselves to have such awareness, a technique known as lucid dreaming. We could learn to "awaken" to our nightmares and recognize them as dreams, thereby rendering the fear or threat impotent and changing it into something positive. In the same way, after dying, when we are in the bardo, if we could recognize our experiences in the bardo as illusions, all frightening experiences would become ineffective or even transform into positive effects.

It is said that if we are trained in dream yoga, we will be able to recognize the afterdeath states (the state of ultimate nature and the bardo, or transitional passage) for what they are—unreal and illusory. It is also said that if we are able to recognize our dreams as dreams seven times, then we will be able to recognize the bardo.[35] In fact, some even say that bardo experiences are easier to change than dream experiences.[36]

According to Tsele, our *thoughts* are the most important thing when we are training to encounter dreams and the bardo.[37] We should make a habit of reminding ourselves that everything we do or see is a dream or a bardo, an intermediate state. If we contemplate deeply on this truth, we will surely succeed in dealing with the bardo after death.

To succeed in our training for dying and afterdeath, the Mahayana (one of the great schools of Buddhism) tells us first to find a reliable, wise teacher. We must then learn the teachings that they give us. We should analyze thoroughly what we have learned and strengthen our experience of the wisdom of the teachings through meditation. We must open our mind and heart to all beings, feeling for them just as we would for our own mother who gave us life and took care of us when we were small and helpless, at her own expense. We should meet all beings with an attitude of equanimity, compassion, loving-kindness, and joy. We must train in the six perfections (Skt. *paramita*): generosity, moral conduct, patience, diligence, contemplation, and the wisdom of realizing the truth as it is. Jigme Lingpa aspires thus:

> In the "passage of life," may I obtain a spiritual life,
> Please the spiritual teachers,
> Rely on the wisdom of learning, analyzing, and
> meditation, and
> Train in renunciation, enlightened attitude, and the six
> perfections.[38]

Dzogchen teachings tell us that it is crucial to know what to do after death when we encounter the "luminous nature" and the "spontaneously present luminous visions" that arise in the passage of the ultimate nature. To know what to do, we must meditate intensively during this very lifetime. We must first understand the teachings about the true nature of our mind, and we must maintain and strengthen that understanding by meditating on it. Then, when we realize our true nature, we will perceive everything that appears before us—whatsoever arises in our awareness, whether in life or in death—as the presence and expression of that same true nature. So Longchen Rabjam advises:

> In the passage of life, this very present moment of life,
> We must ascertain the realization of the wisdom of our own
> intrinsic awareness, as the dharmakaya.
> Then maintain the natural meditative power in the state of
> self-clarity.
> Then all phenomena arise as the energy of spontaneously
> present wisdom.[39]

We have the amazing opportunity in this life, if we pursue the right spiritual path and reach high attainments, to realize our true nature, buddhahood.

We also have the amazing opportunity to transfer our consciousness to a pure land if we have devotion to buddhas and pure lands, such as the Buddha of Infinite Light and Blissful Pure Land. [40] By training in the meditation of phowa, the transference of consciousness,* we could take rebirth in the pure land directly, thereby dispensing with the need to go through the various stages of the passage of dying. Also, another meditator could perform phowa for us while we are alive, dying, or in the bardo, the transitional passage.

If we have not reached any high spiritual attainment, even if we have great accumulations of merits, we will have to undergo the experiences of the passage of dying—the subject of the next chapter.

---

* For details on phowa, see appendix B.

2

Dying
The Crucial Hour of Life

Death comes for all, and it is natural.
Death is the crossroads to our future.
We must handle it with the strength of meditation
  experiences.

I N THIS CHAPTER we will look at the process of dying and ways of
handling death when it comes, including the insights and experiences
of several delogs who experienced the passage of dying and returned to
tell about it.

With the onset of the "fatal sickness"—the illness, injury, or other
event that causes death—we enter the passage of dying. In the course of
the dying process, the elements that constitute the body, senses, and mental perceptions will all dissolve. For accomplished meditators, the passage of dying concludes with the arising of the ultimate nature. For
ordinary people, it ends with the cessation of breathing and falling into
the unconsciousness of death.

Although most people will undergo the experiences of the dying
process more or less as described below, fully accomplished meditators
may not need to do so. When we are about to die, with meditative power
we can unite our intrinsic awareness, which is the true nature of our
mind, with the union of the ultimate sphere and wisdom, which is buddhahood. If we can realize and maintain this union, we have attained buddhahood. If we cannot, then through the meditation of phowa we can
transfer our mind to a pure land of the Buddhas to take rebirth there.

The Process of Dying

As we enter the passage of dying, consciousness gradually disassociates from the physical body as the elements that make up the body start to dissolve. First the vital energies of our body become disarrayed, and then we go through the dissolution of our physical elements and mental perceptions.*

The Elements and Energies of the Human Body

To follow the process of dissolution that is described below, it will be helpful to understand a few details about how the human body is viewed according to esoteric Buddhism. Every particle of our body is made of four elements or a combination of them: earth, water, fire, and air. Earth makes up the solid parts of the body, such as bone and flesh. Water constitutes the fluids such as blood, lymph, and urine. Fire is associated with bodily heat and metabolism. Air is breath, as well as the movement of substances and energies in the body. There is also a fifth element, space, which contains the other four. Physically it corresponds to the hollows and orifices of our body.

In addition to the physical aspects of the human body, there is an inner, subtle system of energy. The three main components of this subtle system are airs, channels, and essences.

The *channels* (Tib. *tsa, rTsa;* Skt. *nadi*) are the network of countless arteries and veins that constitute the body's pathways of vital energy. The three principal ones are the central, right, and left channels.†

The *airs* (Tib. *lung, rLung;* Skt. *prana*) are the forces of vital energy that embody movement through the channels. They are sometimes referred to as winds because of their different activities. There are five main airs,

---

* Various texts use different terms and classifications for the dissolutions of the process of dying (and also for the ultimate nature), though their essential meaning is the same. Unless otherwise indicated in the endnotes, I have mainly followed *Dranpe Melong* (*Dran Pa'i Me Long,* abbreviated DM), by Tsele Natsog Rangtrol, an accomplished master of seventeenth-century Tibet.

† Some writers speak of the three channels as meditative channels that do not exist in physical form. A highly accomplished meditator's body is a body of light and divine form; however, an ordinary person's body is a body of flesh and blood. Similarly, for ordinary people, all the channels are ordinary channels, while for accomplished meditators they are subtle, light, or pure channels.

which represent five different activities of the life energy: (a) life-force (vitalizing) air, which causes breathing; (b) pervasive air, which makes possible the muscular movements of the body; (c) upward-moving air, which is involved in speech, voice, and swallowing; (d) fire-accompanying air, which is responsible for digestive heat; and (e) downward-moving air, which is responsible for urination, defecation, emission of semen, and menstruation.

The *essences* (Tib. *thigle*, *Thig Le*; Skt. *bindu*) are the white and red essential fluids that travel through the channels of the body by the force of air energy. They are described as drops or spheres of vital, creative energy that we receive from our parents at the time of conception. The white essence is the male energy that comes from our father, while the red essence is the female energy that comes from our mother. In the dying process, these two energies begin to converge at the heart. This convergence is the moment of death.

Many esoteric Buddhist teachings employ these physical attributes as crucial means of training. Tsele, for instance, instructs students to "train on the channels as the abode, air as the movement, and enlightened essence as the adornment."[1] Experiencing the boundless bliss of the essence, meditators move their minds and air energies together through the channels, disseminating the blissful essence. As a result, they admit their mind and air into the central channel and secure it there without wavering. The central channel thus becomes far more than a bodily artery. It becomes the meditative path and goal of attainment, the ultimate sphere, free from the limitations of concepts, designations, and dimensions.

The Dissolution of the Elements

When the dying process begins, the airs, or vital energies, first become disarrayed and begin to disperse, and we pass through two stages of dissolution. In the first stage, the *outer dissolution*, the forces of the four physical elements of the body dissolve, and then the sense faculties cease to function. In the second stage, the *inner dissolution*, mental concepts and emotions cease. Each of these stages is accompanied by certain inner experiences.

What is the nature of the inner experiences that occur in the passage of dying? It is important to understand that when we withdraw our outreaching perception inward and focus our total attention one-pointedly on the changes occurring in the body during the process of dying, our whole world becomes that particular happening. For us the whole universe becomes the changes taking place in our body at that moment. That is why changes occurring in even one drop of blood will feel earth-shattering. A single hair on our head might appear like a huge tree. Our habits of fear and other tendencies and emotions will arise in the form of various images of beings, worlds, sounds, and feelings. These are some of the experiences we will find described in the delog accounts later in this chapter.

First, the earth element of our body dissolves into the water element.[2] At this time we feel that we are losing energy or connection with our body's earth element, which has the qualities of solidity, strength, anchoring, and grounding. Our complexion pales as the energy drains from the body. We might feel that we are falling or sinking, and that the ground under us has given way. We can't get up or stand, we lose our balance, and we feel as if we are under the pressure of a heavy weight. That is why dying people often ask, "Please pull me up. I feel as if I'm sinking." We may feel cloudy and see mirage-like appearances.

Second, our body's water element dissolves into the fire element. At this point we might feel that we are losing water energy or connection with the water element, which is wet, fluid, and sustaining. We might feel very thirsty. Saliva drips. Tears fall and then dry up. That is why dying people often ask, "Please give me some water. I am thirsty." We may also feel suffocated and irritated, and witness visions of smoke-like appearances.

Third, our body's fire element dissolves into the air element. At this point we might feel that we are losing the fire energy or connection with the fire element, which is warm, maturing or ripening, and burning. If the dying person has been a devoted meditator and led a meritorious life of compassion and service to others, the dispersion of heat from the body starts at the lower end and moves up toward the heart. If the dying person has led a negative, destructive, and selfish life, the dispersion starts from the upper body and moves downward toward the heart. In both cases, however, the heat finally disperses from the heart.[3] The person can no longer see objects; everything looks full of red sparks against a dark background.

Fourth, our body's air element dissolves into consciousness. At this time we feel the loss of the air energy or connection with the air element, which is light and mobile. We struggle to breathe. Inhaling becomes shorter and exhaling becomes longer. Then the "outer breathing" ceases,[4] and the eyes roll up inside the head. At this time, people who have led negative lives may see illusions in the form of various fearful visions, while virtuous people may see joyous visions. We may also see lamplight-like appearances.

Fifth, consciousness (Tib. *nam-she, rNam Shes*; Skt. *vijnana*) dissolves into space (Tib. *namkha, Nam mKha'*; Skt. *akasha*). At this time, the cessation of "inner breathing" occurs.

Different sources give somewhat different timings for the cessation of the outer and inner breathings. They occur differently for different people because of their individual natures. Basically, when the breathing of the lungs stops after three long breaths, that is the cessation of outer breathing. Total separation of mind from the body (or unconsciousness, according to some texts) is the cessation of inner breathing.

If our death is due to our karmic debts, it will be very difficult for us to reverse it. If our death is due to some accidental circumstance, not a karmic debt, then we might still be revived by medical or spiritual means. But in normal cases, we cannot be brought back to life if we have gone beyond this fifth stage. There are, however, extraordinary circumstances, such as those who returned as delogs. They have gone much further than this point and yet have come back to life.

Three Inner Dissolutions

Now that our inner breathing has stopped[5] and our mind has lost its connection with our physical elements, the channels, the airs, and the essences of our gross body will also be dispersed. Our breathing merges into space. As the result, during that time, three stages of subtle, more subtle, and most subtle inner dissolutions or withdrawals will take place:

1. *Consciousness dissolves into "appearances."*[6] At this time, the white essence that we received from our father descends from the top of the head through the central channel. We see everything as "whitish." It is not luminous or bright white like daylight, but a whiteness like moonlight in a cloudless sky. All thoughts of anger and hatred will cease.

2. *"Appearances" dissolve into "increase."* At this time, from the bottom of the central channel at the navel, the red essence that we received from our mother ascends through the central channel. Everything looks "red-

dish,"[7] like the light of the setting sun in a cloudless sky. All thoughts of attachment and greed will cease. However, some people experience the reddish vision first and then the whitish vision.[8] According to Tsele, this is the best time to perform phowa.[9]

3. *"Increase" dissolves into "attainment."* At this time, our intrinsic awareness, moved by the force of air, becomes enveloped between the two parental essences, and everything becomes "blackness," like the cloudless sky of a dark autumn night. Here our thoughts of confusion will cease.

Now air, essence, and mind gather at the heart level. This is called the dissolving of space into luminosity. The arising of the "luminosity of the basis" will take place next, heralding the entry into the next passage, the state of ultimate nature, which is discussed in the next chapter.

Following the dissolving of space into luminosity, ordinary people will fall into unconsciousness, but there are different interpretations about what happens when the luminosity of the basis arises. According to Karma Lingpa, between the cessation of outer and inner breathing, if we are advanced meditators, we will see the luminosity of the ultimate nature when the air of our body is admitted into the central channel.[10] Ordinary people become unconscious instead. Jigme Lingpa writes that after air dissolves into consciousness, we will become unconscious and inner breathing will stop.[11] Then the luminous nature will arise. Jigme Lingpa also writes:

> When the blackness arises, you will fall unconscious in the
> universal ground.
> Then the eight life forces* arise again and unconsciousness will
> fade away.
> At that time, the original brightness of the primordial state will
> arise.
> It is clear and unceasing, like the autumn sky.
> You remain in emptiness and clarity, free from obscurations and
> coverings.[12]

Kyabje Dudjom Rinpoche says that when air dissolves into consciousness, "mind falls into a prolonged state of unconsciousness. But for those who are accomplished masters or experienced meditators, the conscious-

---

* This refers to eight aspects of the life-force air, one of the five airs.

ness will, after two minutes or so, dissolve into space, and space will dissolve into luminosity."[13]

It is very important to know that not all dying people have the same experiences or have them in the same sequence. Tsele writes that explanations of dissolution "are merely general indications of how people go through the experiences. But there is no certainty [that all will have similar experiences]. Each person possesses a different kind of physical channel, air, and essence, and they will be facing different kinds of sicknesses, negative forces, or accidents [when they die]. So the dissolutions could happen to people in different sequences, or they could occur simultaneously."[14]

How long do the experiences last? Tsele writes that the duration of the outer and inner dissolutions are different.[15] For most people, each experience might last a moment, and the three inner dissolutions especially will not last more than a moment.

What Should We Do When Dying?

How should ordinary people handle these dissolution stages? First, we must try to realize that we are in the process of dying. We should try to take the experiences of dissolution as peacefully as possible, without panicking. We should try to remember that all the transitional appearances and experiences are reflections of our own mind and emotions, like dreams. We should not be attached to them, get irritated by them, or be afraid of them. Rather, we should see and feel everything as the path of our spiritual journey. Anchoring ourselves in calmness, we should peacefully let any situation come and go.

We should remember to employ any spiritual approach or experience with which we have been acquainted in our lifetime. The spiritual approaches with which we are familiar will be more effective and easier for us to rely on.

We should remember our source of blessings, such as buddhas, masters, positive mental objects, teachings, and meditation experiences, and use those experiences and memories as our spiritual supports. Try to remember your own spiritual practices and all your spiritual experiences and energies, and unite with them. To unite with them means to feel that the buddhas, teachers, and deities are present with you all the time and that they are protecting and guiding you. From them, let the light of peace, openness, strength, and joy come to you, fill you, and transform your body into a rainbow-like light-body emitting blessings of peace, joy, and strength. Then try to relax in that spiritual body, again and again, throughout the dying process.

We must repeatedly remind ourselves: "I must stay with my spiritual experience." Such a message makes a great impact and in fact helps us remember the experiences even on the difficult journey of dying. If we stay with our experience, our journey along the road of dying will be smoother and will lead us to a pure land or to a rebirth that is peaceful, joyful, and healthy.

If we experienced the true nature of the mind while we were alive, we must try to remember to remain in the awareness of that nature. Whatever occurs, try to see all happenings as merely the expression of that nature, instead of running after and grasping at thoughts and experiences with attachment or hatred.

If we have been introduced to and trained in the ultimate nature of the mind and its luminous visions, then this is the time to remain in that experience. This is also the time for meditators to remind us of the experiences that we are going through.[16] Longchen Rabjam advises:

> In the process of dying, the physical elements will be
> dissolved.
> You will witness wobbling, fuzzy, and blurry illusions.
> Then earth, water, fire, air, and space [of your body] will be
> dissolved.
> The functioning of your sense faculties will cease.
> At that time, you should remind yourself:
> "Now I am dying, but there is no need to worry."
> Then just look at: "What is death?" "Who is dying?" "Where does
> dying exist?"
> Dying is a mere [sign of] returning your four borrowed inanimate
> elements [to themselves].
> The intrinsic awareness [of your mind] has no birth or death.
> In the state of original purity, dying is [the union of] emptiness
> and intrinsic awareness, the natural mode of the Ultimate Body
> [dharmakaya].
> Just look at: "What is death?" "Who is dying?" "Where does dying
> exist?"
> As dying exists nowhere, it is absolutely unreal.
> Generate courage and confidence in this [understanding].[17]

Jigme Lingpa writes that in the process of dying, the best thing to do is relax naturally in the ultimate nature.[18] The next best thing is to transfer your consciousness to a pure land. At a minimum, seek the refuge of the Three Jewels: the Buddha, the embodiment of enlightenment; the Dharma, the truth he expounded; and the Sangha, the community of followers of the Dharma. Pray to your spiritual teacher, and unite your mind with his or her enlightened mind.

Guru Rinpoche advises us to practice, to pray not to get attached to anything at the time of death, to remember the teachings, and to meditate on merging the ultimate nature of our minds with the ultimate sphere:

When the "passage of dying" is dawning upon me,
Abandoning attachment to and grasping at anything,
I will focus on the clear instructions without wavering,
And transfer my unborn intrinsic awareness [true nature of the
mind] to the state of the ultimate sphere.[19]

These instructions of great masters on dying and death are crucial points to remember and apply, not just during the passage of dying but also during all of life's four transitional passages, including this current life.

DELOG ACCOUNTS OF THE EXPERIENCE OF DYING

To illustrate what happens when we cross the gates of death, I summarize eleven delog accounts. These stories are the experiences of particular individuals, of course. Remember that people will have different kinds of dying experiences because of variations in their mental and physical nature, karmic causes, cultural influences, habitual tendencies, and circumstances of death.

As we have noted, delogs are very devout people, and many are accomplished masters. They came back to life because they had uncompleted services to perform. Some parts of their experiences may be different from what you or I will encounter at death, yet there could be many similarities for people with comparable mental, emotional, or cultural backgrounds.

In these accounts, we focus on the passage of dying. We will return to most of these delogs in chapters 3 and 5, to see how their afterdeath experiences continued into the passage of ultimate nature and the bardo.

Dissolving Energies: The Experience of Karma Wangdzin

Karma Wangdzin was dead for seven days.[20] Born in Lhotrag, Southern Tibet, she was educated and pious. Her husband was Depa'i Drung, the Chief of Oktra. She visited Traphu Hermitage to study the Dharma with Lama Norbu Trashi, and she saw pure visions of both White Tara and Guru Rinpoche.

Karma had undertaken a year's retreat for prayer and meditation. One day, she suddenly fell seriously ill, lost her appetite, and hardly recognized her friends. The next day, a friend of hers told her, weeping, "Elder sister, your eyes are sunken and the bridge of your nose is crooked [signs of death]. Wouldn't it be best if I summoned your husband, the Chief?"

Karma thought to herself, "If I cannot bear even a little sickness, what point is there in my being a devout person?" To her friend she said, "Wait till tomorrow." But that very afternoon, she started to feel cold. She experienced a great thirst, but when she tried to swallow water, it just came out of her nose.

The signs that the energies of her physical elements were dissolving started to appear to her. She kept feeling that her body was sinking, even though her friends kept pulling her up. That was the sign that the energies of flesh were dissolving into the earth element. Her mouth and nose dried up from dehydration, but despite severe thirst she couldn't drink. That was the sign of the energy of blood dissolving into the water element. She was shivering with cold, even though she was covered with warm blankets. That was the sign of the heat of her body dissolving into the fire element. She was struggling to breathe, and it was hard to inhale or retain her breath. That was the sign of her breath dissolving into the air element.

As the light started to fade from her vision, she couldn't see or recognize those around her. As her hearing began to fade, she couldn't hear what friends were trying to tell her. As she lost control of her nervous system, she couldn't utter a word. She was close to losing touch with this world and was ready to see the world she would be going to.

Yet through all this, Karma's mind was lucid, like a fish in clear water. She distinctly remembered all her loved ones but realized there was nothing they could do for one another anymore. For her, the time had come to go it alone. Karma was not confident that she had achieved any reliable Dharma experience. Memories of all the bad things she had ever done in life kept flashing through her mind, and this caused her heart to weep.

Next came a loud crackling noise. With that her breathing totally stopped. She was immersed in complete darkness, as if a candle had suddenly been snuffed out. All her mental energy withdrew to her heart, and she fell into unconsciousness. Karma remained unconscious for a while, and was not aware of grasping at either the pain of death or the eagerness to live.

Make Merits for Me: The Experience of Lingza Chokyi

Lingza Chokyi was born in Kham, Eastern Tibet.[21] She had been seriously ill for sixteen days, and neither religious rites nor medications could help her. She thought, "I might be dying now. When I was young, I wanted to become a nun, but my family prevented me from leaving home. I received some Dharma teachings, but I have very little experience, as my meditation has been minimal. I haven't done any charitable giving either. Alas, I wasted my whole precious human life, which is so rare to attain and so full of potential. Now I am leaving the human world of great potential empty-handed. It is too late to feel regret."

Then she thought, "In the past, my family has been involved in killing twenty to thirty yaks and sheep every year." This worried Chokyi because taking the life of any living being is one of the ten major misdeeds in Buddhism, creating negative karmas that become the cause of suffering and hellish rebirth for the perpetrator. She further worried, "Now they will not sponsor any Dharma services for me. That means I will have to face the consequences of only evil deeds, with no benefit of any virtuous deeds or merits. My husband and children love material possessions. They are tight-fisted and have very little faith. But despite all this, I must ask them what Dharma services they might sponsor for me."

Chokyi called her family to her side and told her husband, "I won't survive this sickness. Now I have my last few words to tell you. I haven't accumulated any merits in my life. Instead, I committed many evil deeds here and there. Please spend one-third of the family property to make merits for me." In the Tibetan Buddhist tradition, survivors of a deceased person spend a large portion of the family's property to sponsor ceremonies, prayers, meditations, feeding of the poor, ransoming life (for example, by buying and freeing domestic animals, birds, or fish), building religious monuments, or making offerings to monks and nuns. They believe that such deeds will create merits, or positive karma, which in turn becomes the source of a peaceful and joyful journey and rebirth for the deceased.

"Half my jewelry should go to our daughter," she continued, "and the other half should be spent on making merits. Whatever services you sponsor for me, please make sure they are done in a pure Dharma way. All of you must do some Dharma practice if you can. Otherwise, regret will torment you when you die. At least let my two sons do some Dharma practice. Please, don't let my three children suffer at the hands of another woman by remarrying. Promise me these things!"

At this her husband said, "If we spend one-third of the property for you, what will we eat? Our daughter will need your jewelry for herself. After your death, I will have to marry again in order to keep up the household. The children are too young to stand on their own feet. I will spend something for you, but I can't promise how much."

Chokyi thought, "Now he won't sponsor any big Dharma service for me. Why didn't I make some merits myself, when I had the chance and the ability? He is going to remarry, and the children will suffer. How pitiful they are!"

This exchange made Chokyi sadder. The sadness brought a feeling of dizziness. Next she felt she was being pulled down into the earth, and she began to go through a number of frightening experiences. She felt that she was being pushed down by the force of many people, wobbling here and there in a big space, and shivering with freezing cold. Then she suffered from the sense that her body was being burned at a cremation ground, seeing the sparks of fire and hearing the roar of flames. When that feeling subsided, she was blown away by a strong storm. Then she felt her body being cut into pieces by many people with various tools. All these apprehensions were merely the result of the dissolving of the elements of her body.

After all these feelings, she experienced the visions of redness, whiteness, and darkness. This was followed by a feeling of absence of recollection or consciousness, which was a steady state of blissfulness. Later, after reviving, she could not remember how long that experience had lasted.

Have the Lords of Death Come to Fetch Me?: The Experience of Denma Sangye Seng-ge

Sangye was born near Chabdo in Kham province of Eastern Tibet.[22] He studied with many teachers, including the fourteenth Karmapa (1798–1868).

One day, at the age of fifty-five, Sangye was struck by serious pain in his heart as if he had been hit by a bullet. He started to have amazing hallucinations. He lost his appetite and sometimes felt as if his body was about to expel all his organs. He experienced the nerves of his limbs being pulled toward his heart.

Sangye feared that death was imminent. But he could do nothing to keep himself alive. He became sensitive to everything, so that whatever happened to him caused great anxiety. His breath was becoming shorter and shorter. He was suffering and felt as restless as a bird being squeezed in a person's fist or a fish being thrown onto dry land. The lights from his eyes rapidly dimmed. Then suddenly all appearances became darkness.

Sangye went through a series of painful experiences as the energies of the elements of his body started to dissolve. Sometimes he felt a severe thirst, as if his insides were being burned in a flame, and he craved a drop of water. At other times he felt he was being crushed under a heavy object like a mountain. In the next instant he would feel he was being violently blown about like a feather in a storm. Now and then, he would feel that the sun and moon were falling to earth. He heard loud noises like thousands of simultaneous thunderclaps and repeatedly witnessed thousands of lightning flashes striking the earth simultaneously. Then he felt that an old house, which in fact was his body, was breaking down. But no sooner would those visions and feelings arise before him than they would vanish like a mirage.

Then Sangye witnessed various sparks of light like fireflies in a dark sky. Sometimes they were clearly apparent and at other times they were not.

Sangye recognized, "These appearances must be the experience of the energies of my physical elements dissolving in the process of death." But then, as human nature would have it, he grew frightened. Many questions started to rush in: "Am I experiencing the dissolution of the energies of the four elements of my body? As in my numerous past lives, has the momentous time of death arrived for me again? Have the Lords of Death come to fetch me? Will I not be able to live any longer?"

He felt trapped in a very dark place, which was in fact his own body, as it had now lost all access to light. There he saw nine openings that would provide him a way out of that dark place—mouth, two ears, two eyes, two nostrils, anus, and genitals. He looked through the opening that led straight upward and shouted the syllable HIK three times as he had been taught in the practice of phowa. That got him out through the tenth opening—the cranial aperture at the top of his head.

According to Buddhism, at the time of death the mind will experience exiting through one of these ten "doors" or openings of the body (anus, genitals, mouth, two nostrils, two ears, two eyes, and the cranial aperture). If your mind exits through the doors of your upper body, this will help you to take rebirth in a higher realm. Meditators are taught to block the lower nine doors, especially the lowest ones, with the visualized images of sacred HUM syllables. They then move straight up through the central channel with the force of meditative energy and exit through the cranial aperture, the opening at the upper end of the central channel, in the top of the head.

Cloudless Sky–Like Luminosity: The Experience of Dagpo Trashi Namgyal

Dagpo Trashi Namgyal came from Central Tibet. He was dead for five days.[23] He had been having pain in his head and upper body. Realizing death could be approaching, he wanted teachings on the bardo.

As the physical elements of his body gradually started to dissolve, his outward-looking perceptions began to turn inward. He saw visions of a five-colored light. This was not an external form of light; he was observing with his mind's eyes a mass of light within himself.

First he lost his perception of the five sense objects: form, sound, smell, taste, and texture. As his vision became blurred, he was unable to recognize people whom he knew. His ears couldn't hear sounds. His nose couldn't smell odors. His tongue couldn't taste anything. His body could not feel any touch.

The earth element of his body dissolved into water, and his body became heavy. As the water element dissolved into fire, his mouth and eyes felt dry, and he became thirsty. It seemed as if his arteries had been rolled up like a ball of thread. Then the fire element dissolved into air, and his body heat was dissipated by wind.

Since the air element is the essence of intrinsic awareness, when his outer breathing ceased, his consciousness dissolved into the nature of luminosity. When his outer breathing merged with his inner breathing, the first of three experiences arose.

First he experienced the "appearances." As the inner sign, his senses became clear. Outer appearances became whitish, like moonlight. His senses became free from momentary changes, and he felt vivid and clear.

Then "appearance" merged into "increase." As the inner sign, he saw firefly-like sparks. As the outer sign, he saw a reddish glow like that of the rising sun.

Then "increase" merged into "attainment." For a few moments, his senses remained clear. He saw flames and lamp-like lights. His ignorance about the nature of reality ceased. Then there arose the cloudless sky–like luminosity. In other words, he began to experience the luminous absorption, which is very clear like the cloudless autumn sky, a state with no gross perception or duality of subject (the senses) and object (the sense objects).

Perceptions of Dying: The Experience of Samten Chotso

At the age of nineteen, Samten Chotso of Kham in Eastern Tibet had a delog experience for seven days.[24] Suddenly the elements of her body became stirred up, and she prepared to die. Delusions came without any break. She realized that she was actually dying, and she started to have the following delusory perceptions.

First her body's physical elements and senses began to dissolve: as the arteries of her heart stopped functioning, she felt as if a mountain had been turned upside down. Then the vessels in her eyes stopped functioning, and she felt as if the sun and moon had fallen from the sky. Then the capillaries of her tongue stopped functioning, and she felt that space was illumined by lightning. Then the capillaries of her ears stopped functioning, and she heard thousands of thunderclaps roaring simultaneously.

Unique Among Delogs: The Experience of Dawa Drolma

Dawa Drolma (1910–1941) was born in Washul Thromtha, in the province of Kham, Eastern Tibet. One her sons was the late Chagdud Rinpoche (1930–2002), who lived and taught in America and Brazil for decades. Dawa Drolma is unique among delogs because she knew she was going to have a delog experience beforehand.[25] She thus prepared herself and those around her. Her delog journey lasted for five days.

In 1924, at the age of fifteen or sixteen, Dawa Drolma kept having experiences of deep meditative absorption. One day she beheld White Tara in person and received this prophetic advice: "Soon you will fall ill and die. However, if you follow certain instructions, after five days you will revive as a delog and benefit many beings." Dawa's teacher, Chogtul Rinpoche, reluctantly consented to her wish to prepare for and undergo such an extreme experience. He gave her his blessing and reminded her, "Remain in the uncontrived nature of the mind, as it is, without falling into delusions. Maintain pure perception of and devotion to your spiritual teachers and your guardian deities. Maintain love and compassion for all your mother-beings."

Then Dawa Drolma became extremely sick. She asked Chogtrul Rinpoche and others who were there to observe the following conditions: "Remove all food and water from my room. After my death, my body should be washed with blessed saffron water in the presence of a girl named Drolma. To symbolize my buddha family,* my head should be wrapped in a blue turban. The door of my house should be padlocked. Then wrap the lock with a blue cloth and seal it with the design of a scorpion. A person dressed in blue should sit outside to guard the house. Then, for five days, while I am dead, no one should enter my room or make any noise around the house. When I return, I will need a dress of blue cloth that is not made of animal skin. I will need blessed water to wash my mouth." She also asked the lamas to keep performing various ceremonies, such as the feast offering of Yumka (a female buddha)[26] and the Long-Life Sisters,† and prayers to Guru Rinpoche.

She and her teachers performed the feast ceremony of Yumka for the twenty-fifth day of the Tibetan lunar calendar. Her teachers reminded her once more: "Let your mind calm down and be without distractions from wild thoughts. Let your mind unite with its own ultimate nature, as mind naturally does at the time of death."

When the time came, Dawa Drolma relaxed her mind in its natural state. She experienced it as a totally clear and immaculate state of spaciousness and great bliss. All conceptualizing had subsided. She wasn't

---

* See the glossary for a full definition of the five buddha families.
† The Five Long-Life Sisters are local land deities (spirits) of Tibet. They were converted to Buddhism in the presence of Guru Rinpoche, who made them Dharma protectors. Later they also became the spiritual support of Milarepa, one of the greatest adepts of Tibet.

slumbering in the universal ground, where there is no discursive thought. She wasn't caught in the sensual webs of bliss, clarity, or no-thoughts. She wasn't floating freely through delusions either. Rather, she was in the unceasing space of the natural mind, as it is. So she was in an altered state of consciousness, though she could hear all the sounds and voices around her.

On the morning of the twenty-sixth day, she vividly beheld the presence of her guardian deity, White Tara, before her, within an amazing sphere of light.

Then she saw that from the pure land of Guru Rinpoche, a rainbow light of five parallel beams entered her room. In the midst of these lights, four *dakinis*, in the form of young women with beautiful dresses and ornaments, appeared as Dawa's escorts. They placed her in a palanquin covered with colorful silk cloths. Dawa Drolma and the four dakinis chanted the Vajra Seven-Line Prayer and the mantra of Guru Rinpoche in unison, continuously with great devotion. She was seeing all these appearances in her visions.

Mind Traveling without Hindrance: The Experience of Gyalwa Yungtrung

Gyalwa Yungtrung was from Kham in Eastern Tibet and was a follower of Bon, the indigenous religion of Tibet.[27] When he was forty-nine, his mother died. He invited many lamas to perform ceremonies for forty-nine days, as it is believed that almost no one remains in the bardo for more than seven weeks. He spent all the wealth of the properties he possessed to sponsor the ceremonies. The memories of her love and kindness and his sadness over her death never left him, day and night. Then, one day, when he watched the nature of his mind, he saw that it is uncreated from the origin and is present spontaneously.

Another day he felt, "The world and the body are all emptiness. My mind can travel everywhere without hindrances. I must connect with the consciousness of my mother wherever she has gone." He suddenly felt that he was out of his body.

Gyalwa went through many more experiences, as we will read in chapter 5 on the bardo experiences of delogs. At this stage he doesn't write about whether he experienced the dissolution of the elements. His account of dying simply shows once again that individuals experience this passage in different ways.

Intrinsic Awareness: The Experience of Tsophu Dorlo

Dorlo was an accomplished master. His real name was Dorje Duddul of Khrozur, but he was known popularly as Tsophu Dorlo. He had a delog experience in a hermitage called Pema Sheltrag of Nyag-rong in Eastern Tibet.[28]

It happened in 1923, when sixty-one-year-old Dorlo suddenly got sick, and everyone lost hope of his recovery. To ease the sadness of his disciples, he gave them teachings and reassured them that he would return in his next incarnation. In a pure vision his principal lama, Zhingkyong Rinpoche, blessed him and told him, "This is not the time for you to enter the pure land. You must go and serve the beings in the hell realms." The lama gave him a huge handheld prayer wheel to take with him.

On the evening of the fourth day, the signs of his death began to appear. Again and again Dorlo kept refreshing his mind about the teachings and instruction that he had received from his teachers. He especially kept his mind united with the wisdom-mind of his lama and remained in the state of oneness without wavering. For a long time, he remained in the intrinsic awareness, the pure nature of his mind. It is the uncontrived presence and unwavering state of the union of clarity and emptiness of the mind.

Soon the dissolution of the elements of his body began. As the sign of flesh dissolving into earth, Dorlo felt that his body was falling and sinking into the ground. As blood dissolved into water, he lost the energies of his body. His nose and mouth started dripping, and his tongue dried up. As heat dissolved into the fire element, his body lost heat. The clarity of his mind turned on and off. His eyes started to roll upward. He couldn't recognize people. As his breath dissolved into the air element, his breathing became heavy, and his limbs started to waver. His mind felt suffocated, and he saw fuzzy, mirage-like visions.

After the dissolution of the gross elements, he started to experience the dissolution of his subtle energies. As the essence of fire, the red essence moved upward, the "appearances" dissolved into "increase," and everything became reddish. As the essence of water, the white essence moved downward, and "increase" dissolved into "attainment." Everything became whitish. Then, as the most subtle life-force ceased, "attainment" dissolved into "luminosity." Everything became blackness.

Her Wisdom-Mind Became Clear: The Experience of Shugseb Jetsun Lochen

Shugseb Jetsun Lochen (1865–1953), also known as Jetsun Rigdzin Chonyi Zangmo, was one of the greatest female teachers of twentieth-century Tibet.[29] She was born in India but studied in Tibet and then lived for the last many years of her life at Shugseb near Kangri Thökar, the hermitage of Longchen Rabjam, a great fourteenth-century master of Dzogchen.

Jetsun experienced the delog state for many days while observing a meditation retreat in seclusion at Zangyak Trag in Drigung Valley of Central Tibet. She attained amazing meditative realizations and experiences. She was able to physically pass through walls without hindrance, and many times she also became invisible to her companions. Occasionally, she was able to reach places by mere thinking. She had visions of deities as well as all kinds of other beings who were invisible to others.

One day Jetsun's life-force energy entered her central channel. As a result, uttering all sorts of sounds, leaping and dancing, she kept running in and out of her meditation cell. Then, suddenly, she collapsed on the ground like a piece of rock falling down and remained motionless.

Thinking that she was dead, her friends wept and began to discuss her funeral arrangements. But her mother noticed that her face still maintained the complexion of a living person, so she insisted that her daughter's companions check her carefully. They detected a little heat, like the temperature of a bird, at her heart. Because of the unusual power of her life in general, her friends concluded that she might not have departed for good. So they started to perform a feast offering ceremony.

For Jetsun herself, although her body could not move, her wisdom-mind became many times clearer than ever. She was able to hear distinctly all the conversations of her friends and other people around her.

The Dark Demon Departs: The Experience of Tagla Konchog Gyaltsen

Tagla Konchog Gyaltsen (1856–1946) was born in Ma Valley, among the Akyong Ponmotsang tribal group of Golok in Eastern Tibet. He became a well-known master. He had a delog experience for many days at the age of eighty-eight.[30]

In 1932, Tagla was staying in the spectacularly beautiful Ma Valley under the ever-watchful guard of the great sacred mountain range Amnye Machen. One day, Tagla was stricken by a serious sickness that rendered him neither dead nor alive. In the sky before him, he suddenly had visions of clouds of colorful light. In the midst of them, he beheld Guru Rinpoche surrounded by many enlightened ones in peaceful and wrathful forms and by great masters of the teaching lineage. He heard the Buddha of Compassion saying to him, "Son, don't be distracted. Concentrate upward here. With devotion sing the Six-Syllable Mantra, OM MANI PADME HUNG. You are about to witness the experiences of the transitional passage [bardo]."

Soon, from the south, riding on white clouds, the White Guardian Deity with white complexion and youthful appearance came floating toward Tagla. He was attired in white silk robes, and his hair had been tied up in a topknot. He was carrying a white silk pouch over his shoulder, and suspended from his waist was a single die made of conch (that is, one of a pair of dice, a Tibetan divination tool).

Then, riding a cyclone, the angry Dark Demon of black complexion also arrived. He was attired in a dark gown and had his hair loose and flowing. He carried a black pouch over his shoulder, and a black die made of coal was suspended from his waist.

The White Guardian Deity said to Tagla, "I am the White Guardian Deity. I take care of virtuous beings. I have come from the court of the Dharma King of the Lords of the Dead to fetch you. What confidence do you have to deal with the bardo, the transitional passage? I keep the accounts of the virtuous deeds that people have accumulated."

Full of confidence, Tagla narrated all his meditative experiences, his realizations, the numbers of prayers he had recited, and the kinds of services he had performed for others. He expressed his great joy in entering the journey of the bardo and meeting the Dharma King. Then Tagla invoked his refuges, the buddhas and lamas, for the support of their blessings. At this, all the refuges appeared before him, filling the sky. They all joined Tagla in singing the holy Six-Syllable Mantra with most enchanting voices and melody. The sound filled the whole atmosphere.

After giving teachings on the transitional passage, Tagla's principal teacher, Pema Dechen Zangpo, said, "Now please go. Your own innate virtuous nature is appearing as the White Guardian Deity, who will lead you." Tagla saw a beam of rainbow-like light that extended toward the west as the path that leads to the Blissful Pure Land of the Buddha of In-finite Light. But his principal lama added, "The time of your going to the Blissful Pure Land has not yet arrived."

Outraged, Dark Demon approached Tagla. He dismissed Tagla's vir-tuous deeds as if they were impure and accused him of committing nu-merous evil deeds. He tried to intimidate Tagla by describing the terrifying bardo journey that he was facing. Then the actual messengers of the court of the Dharma King appeared. They included the Ox-Headed Awa, the Snake-Headed Harmful One, and the Monkey-Faced Coward.

At first Tagla was scared, but soon he regained his confidence and said, "Dark Demon! Listen to me! In order to defend the honor of virtu-ous deeds, I must refute your accusations." Listing all the virtuous deeds that he had accumulated while he was alive, Tagla concluded, "I have no reason to be intimidated. You, Dark Demon, shut your mouth!" With that, the Dark Demon vanished in a storm.

Then, in a flash, Tagla saw his real body lying dead in his bed at home, surrounded by friends in mourning. Thinking, "Now there will be no way of regaining my life," Tagla's heart sank in sadness. At this, the White Guardian Deity approached and said, "You will be dead only for a while. Soon you will return to life." Then, accompanied by the White Guardian Deity, Tagla set out on his transitional journey.

Don't Panic!: The Experience of Changchub Seng-ge

Changchub was born at a place called Lho Gyalwa.[31] His father was from Kham, and Tagla refers to him as Nyagtrug, so he is probably from the Nyag-rung area of Kham, Eastern Tibet.

Changchub was sick. He could barely get out of bed to get a drink of water. Suddenly he felt that he was floating in the sky. His house was col-lapsing. The root of every hair of his body was piercing him like a sharp instrument. Mountains and houses seemed to be collapsing upon him. The current of a huge river was carrying him away. He was burning in a mountain of flames. A forceful storm was blowing him away. Thousands of suns were rising and burning him. He was hearing thunderous threat-ening shouts. It was as if each experience lasted for thousands of years. They were all signs of the elements of his body dissolving and the ceas-ing of his inner breathing. When his inner breathing had ceased, five lights arose. Suddenly Changchub had a vision of clarity, like the sun rising at midnight. Awareness was so clear that it was like a lamp, but it was unstable, like a lamp flickering in a storm. He was also able to see fragments of his past and future births.

Then attachment to mental objects arose in him, and suddenly he felt that he was being crushed beneath a boulder. A thought came to him: "Oh, I have to go into a castle." Suddenly he was bathed in a red light. That frightened him, as he thought that his face might have been injured. At that point, from the red light two beams of five-colored light unfurled. The upper beam of five-colored light was very clear, shining, bright, and active. The lower beam was pale. At this part of his narration, Changchub gave his instructions for others: "At that point, do not get scared of the upper beam of light. That is the light of five primordial wisdoms. The lower beam of light is the light of five poisonous emotions. Do not get lured by the lower beam of light."

Changchub is notable for such guidance. His tale is a treasure trove of advice on what helpers should tell dying meditators as an introduction to or reminder of their meditations. And so, when the lights described above appear, Changchub advises:

This is the time for ordinary people to perform phowa and for highly accomplished meditators to perform the introduction.

Regarding the introduction: If a [dying] person rolls his or her eyes upward, and if there are no breathing movements through the nostrils, that is the sign of the ceasing of the outer breathing. At that time [helpers should] call the person by his or her name. Slowly pull up the hair at the crown of the head a little. Do not allow loved ones to remain nearby if they are moaning and crying.

Give the dying person the following instructions about the signs of the dissolution of the physical elements: "You might feel as if your house is collapsing, but that is not so. That is the sign of your outer breathing ceasing. Do not let your mind waver! You might feel that sharp instruments are piercing through the root of every hair of your body, but that is not so. That is the sign that your arteries have stopping working. Do not be afraid!"

When the complexion is yellowish, say, "Now you might feel as if the house is collapsing on top of you, but that is not so. That is the sign that the energies of your flesh are dissolving into the outer earth element. Don't worry!"

When the complexion turns reddish, say, "Now you might feel that you are burning in a mountain of flame, but that is not so. It is the sign of your inner heat element dissolving into the outer fire element."

When the complexion turns whitish, say, "Now you might feel that you are being carried away by a huge river, but that is not so. It is the sign of your inner blood element dissolving into the outer water element. Do not be frightened."

When the complexion turns greenish, say, "Now you might feel that you are being carried away by a huge storm, but that is not so. It is the sign of your inner breathing dissolving into the outer air element.

When the complexion turns bluish, say, "Now you might feel that you have drowned in the ocean, but that is not so. It is the sign of your inner elements dissolving into space. Don't panic!"

Changchub's account is distinctive for the way he goes back and forth between the end of the dissolution and the arising of the ultimate nature as well as the beginning stage of the bardo. Usually, people pass through the stages of dissolution, then experience glimpses of the luminous nature, and then go to the bardo. But in this case, even after the glimpses of the luminous nature, Changchub again had dissolution experiences. So, apparently, some dying people go back and forth before they depart for good, because of their mental, emotional, and karmic nature. Or perhaps they are fighting to remain alive.

Don't Be Afraid—Be Prepared

You might be feeling worried after reading this chapter. A Tibetan woman once told her teacher, a lama, "When I hear about the rewards of good actions, I become hopeful for liberation—even for me. But when I hear about the consequences of bad actions, I have doubts about liberation—even for you."

While it is not helpful to be paralyzed by the fear of what comes after death, it is very good to be concerned and careful before it is too late. The good thing about karma is that we can always improve it. If we are not on the right path, we can turn our lives around. If we are already on the right path, we can improve. We control our destiny. There are hundreds of different teachings and compassionate ones to help us help ourselves.

But the first step is to know and accept the inevitability of death and the consequences that are waiting for us—while there is still time. That way, we can do all the preparations necessary while we are still alive. We need to develop positive attitudes and serve others with beneficial deeds. If we do not prepare this way, death will be a sorrowful occasion that not only marks the end of our days of life, but also presents the danger of a painful or even hellish future.

If we handle our lives well, however, death is certain to be a time of celebration. It will mark the end of old age and sickness, and the dawn of happiness. Some of us may see enlightened beings of boundless compassion and omniscient wisdom leading us to joyful paradises, such as the Blissful Pure Land of the Buddha of Infinite Light, discussed in chapters 7 and 9. If we are highly accomplished esoteric meditators, moreover, we may even attain enlightenment at death in what is known as the passage of ultimate nature, as the next chapter shows.

But the point is that we need to prepare for death and afterdeath now, without delay. If we exhale and cannot inhale, death will have arrived. That's how close we are to the day when we celebrate or sob.

3

The Ultimate Nature
Glimpses of the Luminosity

It is the basis of mind, the wisdom of ultimate peace and its
  luminosity.*
We must prepare to recognize it when we see it nakedly at death.
Even if we cannot maintain it, the mere memory of the luminosity
Will ease much pain and confusion.

A FTER WE STOP BREATHING, the true nature of the mind arises and
we go through what is called the arising or passage of the ultimate
nature. This passage (Tib. *chonyi, Ch'os Nyid*) presents a number of significant opportunities to attain liberation, but to realize these opportunities, we need to be accomplished in advanced esoteric meditative
training such as the Tibetan Buddhist practice of Dzogpa Chenpo
(Dzogchen). The experiences described in this chapter may thus be had
only by highly accomplished meditators. Ordinary people instead fall
unconscious through part of the passage of ultimate nature and then
awaken to gross concepts and emotions. Readers who find this chapter
too complex may safely move on to chapter 4.

THE ULTIMATE NATURE EXPERIENCED AT DEATH

For accomplished meditators, the passage of ultimate nature starts
when the luminous nature of the basis, the true nature of the mind,

---

* Some writers translate the "luminosity" (Tib. *osal, H'od gSal*) as the "clear light."

arises as it is. It ends with the dissolution of the spontaneously present visions. In some traditions, as Tsele explains, the luminous nature of the basis is considered to be part of the passage of dying.[1] But in Dzogchen, it is considered to be a passage in its own right. I follow the latter tradition in this book.

According to esoteric Buddhism, every being possesses buddha-nature or enlightenment in his or her true nature. So when all concepts and emotions dissolve into the primordial purity at death, the luminosity of the innate wisdom shines forth for every being. The mind of even the tiniest insect will experience, for at least a split second, its own innate awareness, the luminous nature, and its own spontaneous presence, the luminous visions.

If we are highly realized meditators on the ultimate nature of the mind, and if we are ready to attain enlightenment, we can realize and maintain the ultimate nature and its visions as they are, at any stage of this period. When the true nature arises, for instance, if we can recognize it and perfect or maintain that realization, we will be liberated and enlightened right then. The same applies to the arising of the luminous visions that follow—the lights, sounds, forms of peaceful or wrathful beings, and joyful or painful worlds. If we can see them as self-appearing visions that spontaneously arise from the luminous nature, and if we can maintain that realization, we will attain enlightenment. At whatever stage we recognize the truth and maintain that realization, we attain enlightenment, and there will thus be no need to travel any further . through the bardo.

Although attaining enlightenment during the passage of ultimate nature requires advanced esoteric meditative training, even modest familiarity with the nature of the mind can help us during this passage. We could have flickers of realizing the truth. Although this will not translate into liberation, the power of having even a brief experience of the true nature and its visions will greatly ease our fears and pains as we progress through the bardo. It will bring peace and joy, create meritorious karma, and lead us toward a better future life.

If we have very little or no meditative experience, however, we may not even notice when the true nature arises, as it may be too foreign, momentary, or invisible to us. Or, if we do notice it, we may experience it for but the briefest moment. So the ultimate nature flashes by without our recognizing it, and most of us fall into a deep unconsciousness.

When we regain consciousness, we start experiencing all kinds of visions, appearances, sounds, and feelings—some attractive and beautiful, others terrifying and ugly. Without training in meditation, we grasp at our visions subjectively and objectively, see them as real, and become afraid or attracted. If so, we are bound to continue through the whole cycle of the bardo, the transitional passage, and rebirth, as almost all of us do.

For realized meditators, Tibetan Buddhism presents a detailed portrait of the experiences and opportunities they can have in the passage of ultimate nature. The particular sequence and shape of these experiences can vary from person to person, as delog stories show. Tsele says that this is because different people have different mental, emotional, and physical makeups. But generally, the passage of the ultimate nature has two major stages: (1) the pure luminous nature of the basis and (2) the spontaneously present luminous visions.

The pure luminous nature of the basis has four substages:[2]

1. *Space*[3] *dissolves into (becomes one with) luminosity.* This is also called the dissolution of "attainment" (or blackness) into "luminosity."[4] At this point, our inner breathing has already stopped, mind and body have been separated, and the awareness of our mind has shot up like a spark into space. Our consciousness has exited the body. At this moment we experience the luminosity of the basis. This is the luminosity of dharmakaya. It is the union of clarity and openness, like the pure, cloudless sky of an early autumn morning. Karma Chagme Rinpoche, a great seventeenth-century master, says that when the blackness disappears, the luminosity of the basis arises.[5] If we could recognize that luminosity of the basis, as it is, and could maintain that realization, we would attain enlightenment.

All our perception of the external world—of things such as earth and stones—will fade away. The inner luminous visions of the ultimate nature will arise. All visions will shine as the lights of the five primordial wisdoms.

2. *Luminosity dissolves into union.* This stage is the union of openness (emptiness) and appearances. This is the luminosity of the sambhogakaya. We will see spontaneously present forms of the wrathful deities. We will hear the loud roars of natural sounds like thunder. We will witness a rain of weapons of rays and light. The lights of these luminous appearances are the natural power that arises from the purity and openness nature of our own mind. The sounds are the natural expression of our

own natural mind. If we are not realized, however, we might faint from fear of these forms and sounds.

Further, the whole universe might appear as a world of radiating lights, with the beautiful light images of the peaceful deities in infinite circles of five-colored lights. Chains of light with numerous rays emanate from our heart and meet the hearts of the deities. Then all the deities merge into us, for in reality, they are aspects of our own enlightened nature. We attain liberation by recognizing them without fear or attachment as self-appearance.

3. *Union dissolves into wisdom.* From our heart extend broad, beam-like paths of light in blue, white, yellow, and red, one stacked above the other. Each beam-like path is adorned with a circle of light of corresponding color the size of a mirror,* which is again decorated with five circles of light the size of peas. These are the lights of the wisdom of the ultimate sphere, mirror-like wisdom, wisdom of equanimity and discriminative wisdom. Above that, we will see a parasol made of lights of five colors, or five wisdoms, like a parasol of peacock feathers.

At this point we could attain three liberations. As our grasping at the "self" of the body has been released, we remain in the essence of ultimate nature, which is the liberation of the body into luminosity. As we have been free from gross and subtle elements, our perceptions have been liberated as the luminosity of great bliss. As we have been free from both gross and subtle defiled emotions, we recognize the natural face of liberation by uniting with the intrinsic awareness.

4. *Wisdom dissolves into the state of spontaneously present knowledge-holder.* At this stage, the visions of wisdoms, the four beam-like paths of light, merge into the parasol-like lights above. Then the following symbolic images appear like a reflection in a mirror: We feel that we are seeing the appearances of the dharmakaya, the primordial purity, symbolized by the cloudless pure sky above in space. Below that, we see the pure lands of the sambhogakaya, the spontaneous accomplishment, symbolized by figures of peaceful and wrathful deities. Below that, we see the pure lands of the nirmanakaya in various manifestations. At the bottom of all these, we see the world of six impure realms. As all arise spontaneously and are present equally, and as all arise in the compassionate nature, the omnipresent power, there is no discrimination be-

---

* An Asian ritual hand-held round mirror.

tween samsara and nirvana. At this time we may also experience many buddha-wisdoms, such as foreknowledge. Finally, all those spontaneously accomplished visions dissolve or merge into the nature of the intrinsic awareness itself, like the light of a crystal dissolving into the crystal itself.

At this stage it is important to use two key meditative tools. First, we must recognize the intrinsic awareness, the nature of our own mind, as it is, as if we were meeting a close old friend again. If we do this, we will realize the true nature of everything. We will transcend the very concepts of "existing" and "not existing" and will attain buddhahood, the ever-liberated state.

In this second stage of the passage of the ultimate nature, the spontaneously present luminous visions, we must recognize the visions of various forms and sounds as the spontaneously present energies of our own enlightened mind. Then the visions will arise as the spontaneously present five wisdoms and the buddha-mandalas, inseparable from the enlightened mind itself. But if we see the light forms and sounds as objects separate from the mind itself, our grasping at the "self" of the visions with dualistic concepts will cause them to arise as various phenomena of gross perceptions and emotional afflictions and the world of five gross elements. We might faint from fear or be attached to them. Then they will become the fuel of more samsaric cyclic existences. Guru Rinpoche advises:

When the period of ultimate nature is dawning upon me,
Abandoning all fear and terror,
I will recognize all the happenings as self-appearances of the
    intrinsic awareness itself.
And I will realize them as mere appearances of the ultimate nature.[6]

Jigme Lingpa advises:

If you analyze the state of ultimate nature,
There are many aspects to be analyzed.
But, instead, if you just analyze the analyzer itself,
You will find that nothing exists anywhere.
Then liberate the concept of "not existing" also.
This is the ever-liberated state.[7]

Longchen Rabjam advises:

> Through the mode of ceaseless arisings* of intrinsic awareness,
> The earth, water, fire, and air dissolve into space.
> Then the space dissolves into luminosity.
> At that time, the six senses and universal basis dissolve into the
>   ultimate sphere.
> Your mind will be separated from your body.
> Your intrinsic awareness will be free from phenomena.
> The ultimate body, the great original purity,
>   free from all concepts, will arise.
> At that time, if you could recognize [the realized state of] the
>   meditative trainings that you are experiencing,
> Then without any hindrance, you will directly be liberated in a
>   single instant.
> This is the attainment of the ultimate body with twofold purity.
>
> However, if you cannot recognize the arising [of the ultimate
>   body],
> Then the arising of the luminous visions, the arisings of the
>   universal basis, will appear.
> Space will be filled with sounds, lights, and rays as well as with the
>   [forms of] peaceful and wrathful deities.
> If you can recognize them as self-arising,
> You will be liberated into the original state, the attainment of
>   enlightenment.
> So, it is crucial to know that all the appearances are self-arising
>   [your own light].
> By recognizing their nature as they are, you will attain
>   buddhahood.[8]

Longchen Rabjam writes:

> A yogi who is attaining liberation in this very life
> Dissolves the earth element into water, water into fire, fire into air,
>   air into consciousness, and consciousness into luminescence;
> Then, uniting with [the union of] wisdom and ultimate sphere,
> The yogi secures permanence in the primordial state.

---

* Ceaseless arisings: Tib. *tsal, rTsal,* power of intrinsic awareness.

For the benefit of others, like a dream, with wisdom and two
    buddha-bodies,*
The yogi will appear before sentient beings as the buddha-
    activities to serve them.[9]

A helper who is assisting us in our passage through the ultimate
nature could remind us about our meditations, if we are meditators of
esoteric teachings. Chagme Rinpoche writes:

[The helper] should call to you near your ear
And repeat three times, saying,
"The luminosity of the basis has arisen in you,
So remain in your contemplation. . . .
Embodiment of all the Buddhas:
Your lama and the ultimate nature of your mind have become one.
Now look inwardly at your own mind.
The emptiness essence of it is the lama, the ultimate body
    [dharmakaya].
The clarity nature of it is the lama, the enjoyment body
    [sambhogakaya].
The arising of various manifestations is the lama, the manifesta-
    tion body [nirmanakaya]."[10]

The helper could also explain the visions of the ultimate nature.
Chagme Rinpoche writes:

The four directions, in between, up, and down are filled with
    lights, rays, and spheres of light.
The sky is filled with hosts of peaceful deities
Who radiate clarity, sparks, glory, and majesty.
From the hearts [of the deities] the paths of five wisdoms
With rays of bright and sparkling lights are touching your heart.
Accompanying these [lights] are also the paths to the six realms
    of samsara
[Which are also in the form of five-colored lights] but without
    their brightness.

---

* Two buddha-bodies: the formless body (dharmakaya) and the form bodies (sambhogakaya and nirmanakaya).

When you see them, do not go along the [dull lights] path of the
    six realms.
Go along the five [bright] light paths of wisdoms.
Pray respectfully to the buddhas of the five families.
After that, your personal deities, dakinis, and dharma protectors
    will come
With eight cemetery costumes and nine expressions,
With musical sounds, the thundering of HUNG and PHAT,
They shake and make the whole world tremble.
They have come to welcome you to the stage of the transitional
    passage.
Don't be scared or frightened by them, but see them as your
    personal deities.
They will lead you to pure celestial lands.
After that, hosts of blood-drinking wrathful deities
Will come to welcome you to the stage of the transitional
    passage.
They are frightening and unbearable to look at, and are
Roaring HUNG and PHAT like thousands of simultaneous
    thunderclaps.
The whole sky, space, and earth will be filled with these wrathful
    deities.
Shouting *Kill, kill* and *Beat, beat,* they shower weapons of
    light rays.
They will surround you like a captured criminal, and you will have
    nowhere to escape.
However, they do not come from somewhere else.
They are hosts of deities of your own body.
Do not get scared or panicked by them,
Mistaking your welcoming forces as your enemies.
At this crucial junction,
Do not flee, but generate devotion to them.[11]

In both the passage of dying and the arising of the ultimate nature, we
witness various kinds of lights and phenomenal appearances. Realized
people see and feel them at a level of oneness, not in a subject-object mode
of perception. They can see and experience hundreds of things simultaneously, not necessarily through their eyes and ears, but with totality,

with everything vividly before their awareness at once. All appearances are of peace, joy, oneness, and openness, whether they are in peaceful or wrathful forms. There is no discrimination of good versus bad, no limits of this or that, no conflicts of wanting or hating, no pain or excitement. The higher the realization, the more fully one can see things simultaneously. By contrast, most ordinary people experience things with limitation, confusion, pain, and fear in these passages of death.

The length of time that ordinary people witness the various visions of the ultimate nature, if they do at all, depends entirely on their individual disposition and meditative experience. Tsele writes, *"Liberation by Hearing* [sometimes called the *Tibetan Book of the Dead*] and other texts talk about the dying seeing the five buddhas families such as that of Akshobhya Buddha with retinues during the first night [or first week of death] and Ratnasambhava during the second night [or week]. Many people accept this as the ordinary cycle of day and night. In reality, however, seeing these buddhas is part of meditative absorption, and ordinary people will see them for only a moment."[12]

When we read about light in these afterdeath descriptions, many of us might think, "Oh, yes, these must be beams of light or sunlight-like phenomena coming from somewhere." But in true realization we are not perceiving those lights as objects—the objects of eye-consciousness—or phenomena produced by a particular source or coming from somewhere else. Light is clarity and luminosity, which is also peace, joy, bliss, openness, oneness, and all-knowing wisdom. We are the light, and the light is us: all are one. This is the union of the spontaneously present wisdom, which is luminosity of the ultimate nature and of the spontaneously appearing luminous visions of the wisdom. Thus, this light is also called wisdom-light. The extent of clarity, peace, openness, and omniscience of the wisdom-light that we experience depends on the degrees of our past virtuous karma and the depth of our realization. This principle is the very basis from which esoteric Buddhism speaks of such concepts as nonduality, natural light, wisdom-light, clarity, spontaneous arising, self-arising, spontaneous presence, self-present, self-arisen, buddha and pure land, unborn state, and fully enlightened state.

We all have the potential to become enlightened during the passage of the ultimate nature if we can realize, perfect, and maintain the true nature of primordial purity—the union of openness nature and the spontaneously arisen appearances, the intrinsic light. But to attain such realization will be impossible unless we have achieved it in our lifetime through meditation. So the time is now, while we are alive, to prepare for our great journey.

DELOG ACCOUNTS OF THE PASSAGE OF ULTIMATE NATURE

In their first-person accounts of dying and death, many delogs do not mention their experiences of the ultimate nature. It is not clear whether they did not recognize it because their meditation experience wasn't advanced enough or they chose not to mention it because such experiences concern only highly accomplished meditators. The following accounts are exceptions: they *do* describe the experience of the ultimate nature; yet instead of attaining enlightenment, these delogs all continue on to the transitional passage, the bardo. Perhaps they could not maintain the ultimate nature because their realization wasn't yet perfected, or they may have chosen to enter the bardo in order to help others there. The interesting thing is that these delog accounts differ in their details of the experience, so obviously the narrators are not simply repeating something that they studied. This demonstrates that even a meditator will not necessarily see and recognize everything exactly as described in the teachings.

Spontaneously Present Light: The Experience of Lingza Chokyi

When we left off Chokyi's account in chapter 2, she had undergone the experiences of dissolution and then entered a state in which there was no conceptual recollection. When she emerged from it after an undetermined period of time, she witnessed a five-colored light in the form of a helmet over her head. From the center of that light, rays of red light projected outward. At the end of each ray, there was a being in a human body and the head of an animal, each dressed in different garb. Their wide-open eyes were as huge as the sun and moon. They were brandishing all kinds of weapons and thundering, "Beat! Beat! Kill! Kill!" Chokyi was absolutely terrified.

At that point, she remembered that a lama had taught her: "The lights that you will see are self-lights, the spontaneously present lights of yourself. Rays are self-rays. Images are self-images. Sounds are self-sounds. All are the self-radiance of your own mind." She thought, "So they are not real!" At that very moment they all disappeared. All her fears were pacified.

A Bodiless Body of Light: The Experience of Dagpo Trashi Namgyal

We read in chapter 2 that Dagpo saw the arising of the luminous state, clear like the cloudless sky. If he had recognized it, it would have been the attainment of buddhahood. The sky-like freedom from elaboration* was the dharmakaya. The pure luminosity was the sambhogakaya. The five afflicting emotions had arisen as the five wisdoms. Then he would experience flawless bliss so vast that it could not fit in the sky.

However, Dagpo's mind became deluded, and he saw the lights as objects. He saw all kinds of white, yellow, red, and green lights. His own body wasn't the same as it used to be; it had become a bodiless body of light. Everything was joyful and swift. He could travel to any place he though of just by thinking of it.

Five kinds of lights accompanied him. The light at his right was white. The light at his left was dark in color. The light in front of him was yellow. Wherever he went, these lights were there with him.

Then he saw a house and went in and sat in it. It had nine entrances: seven doors plus one entrance up and one down. Fears came into his mind as he thought, "This must be my own body." Then he performed phowa and shouted HIK! Instantly he exited from his body and reached a celestial pure land.

Visions of Ultimate Nature: The Experience of Tsophu Dorlo

At the end of his account in chapter 2, Tsophu Dorlo had entered a state of blackness. Next his consciousness dissolved into luminosity, and he experienced an innate joy. Then the luminosity of the path and the luminosity of the basis—known as the mother and child luminosities—were united as one. He remained in the spontaneously born innate primordial wisdom for a long time.

At that time the visions of ultimate nature spontaneously arose in him. All the perceptions became buddha-forms and lights.

---

* True nature is utmost simplicity and oneness. Anything more is an "elaboration" (Tib. *trotral*, s*Pros Bral*)—a fabrication and a distraction.

Space became blue-colored light. In the center and in the four directions, Dorlo witnessed the visions of the five buddha families and their pure lands. Buddhas were accompanied by disciple bodhisattvas, door guards, the six buddhas,* and many dakinis and masters. He also witnessed the visions of five wrathful buddha families with their disciples. Finally, the visions of the ultimate nature ceased.

In the Womb of a Body of Light: The Experience of Samten Chotso

Nineteen-year-old Samten Chotso experienced the white and red essences of her body gathered at her heart and her consciousness encapsulated between them. Instantly, there arose the wisdom that is free from sensuous joy. Because she recognized it and remained in it without wandering, her delusions were cleared.

She felt that she had attained the state of the Buddha of Infinite Light. Then she experienced the cloudless sky–like clear luminosity. She wrote in her account: "If beings recognize this luminosity, they will be enlightened. But it is sad that by not knowing it, they have been caught in the delusory wheel of samsara."

That instant her body became a body of light. The appearances became a mass of five colored lights. She felt that she was in the womb of a body of light. There were nine windows in the body, from bottom to top.

Next she heard the voice of Guru Padmasambhava singing his mantra. From the "top window" (the cranial aperture), descended rays of light, mainly white in color. "There I saw Guru Padmasambhava in the midst of the lights," she reported.

---

* Door guards and the six buddhas: In many esoteric Buddhist mandalas, there are four door guards protecting the gates. The Crow-Headed Door Guard of the East represents loving-kindness, the Pig-Headed Guard of the West represents compassion, the Dog-Headed Guard of the South represents sympathetic joy, and the Owl-Headed Guard of the North represents equanimity. In some mandalas there are also six buddhas, who are the teachers or saviors of the six realms. They are the buddha who pacifies arrogance, the karmic cause of taking birth in the god realm; the buddha who pacifies the jealousy of the demigod realm; the buddha who pacifies the greed of the human realm; the buddha who pacifies the ignorance of the animal realm; the buddha who pacifies the miserliness of the hungry ghost realm; and the buddha who pacifies the hatred of the hell realm.

Instructions to Helpers: The Experience of Changchub Seng-ge

How can we help people going through the passage of the ultimate nature? We can consult Changchub, whose delog tale gives step-by-step advice. He says that, when the inner breathing of the dying person has ceased and they have started to see the luminous nature of the basis and the luminous visions of the ultimate nature, the helper should talk to the dying person as follows:

For accomplished meditators, say, "Sir/Madam [or name], please stay with your meditation without distraction. The time of death has arrived for you. Please do not waver from your meditation. Now watch your mind. Has your mind any form, any shape, or any color? No. Your mind does not have any form, shape, or color. Your mind has nothing to grasp at. That nature is the union of clarity and emptiness. Please stay mindfully in that union without wavering. All the sounds that you hear are self-sound. All the lights that you see are self-light. All the rays that you witness are self-rays. Please do not be frightened or irritated by those sounds, lights, and rays. Remain in meditation without wavering."

Then say prayers to invoke the blessings of the buddhas and lineage masters. The introduction and these prayers will help the dying meditator to attain enlightenment.

For ordinary meditators, say, "O child [or name], you might be experiencing a house falling down. But that is not so. It is the sign that your inner breathing is ceasing and your mind is exiting your body. As soon as your mind is out of your body, you will see the light of five colors surrounding you. Do not be scared of them or become panicked. If you recognize them, they are the lights of the five buddha families. If you can't recognize them, they are the lights of the Lords of the Dead. So don't be frightened.

"Please listen carefully. Among the lights that you will see, there are five kinds of lights. In the midst of blue light, your ignorance will arise in the form of a Bear-Headed Person. Don't be scared of him, but have devotion to him. He is Vairochana Buddha. Please recognize him as such.

"Again, in the midst of white light, your anger will arise in the form of a Serpent-Headed Person. Please don't hate or dislike him. He is Vajrasattva Buddha. Please recognize him as such.

"Again, in the midst of yellow light, your arrogance will arise in the form of a Tiger-Headed Person. Please don't get scared by him. He is Ratnasambhava Buddha. Please develop devotion to him.

"Again, in the midst of red light, your attachment will arise in the form of an Eagle-Headed Person. Don't be terrified of him. He is the Buddha of Infinite Light. Please develop devotion to him.

"Again, in the midst of green light, your jealousy will arise in the form of a Monkey-Headed Person. He is Amogasiddhi Buddha. Please recognize him as such.

"These five lights are the lights of the five buddhas. If you are afraid of them, they will become the paths that lead to the inferior realms. Please don't be scared of them or run away from them.

"O child of good family! You might feel that [instead of the paths of lights] you must take a narrow path,[13] but please don't go that way. That path will take you to birth in the hell realm. You might also find a river of hot ashes. That will take you to birth in the hungry ghost realm. You might find a swamp of filth. That will take you to birth in the animal realm. You might find an opening to a brass tube–like path filled with odors of food. That will take you to birth in the human realm. You might find a path filled with shining weapons. That will take you to birth in the demigod realm. You might also find a path with many gates and wheels of sharp weapons.* That will take you to birth in the god realm. Please don't follow these paths.

"Instead, please come up through the central channel of your body, which is wide open at the top. Above your head is Vajradhara Buddha with blue complexion."

As the helper, you should meditate on uniting your mind with the mind of the deceased. Then, loudly shouting PHAT many times, merge the united mind into the wisdom mind of Vajradhara Buddha. Then contemplate in oneness with Vajradhara Buddha. Remain in that contemplative state as long as possible, again and again. At the end, say aspiration prayers.

A Supremely Blissful State: The Experience of Dawa Drolma

Dawa Drolma mentions her experiences of the ultimate nature in two lines. She says, "As the result, my mind opened into a supremely blissful state, the ultimate nature, which is free from imputations, like the sky." In

---

* The wheel of sharp weapons is an ancient weapon in the form of a wheel with sharp spokes, which was usually hurled like a discus.

other words, just as the sky is free from impurities, the ultimate nature is free from conceptual and emotional designations. This must have been the experience of the luminosity of the basis as it is. Then she says, "A ceaseless power of that state, the luminous basis, spontaneously arose in the form of totally pure display." This must have been the experience of the luminous visions.

Then Dawa Drolma felt a sensation like climbing up higher and higher into a vaguely defined space, swiftly like a vulture soaring through the sky.

A Feeling of Sadness: The Experience of Karma Wangdzin

Karma remained dead for seven days. Her delog story is more philosophical than some of the others. It explains that the fearful visions and feelings are mere perceptions reflected by one's own insecure mind. As we will see in her reported experiences of the bardo in chapter 5, she describes in detail a place where people are waiting their turns to be called for judgment.

Karma heard the voice of a woman calling her: "O Karma Wangdzin!" Though Karma Wangdzin was her Dharma name given by a lama, everybody called her Lhawang Putri, the name given her by her mother. However, at this juncture, she was called by her Dharma name. The voice continued, "O Karma Wangdzin, you have now reached the next world. The impermanence of life, the experience of death, has happened to you. Aren't you aware of it? Do not be attached to or crave your illusory body. Raise your mind upward to the ultimate nature."

Thinking, "I am dead!" Karma looked up. Above her she saw an open hole with light coming through it, as if she were in a pot and viewing a hole at the top of the pot. Merely by seeing the open hole, she instantly got out of a dark place through the hole. She didn't even have to think of moving up or getting out; it just happened. As she was lifted out, she felt that she emerged from a cave surrounded by trees. In fact, she had exited from the cranial aperture of her head surrounded by hair, but she wasn't aware of that.

In the sky about two feet above the "cave," she saw a white ball of light wrapped in colorful lights, like the eyes of a peacock feather. From it, rays of light were emanating in all directions. As soon as she saw it, a feeling of aloneness or sadness coursed through her.

Our Sublime Potential

The ultimate nature is our birthright, the foundation of each of our minds. Most of us, however, can hardly conceive of its splendor—let alone of the possibility of uniting with it after death. This chapter has, I hope, offered a glimpse into our sublime potential to realize the truth at death if we devote ourselves to meditating on the nature of the mind. Those who achieved the attainments described here started out as ordinary people, like us. They then devoted their lives to contemplating and maintaining the realization of the ultimate nature.

However, doing even a little meditation will greatly help us when we die. If we could glimpse the ultimate nature while we are alive or at death, that would create enormous merits to propel us toward a peaceful and joyous future.

Even simpler meditations and prayers penetrate into deep layers of our minds. As layers peel off when we die or enter deeper states of consciousness, the fruits of our meditation emerge.

Pema Ozer, a Western lady, had been practicing Buddhism for only a few years when she was hospitalized for major surgery. As a child, her happiest moments had been riding along country roads with her grandfather in his horse-drawn buggy. After his death, she had always imagined that when her time arrived, he would meet her in his buggy. Sure enough, as her consciousness began to drift away on the operating table, she saw her grandfather waiting at a crossroads in his buggy. She was about to join him when the Buddha appeared. Walking back and forth across the road to dissuade her from reaching her grandfather, the Buddha encouraged her to keep breathing. She did, and is healthy today. The key is that her meditation experience emerged even though she had spent a relatively short time practicing at that point.

So it is essential to meditate on the nature of the mind as much as possible while we are alive.

4

The Bardo
The Momentous Transitional Passage

There is no longer a physical structure that controls us.
Our negative mental habits appear as the world of delusions
and fear.
Our positive habits arise as the world of peace and joy.
So we must remember to generate and maintain spiritual
qualities.

FOR ORDINARY PEOPLE, the bardo, the transitional passage, starts when consciousness is regained. It ends at the conception of the next life. For experienced esoteric meditators, it starts with or at the end of the spontaneously present luminous visions.

During the passage of dying our mind is joined with our body. The next stage, the passage of ultimate nature, is often so brief that ordinary people barely witness it. So the bardo, the period between the experience of ultimate nature and our next rebirth, is the major afterdeath event—the most crucial juncture of our lives—and the longest in duration among the first three transitional periods.

Generally, the passage through the bardo lasts for up to seven weeks (forty-nine days), but it could be much shorter, or in some rare cases it might even be longer. During the first half of this transitional passage, we may feel that we have the body and emotions of our previous life. During the second half, we may feel that we have the body and experiences of our coming rebirth.

Experiences of the Bardo

In the bardo, most of us will feel that we are traveling through narrow paths or tunnels, traversing a desert, crossing bridges over turbulent rivers, being judged by the Lords of the Dead, perhaps persecuted by executioners, and dispatched to hellish regions, higher realms, or heavenly pure lands. All these encounters are reactions of our own physical, cultural, mental, and emotional habits that we have fostered in the past.

We may feel as if we are squeezing out of a narrow, dark tunnel as our consciousness exits the dying body. At the end of the tunnel, we might see a door or a window with light shining through. This could be the cranial aperture or any of the nine openings of the body. Until we can clear the deeply rooted habits that we are harboring and find the exit to total liberation, we will go around in a cycle without end, like a bee trapped in a room.

In the bardo, many beings experience similar kinds of world systems together, because they are all reaping the effects of similar karmas that they produced in the past. But in some cases, the experience will be a purely subjective perception of the deceased person, with no actual participation by others, even though the deceased may feel as if many beings are sharing the experience with him or her. For example, as we shall see in chapter 5, the delog Do Khyentse felt that his sister and others were accompanying him during his visit to the pure lands, but in fact she was alive and busy studying at Yarlung Monastery.

As noted earlier, if we are highly realized meditators who have attained enlightenment in life or while in the passage of ultimate nature, we may have no need to go through the bardo.

If we have accumulated a great deal of merit and achieved some meditative experiences, we will go through the bardo, but with little sense of fear and suffering. By the power of our merits and meditative realizations, we will be able to take rebirth in a spontaneously manifested pure land, or at least in one of the happy realms of the world.

If our mindstream is filled with karmic traces of evil deeds, we will not be able to see the ultimate nature and will be terrified by natural sounds and the visions of lights, rays, and images. We might not even dare to look at the visions, nor will we understand them to be expressions of our own true nature. Instead we will struggle with them as mental objects in the form of conflicting forces. Such negative perceptions of conflict and struggle could lead us to the experience of a hell realm as our rebirth.

In the bardo, our consciousness is totally separated from our body. Our mind has left our cherished form behind as a corpse with no warmth, no breath, and no movement. Our consciousness will be floating around without any gross body to anchor it. We will be able to see without benefit of sunlight or moonlight. We will assume a mental body, most likely imagined according to our past habits. Some texts, however, describe it as a subtle body of soft light. But still we might be thinking we have our previous body and are still alive.

We may go through the following experiences: We will have no sense of stability, as our feelings and the circumstances around us will change from moment to moment, according to the changes in our thoughts and the influences of our karmic forces. We will find ourselves with any person or in any place that comes to our mind, unless the place is beyond our karmic range. If we think of New York City, we will be there instantly, without spending any time or effort to travel there, since our body is a mental, not a physical, one.

Being able to travel is not our problem, but stability is. It is hard for us to stay in one place and to focus on any thought, as we are always moving, flickering, floating, and being driven about. We are constantly running, flying, and moving, like a feather in a storm, with no endurance.

Our mind will be much sharper than it was in life. We will see and hear from many others who, like ourselves, are wandering in the bardo. We will enjoy some degree of clairvoyance, knowing other people's thoughts, but we will have less reasoning or analytic power, owing to the lack of mental focus. From moment to moment, our mind may swing through many changes of happiness and suffering, hope and fear, peace and pain. Sometimes we might feel in danger from the force of the elements, as if we were buried under houses, caves, or collapsed earth; falling and sinking in water; burning in a wood fire or in flaming houses; and being blown about in strong, stormy winds—experiences that are perhaps similar to the dissolutions of the passage of dying, only here they are more naked and direct.

If we see our dead body, we might behold it clearly, as it actually is, and become protective of it. Or we might hate it and not want to look at it. We might not see or recognize our corpse at all. Many times, mysteriously, we might see it in a different form, such as the body of a dog or a snake. Seeing our body might help us realize for a moment that we are dead, but immediately afterward we might have no recollection of that, since there is so little strength of focus for remembering.

That is why it can take a long time before we really understand that we have died. We have little reasoning power in the bardo. So one moment we will realize that we're dead, but the next moment we'll forget and resume our habit of feeling alive.

We might be seeking food all the time, but we are unable to enjoy any food unless it is offered to us spiritually or dedicated in our name. We will mostly be able to enjoy the smell of food rather than the food itself. That is why many texts refer to beings in the bardo as the "odor-eaters."* (In the Tibetan tradition, this is the very reason why the smoke of burning food, or *sur* (*gSur*), is ritually offered to a deceased person for many weeks after his or her death.

We may feel lonely and insecure, ever searching for shelter and stability. Tired of being swept about by karmic, mental, and emotional storms, we will be so desperate for the steadiness of a body that we may care little about what kind of future situation we trap ourselves into.

Some people relive their dying experiences, exactly as they went through them, on every seventh day after their death, again and again, especially if it was a tragic death. That is why every seventh day is observed by survivors with prayers and dedications.

We might approach our friends, but to our surprise, they will ignore us. We might sit down at the dining table, but no one will offer us a chair or serve us any meal. We might ask people questions, but no one will answer us. That might make us sad, thinking that everyone is angry at us and no one cares for us. Maybe we will see others going through our personal belongings and taking whatever they want, and we might angrily conclude that they are robbing us. At such a juncture, the worst thing we could do for ourselves would be to succumb to negative emotions such as anger. So we should learn about the signs of death while we are alive and remind ourselves, thinking again and again, "At the time of death I will not get into negative emotions."

The Court of Judgment and Verdict

After some time, many of us will witness the arrival of the Lords of the Dead (*shinje; gShin rJe*), who come to fetch us. They are the agents of the

---

* Tib. *driza, Dri Za;* Skt. *gandharva:* a class of spirit-beings who are celestial musicians and who live on odors such as incense.

Dharma King of the Lords of the Dead (*shinje chokyi gyalpo; gShin rJe Ch'os Kyi rGyal Po*), who is the highest and final authority in the Court of Judgment for the dead. The Lords of the Dead appear in various forms and play different roles. You might see them arriving to summon you to the court, supervising the deliverance of your judgments, and executing the edicts of the Dharma King.

At this junction, we will leave our old location and go far away on a strenuous journey. It will seem as if we are trekking over amazingly high mountain passes and narrow paths. That will be followed by the feeling of crossing an endless hot desert. Then we make our way over a long, dangerous bridge above a turbulent river. Finally we will reach the court of the Dharma King of the Lords of the Dead.[1] All of these "travels" are the result of the mental, emotional, and cultural impacts imprinted in our mindstream. Now they are manifesting in the form of external images and sounds, feelings and fear, and experiences of law and order, punishment and reward.

The experiences of being judged by wise and powerful ones, prosecuted by opponents, and defended by supporters are the expressions of habits that we harbored while we were alive. That is the very reason why, if we could develop the pure perception of seeing all as buddhas, all would appear to us as buddha-manifestations, for in their true nature, all *are* buddhas in actuality.

For devout people, a Guardian Deity for the dead will also appear, to accompany the dead throughout their journey. The Guardian Deities are enlightened ones, usually in the form of a male or female deity or a spiritual master.

The court of the Dharma King is the place where our next birth will be decided after the records of our past positive and negative deeds have been checked. We will be examined by defenders, who will plead for us by presenting the evidence of our positive deeds. The prosecutors argue against us by presenting the evidence of our negative deeds. For the records of our deeds, they check a mirror in which our deeds appear; notes in which our deeds have been recorded; and pebbles with which our deeds will be measured out on scales. Again, these are mere reflections of our cultural habits of judging, defending, and prosecuting that are ingrained in the depth of our mindstream.

The court of the Lords of the Dead is no place to try to be clever or curry favor for it is not a court of legal professionals but the actual expression of what we are.

In the delog accounts gathered in the next chapter, we will read that the dead travel to different hellish and happy realms. But these delogs are not ordinary people; they are on a mission to gather information in order to inform and serve others. By contrast, as ordinary beings, we will not need to travel around different realms, because the Lords of the Dead will dispatch us straight to whatever realm is dictated by our karmic habits.

Hints of the Rebirth Awaiting Us

In the later stages of the bardo, we will start seeing lights of different colors. These represent the energies of our karma and emotions, and indicate the rebirth realm awaiting us.[2] We will see a white light if we have done some virtuous deeds but our dominant emotion is arrogance or desire, thus propelling us to take rebirth in the god realm or human realm, respectively. We will perceive a soft yellow light if our dominant emotion is jealousy or ignorance, causing us to be reborn in the demigod realm or animal realm, respectively. Alternatively, some might see a blood-colored light for the animal realm and a snowstorm or rainstorm color for the demigod realm. We will witness a smoky light if we have committed unvirtuous deeds and our dominant emotion is miserliness or greed, thus impelling us toward the hungry ghost realm. Lastly, the light will look like a piece of log or floating black wool if our dominant emotion is hatred and we are heading for the hell realm.

However, different texts give different colors of lights as the signs of birth in various realms.[3] Tsele writes that the colored lights of the realms may not be certain in all cases.[4]

The realm of our birth might also appear in symbolic images. If we are going to take rebirth in the god realm, we might feel we are on a high floor in a mansion. If we are being propelled toward the demigod realm, we might feel that we are in a wheel of fire. When headed for the human realm, we may perceive ourselves to be in the midst of many people. Or instead we might feel that we are approaching a lake with swans, horses, or cows, or entering a house, city, or crowd.[5] If we are moving toward the animal realm, we may feel that we are in an empty cave or hut. If we are entering the hungry ghost realm, we may sense that we are in a dry cave. Those going to the hell realm may go there immediately if they have committed grave offenses, so they may see no particular image in the bardo.

When the time arrives for our conception in, say, the human realm, we will see our parents engaged in sexual intercourse. If we are going to be born as a male, we may feel jealousy toward our father-to-be and desire for our mother. If we are going to be born as a female, our desire will be for our father and our jealousy toward our mother.[6] That emotional feeling, in fact, will become the trigger point for us to be admitted into the womb of conception. Womb birth is one of the four ways of taking birth. The others are egg birth, moisture birth, and miraculous or instant birth.

If we are devotees of the Blissful Pure Land and are able to focus our mind on the Buddha of Infinite Light and his abode, we might soar to the pure land like an eagle through the sky as soon as we are out of the body. At that moment, we might see or hear our loved ones or enemies calling us back. They are not really our loved ones, but our own emotions tricking us as obstructions. So we must focus totally on the pure land. Chagme Rinpoche says:

> While you are on your way to the pure land from here,
> You might hear your parents, relatives, or friends saying,
> "It's me. Don't leave me. Come here."
> They might call your name, crying and lamenting.
> But they are negative forces who are obstructing your
>   liberation.
> Do not look back or answer them at all.
> With the exception of the Buddha of Infinite Light,
> Do not contemplate anyone—
> Only the happiness and joy of the Blissful Pure Land.
> Do not be attached to anything.
> Then it is certain that you will reach the Blissful Pure Land.[7]

Chapter 7 gives some descriptions of the Buddha of Infinite Light and his Blissful Pure Land, based on the sutras, the teachings of the historical Buddha, Shakyamuni.

WHAT SHOULD WE DO IN THE BARDO?

How should we handle the bardo? First, it is very important to verify whether we are really dead or not, so we must look for certain signs:

- Look into a mirror or water. If you don't have a reflection, you are dead.
- Walk on sand or in snow. If there are no footprints, you are dead.
- Go into the sun or walk in the light. If there is no shadow beside your body, you are dead.
- If people are not responding to you, if they are not even looking at you, or if they are not serving you any food, that is not their fault, nor are they are angry with you. It is because you are dead.

After realizing that you are dead, try not to feel sad and shocked, for this will not help and will only hurt. Try to react to death in the three following ways:

1. *Realize that you are at the most crucial juncture of your life.* For the sake of your future, you cannot waste a moment. This is your greatest opportunity to advance.

2. *Remember and feel happy about whatever spiritual path you have pursued in your lifetime.* That will be the great source of peace, joy, and strength for you.

3. *Remember any one of the following three practices, according to your ability and experience.* Then try to stay with that practice without distraction.

(a) When you see the forms of male and female beings, as mentioned in *Liberation by Hearing*,[8] recognize them as male and female buddha families and pure lands. Realize them as the reflection of your own buddha-mind. If you try to see them with positive perception, you will find them to be the source of blessings, as they are all mere impressions of the mind in the bardo.

Remember the feelings of devotion to the buddhas, to your spiritual teachers, and to your meditation. If you have any experience in esoteric meditation, try to realize the oneness of everything that happens, for all happenings are one in their true nature, according to the esoteric path. You must try to see and feel that all the peaceful or wrathful forms, sounds, and feelings that you might be encountering are merely the manifestational power of that oneness. See the lights as wisdom-lights, or turn them into lights of wisdom through meditation techniques that are familiar to you. Do not grasp at or struggle against them, taking the attitude of subject versus object; instead, open to them and be one with them. Relax in the awareness of that oneness state. Rest in it again and again.

(b) If you are not a realized or experienced meditator, but a spiritual person, first you should try to calm down your mind and be stable. Then try to remember your spiritual support, whether it is a divine presence, a master, or a positive experience that is present to you and in you. Try to keep your mental focus on it again and again, instead of being distracted everywhere. Try to have compassion for others, instead of pitting yourself against them. Try to see all as divine manifestations instead of sources of fear and pain. Try to say prayers and mantras and hear all sounds as words of devotion and compassion, instead of lamentations. We must try to stay in such a spiritual atmosphere throughout our transitional journey. Positive memories, devotional prayers, and compassionate openness will become a source of powerful protection, soothing experience, and wisdom-light that makes the transitional journey a joyful ride.

Experienced spiritual people are able to perform services for others. Through the power of prayers, merit making, devotion, and/or contemplation, they can bring our mind to an image (or an object) and stabilize it. Then they can give us teachings, invoke the compassionate blessings of deities, and bestow empowerments in order to lead our mind to buddhahood or at least to a good rebirth. If we have some virtuous karmas as the cause, these meditative services will function as effective conditions, and the service will be most beneficial. Such service could become a real turning point for us in our transitional journey.

Whatever positive memories or experiences we can muster, they will generate and strengthen the force of peace, joy, devotion, love, pure perception, and wisdom. That force will lead to the attainment of enlightenment or to a better rebirth—just as the force of negative emotions causes us to be born in a hell realm. Such a positive force could divert us from the path of rebirth in the hell realms, even if we have been destined for them. Whatever spiritual experiences and strength we have acquired in our lifetime will certainly bear their fruit at the right time. However, it is prudent to activate the force of our positive karmas instead of giving the negative karmas that we also have the chance to dominate our life. Longchen Rabjam advises:

> Although arisings [of the ultimate nature] have appeared in that
>   manner,* if you cannot recognize them,
> The bardo of transitional passage, like a dream, will appear.
> Then, by remembering buddha pure lands, and
> Seeking refuge in your spiritual masters and tutelary deities,

---

* In the manner described in chapter 3, "The Ultimate Nature."

You might take rebirth in pure lands and attain liberation.
Many, instead, may take rebirth as human beings with sevenfold
     qualities, and
The attainment of liberation will be assured in their next birth.[9]

(c) You might be going through the delusory hallucinations of the
bardo without having had much spiritual and meditative experience. If
so, you must try to remember not to become angry, upset, or afraid, but
strive to see all the appearances as unreal, like a dream. No one is putting
together a show of these transitional arrangements for your benefit, for
they are just illusions imagined because of your own past mental habits,
fueled by afflicting emotions. Try to make your mind open, positive, stable, and peaceful, instead of adopting a grasping or negative perception
with emotions of hatred, desire, or confusion. Try to feel compassion for
others who are also being buffeted about in this scary transitional journey. If you can generate and maintain such a positive state of mind, purified by the wind of devotional or compassionate energies, your mind will
be in great peace, like the immaculate cloudless sky. No dark clouds of
negative karmic energies will come to cast shadows of confusion or pain.
Sun- and moonlight-like joy and peace will prevail throughout your experience of whatever phenomena arise, ensuring an abundantly happy
journey.

In addition to the above three practices, we might also remember how
to "reverse" the process of taking birth in inferior realms, if we face any
of them. If you see indications of an inferior birth—the soft lights and
signs, or your future birthplace or parents—the most important thing is
not to fall into negative thoughts or emotions, such as grasping, craving,
attachment, hatred, jealousy, fear, or confusion. Try to see them with a
spiritual mind, a mind of peace, oneness, and openness. You could try to
see them with a peaceful and relaxed mind by realizing that they are fabrications of your own mind. Or you could try to see them as male and female deities and their pure lands. Pray to the deities and spiritual masters
for their blessings and guidance.

OUR FUTURE JOURNEY

In this life, our mind is relatively stable because it is anchored in this
gross and earthy physical structure. This makes it easier to gain spiritual

views and habits through meditation. But it is also harder to make big changes or improvements, precisely because the mind is trapped and programmed in the system of our rigid, earthly body.

In the transitional journey of the bardo, however, the mind is rapidly changing without any structural restriction. It is therefore easier to change or improve our future journey. But it is also much harder to find a path and focus on it, since there is no anchoring faculty of a physical body. Our bodiless mind lives on with its past habits and floats rapidly without break at high speed toward its future destiny.

Today, fortunately, we are alive and have a solid earthly body to hold on to, so that we can prepare for the bardo and for our next life. If we can enjoy peace, joy, strength, and wisdom while we are alive, then when the day of death comes, we will actually be able to welcome it, thinking, "I am so happy, because I have made all the preparations for this moment. I didn't waste any of my golden opportunities."

In the bardo our mind will be much clearer and more powerful than it is today. Its experiences will be much sharper and more sensitive. If we have gained positive experiences while alive, we will enjoy their effects in this transitional passage very easily, clearly, and effectively. But it will be very hard to start a new mentality and experience, as we need steadiness in order to cultivate new habits.

If the awareness of peace, joy, and openness has become part of our mental character while we were alive, then in the bardo all our mental states and the phenomena around us will arise as positive appearances and experiences. Even the five afflicting emotions of our mind will arise as the five wisdoms, and the five physical elements as the five intrinsic lights, which is the spontaneously present energy-light of wisdom.

Hosts of divine beings, in male and female forms, will lead us on our path. Our mental body will soar away like a falcon through the boundless clear blue sky with a great display of magical offerings, sweetest music, and joyful dances filling the entire atmosphere. We will be welcomed to the most beautiful, peaceful, and joyful pure lands or paradises. We will also enjoy the power to lead many others to those pure lands with great celebration. All these things will only happen because of the spiritual preparations we have made while we were still alive.

5

Tales of the Bardo
Afterdeath Experiences of Tibetan Delogs

B ECAUSE MOST of the delog literature deals with the bardo, I have
devoted this entire chapter to examples of these tales.* The aim of
this chapter is to illustrate the unavoidable karmic consequences that
everyone will face. I hope it will inspire people to behave in the right way
and improve their future.

People often ask why delogs only mention Buddhist prayers and meditation and Buddhist deities and teachers. In a sense, I don't think that the
Buddhist attributes should matter. In my opinion, thoughts and feelings
of peace and joy, and their expression in words and deeds, become sources
of benefit and liberation, whether they are expressed through Buddhism
or any other belief system. Whoever has attained the wisdom of ultimate
peace and joy is equipped with the power of liberating others, whether
they are in the form of Buddhist deities or not. However, the delogs of
Tibet happened to witness the power of Buddhist deities and teachings
because they themselves were Buddhists, and their mental habits and
karmic relations were connected with Buddhist deities and teachings. As
discussed earlier, Buddhists believe that all the appearances before us and

---

* The delog Do Khyentse only provides details of his experiences in the pure lands, but
other delogs elaborate on their long and arduous transitional journey, the judgments
that were passed in the court of the Lords of the Dead, and the various painful world
systems that they witnessed in great detail. Most of the accounts focus on the sufferings of various hells and other inferior realms, and in this regard the details given by all
these delogs are quite similar. I have therefore summarized only those details of the inferior realms from the tale of Lingza Chokyi, to avoid repetition. For the description of
the eight hot hells in Chokyi's account, I have incorporated details from Tsophu Dorlo's
account.

all the experiences that we go through are mere reflections of our mental habits. So whatever belief system we follow, if it has the wisdom of ultimate peace and joy, then it will be a true source of benefit in life and in death. We will see and feel it as the source of liberation. The name and form are not the real issue, as they are only skillful means, or a device to reach the goal. It is the quality that counts.

Recall while reading these tales that different witnesses experience the images, sounds, and activities of the bardo differently, since these images and sounds are their own mental hallucinations or reflections. For example, one person might see the Dharma King in a wrathful form, while another sees him in a peaceful form. Some might observe the Monkey-Faced One taking notes, while someone else sees him reading the mirror in which a person's deeds are reflected. Despite these individual variations, it is notable how many similarities there are in these accounts as well.

Let Her Remember All That She Sees:
The Experience of Lingza Chokyi

Each delog account has a different kind of wisdom and character. The tale of Lingza Chokyi may be closer to the experiences that most ordinary people might have during their death and afterward.

Chokyi found herself looking at her bed, where she saw the dead body of a huge snake wrapped in her own clothing, reeking with a horrible odor of rot. The rotting snake was her own body, but she wasn't able to recognize it. Often the dead person does not see their own corpse in its exact form—if they even see it at all.

When Chokyi's children began to cry, and to hug and kiss the snake, Chokyi's whole perception suddenly transformed. She started to hear loud sounds like simultaneous thunderclaps. She saw hailstorms of blood, and globs of pus the size of eggs started to hammer at her. It was unbearable! But as soon as her children stopped crying, the sounds of thunder and the hammering of hailstones instantly ceased. The whole atmosphere grew peaceful, and all her pain and fear subsided. Her perceptions returned to normal for a while.

Tibetan Buddhists commonly believe that mourning and crying for the dead hurts them. That is one of the reasons why Milarepa expressed these wishes:

There is no one who inquires about me if I am sick.
There is no one who cries for me if I am dead.
If I could die in such a solitude
This yogi's wishes would be fulfilled.

There are no footprints [of kin] at the door [of the cave].
There is no stain of blood inside [from fighting for inheritance].
If I could die in such solitude,
This yogi's wishes would be fulfilled.[1]

Chokyi heard her brother telling the family, "Crying won't do any good. It is better for us to arrange the funeral rites. We must get a lama to perform a phowa, the transference of consciousness. We must invite Thugje Rinpoche and twenty or thirty monks to perform death ceremonies." (A death ceremony might last weeks or a whole forty-nine days, depending on the ability of the family to sponsor it.) "We must also invite the Gomchen [a lama who is a 'Great Meditator'] to preside over the funeral ceremonies, as she has faith in him."

Chokyi could see and hear the family making preparations for her funeral, but somehow she convinced herself that they were planning a ceremony for some other purpose.

When a lama started to recite the *Vajracchedika Sutra*,* Chokyi felt joyful just hearing it. In the afternoon, the Gomchen and about twenty monks arrived. She prostrated herself to the Gomchen and others, and approached to receive their blessings. When they failed to respond, she thought they were angry with her and asked them, "If you are angry, why did you bother to come here?" No one spoke even a word in response. Chokyi could not understand why they didn't see her.

Chokyi saw the Gomchen placing his hand on the head of the "snake" and saying, "Chokyi, death has arrived for you. Don't be attached to your children, wealth, or food. Merge your consciousness with my consciousness. Then we will travel to the Blissful Pure Land of the Buddha of Infinite Light together. We will go there!"

Chokyi thought, "I am not dead. I have my body with me." At the same time, she yearned to go and merge with the lama as he instructed. But from fear of the snake, she pulled back.

At that moment, she heard the Gomchen shouting PHAT! She felt joyful

---

* This classic text, known in English as the *Diamond Sutra*, is one of the Buddha's teachings. It teaches that phenomenal appearances are illusions projected by the mind.

and blissful. Then the Gomchen told the family, "The performance of the phowa is too late. Chokyi's mind has already separated from her body."

Then everyone was served dinner, but no one gave Chokyi any food. The Gomchen told Chokyi's daughter, "Serve your mother her share of the food." So her daughter made a little plate of food with a piece of meat and brought it with tea. Placing it near the snake, she said, "Mother, please eat." Although she was hungry and thirsty, Chokyi could not eat her food because she was disgusted by the snake. Chokyi lost all respect for her daughter for leaving the food by the snake.

After dinner, while mumbling some prayers, the Gomchen burned her share of the food in the fire as a *sur*, a food-burning offering ceremony. Only then did Chokyi feel satisfaction as if she had eaten and drunk. Sur is a traditional Tibetan Buddhist ceremony for offering food, drink, and wealth to the dead or other spirit-beings. The sur materials are blessed with prayers and meditations and then are dedicated to that particular being or beings. The materials are burned to produce an odor, because smell is easier for spirits and beings in the bardo to enjoy.* With this ceremony, Chokyi no longer felt hunger or thirst.

As soon as the lamas finished their altar arrangements, they began to perform an elaborate death ritual. The Gomchen remained in meditation by himself. Chokyi continued to feel sad because she thought everyone was upset with her and because they didn't serve her any food. Since she had no gross body with which to anchor herself, she lacked the stability to remain in one place or maintain a consistent feeling.

Then an idea came to her: "I will take my jewelry and run away." Coincidentally, her children burst into tears again, and a hailstorm of pus and blood started to beat at Chokyi. She could not see anything, and her mind started jumping around even more.

Chokyi wished to run up to Bangar Rinpoche, who was leading the ceremonies, but she thought, "He is a monk. He might not like a woman coming too close to him." So she stayed behind him, hiding. Although the performance of the ceremony was soothing, her fear persisted.

Then she ran to the Gomchen. She saw him in the form of a translucent image of the Buddha of Compassion (Avalokiteshvara). He kept saying, "Nying-je! Nying-je!" (Pity! Pity!). Chokyi understood that the Gomchen was uniting her mind with his mind, which remained in con-

---

* For more about the sur ceremony, see chapter 9, "Ritual Services for the Dying and the Dead," the section "Religious Services after Death," pages 220–225.

templation in an even state. Her fears were eased, and her agitated mind merged into an unimaginable bliss.

After a while she returned to her usual floating thoughts. She saw people having their meal. Again the Gomchen held a sur ceremony, and she enjoyed the food that was dedicated to her in the form of smell.

After a while, she heard a voice coming from outside, saying, "Chokyi, come here!" She went out. Someone was there who she thought was her father. He said, "Come out, I have something to show you. I will let you go back very soon." At this, she thought again, "I have a houseful of lamas. But they are all angry with me. My husband and children are not even giving me any food. So I will follow my father."

As soon as she had that thought, she found herself on a gray barren road bereft of even a single blade of grass or tree. From there she was able to see things at a great distance, and she beheld a vast sandy, flat field. In the middle of the field ran a huge river, but it was hard to tell which way it was flowing. She saw a broad bridge. On this side of the bridge, at the foot of mountains, there was a big city.

The person who had called Chokyi out took her to that city and told her, "First, look around here and see if you can find anybody whom you knew. I will be going to the other side of the river. You should go there too."

This city was filled with so many people that it was as if she were looking into an anthill. Some wore colorful clothes and had good complexions. Others wore ugly clothes and were filthy. But all were sad and crying and had gloomy faces. Thinking, "I might be facing the same situation as these people," Chokyi started to tremble.

In the midst of the people, Chokyi spotted Chogon, who used to take care of her domestic animals. Looking at Chokyi, he said carefully, "Sister, did you get here?" She said, "Yes, I just got here." Then Chokyi peppered him with questions, "Are you living here? Who are these people? Why are they unhappy? Someone asked me to come to the other side of the bridge, and I think I may go there. Who is on the other side?"

Chogon said, "This is the transitional city, the borderland of the living and the dead. We are waiting here because our life span in the world of the living is not yet exhausted. Those who are wearing good clothes and have good complexions are the ones who have accumulated merits in the past. They are waiting for some more merits to be accumulated and dedicated to them by their families in the human world. Those who are wearing filthy clothes and have bad complexions are the ones who haven't accumulated any merit. No one is making merits for them either. As soon as our life span is exhausted, each of us will cross to the other side of the river. Over there the Dharma King of the Lords of the Dead and his executioners are stationed. They will check the karmic records of people. Then they will send the ones who have merits up to higher realms or to liberation. Those who have committed evil deeds will be sent down to the hell realms. In the hell realms, they will suffer unimaginable burning and boiling. Day and night, I worry about what fate awaits me. I went to the other side a couple of times, but they instructed me to wait here, as my life span has not yet ended. Sister, you could go to the other side and listen to what the Lords of the Dead have to say. If you have to wait here, come back."

Judgment by the Lords of the Dead

Soon, Chokyi was summoned to the other side of the river. There she saw a huge wall. On the other side of the wall was a giant golden throne. On the throne was the Dharma King of the Lords of the Dead. His complexion was yellow, and he wore monk's robes with golden designs. His hands were in a contemplative posture. He had a protuberance on the crown of his head. There were silk curtains around him and brocade parasols over his head. All kinds of decorations and offering materials had been arranged around him. So Chokyi saw the Dharma King in the form of the Buddha.

To the Dharma King's right was one of the Lords of the Dead in a human body with an ox's head. He was holding a mirror in his hand. To the Dharma King's left was a monkey-headed Lord of the Dead, holding a scale in his hand. In front of the Dharma King was a deer-headed Lord of the Dead, writing and reading notes. In addition to them, there were all kinds of Lords of the Dead with heads of various animals. Wearing frightening costumes, they were baring their sharp fangs, staring with bulging eyes, brandishing all kinds of weapons, and filling the atmosphere with shouts of "Kill! Kill! Beat! Beat! Ha! Ha! HUNG! HUNG!" They were running and jumping everywhere. It was frightening even to look at. The fate of some three hundred people was being debated.

Among these people there was a monk with a rosary in his hand. The Dharma King was asking him detailed questions about what he had done while he was living in the human world. He enumerated many virtuous deeds. As an evil deed, he mentioned only one thing, the eating of meat.

As ordered by the Dharma King, the Ox-Headed Awa and the Monkey-Headed Lords of the Dead checked the records. They reported to the Dharma King that, with the exception of minor discrepancies what he was saying was true.

At that moment, the White Guardian Deity appeared and pleaded for the monk, saying, "This man has accomplished unimaginable virtuous deeds and has committed no evil acts. He mustn't even be sent to the human and god realms, but only to a buddha pure land." He presented a huge bag filled with white pebbles, which represented the monk's virtuous deeds.

Then the Dark Demon appeared and argued against him, saying, "This man has committed many unvirtuous deeds in his many past lives. So he must be sent to hell." He presented a cup full of black pebbles representing his evil deeds.

After comparing the two, they found that the good deeds far outweighed the bad. The Dharma King remarked, "All his unvirtuous deeds seem to have been canceled out by his virtuous deeds."

The Dharma King then delivered his verdict: "You have achieved the goal of having a human life. Human birth is better than birth in a god realm. So I am sending you to take birth as a son of a wealthy family. There you will pursue the path of Dharma and will make progress." Then the monk disappeared along a dappled yellow path.

Then Lords of the Dead questioned another person. He said, "I don't have any detailed account of virtuous deeds to present to you. I was poor and had very little to eat. My wife wasn't religious either. So, with the exception of paying taxes, I haven't done much charity. I couldn't practice Dharma physically and mentally. I killed a few fish, chicken, goats, and sheep. Under the influence of bad people, I robbed some hermits. I am so sorry!" He was trembling and beating himself. Those Lords of the Dead with their weapons were laughing with joy. Chokyi was scared.

After checking, the Lords of the Dead reported to the Dharma King, saying, "Could they be numbered, the fish that this man has killed? He has also killed twenty-nine chickens, forty-seven pigs, forty-three sheep, and sixty oxen. Look at the number of insects that he has killed by setting a mountain on fire! With four others, he beat and robbed people who were on pilgrimage."

At this the Dharma King said, "You have committed such evil deeds. You have possessed such a rotten heart. Didn't you care a little bit for yourself? Robbing and hurting religious people is even more serious than killing animals." He told the Lords of the Dead, "Now let him suffer in different hell realms. Since he has enjoyed the unvirtuous food of robbing, he must be continuously fed with molten metal."

The White Guardian Deity appeared and pleaded to have the sentence reduced, producing about twenty pebbles to represent the man's virtuous deeds. Then the Dark Demon appeared and demanded his confinement in the lowest hell. He produced a huge quantity of black pebbles the size of Mount Sumeru. Immediately, the Lords of the Dead put a noose around his neck and, catching his heart with hooks, dragged him into a burning iron cell.

Next appeared a priest carrying a medicine bag on his shoulder. When questioned, he listed all the prayers that he had recited and all the offerings he had made. He never let any poor yogis go empty-handed. He was a doctor and treated them all to the best of his ability, having cured many. He never asked for any fees, only taking what his patients offered him. He had never given anyone the wrong medication. He himself never killed any domestic animals, but being a householder he was indirectly involved in such killing.

Then the Lords of the Dead checked the mirror and said, "You are truthful about the virtuous deeds that you claim. But when your brother Chongthar was sick, he came to you for treatment. Because you were envious of his wealth, you gave him the wrong medication and he became sicker for eight months. Finally you cured him, but took a suit of armor of good quality in exchange for your treatment. You also killed one hundred and seventy-three domestic animals."

When they checked the pebbles, the number of white pebbles was slightly larger. However, when they checked the scale, the weight of unvirtuous deeds was greater.

At that, the Dharma King told the priest, "If you hadn't given that wrong medication, you could have earned your next birth in the human or god realm." Then he ordered the Lords of the Dead, "Take him to the boiling poisonous lake. Let him drink boiling poison all the time. Nail a thousand iron thorns to his body. When his unvirtuous deeds are purified, let him go up." The Lords of the Dead caught his heart with iron hooks and dragged him away amid great commotion.

Then a man dressed in blue wool clothes made his confession: "When my first wife left me, I also lost all my two hundred domestic animals. In revenge I burned down two of her parents' houses, burned seventy-five domestic animals, and shot and killed a man and a woman trying to escape. Then I married again and became rich. For the purification of my misdeeds, I went on pilgrimages all over Tibet for two years and met many blessed lamas. Crying, I confessed all my misdeeds before everyone. I received empowerments and instructions from a Great Meditator and meditated on the nature of the mind, the union of clarity, awareness, and openness. I observed many fasts and recited numerous scriptures and prayers."

At this the Dharma King said, "There are many who commit evil deeds, but very few who purify them. Although there is no merit in evil deeds, if you purify them, they can be washed away. That is their merit. If you have done virtuous deeds without evil deeds, you will become a person who will lead all who are connected with you to liberation. But you will take rebirth in the human realm and will practice the Vajrayana or esoteric path, and in four successive lives you will attain buddhahood. So follow the yellow path, which is the path to the human and god realms."

After some time, many of those who had arrived at the court of the Dharma King with Lingza Chokyi had been dispatched up or down. Many had been led up by their teachers. But then new people kept streaming in.

The Dharma King suddenly rose from his seat, saying, "There, he has arrived." On the mountain pass, at a distance, Chokyi saw the approach of a heavily built monk surrounded by about three hundred people. This group was further followed by about three thousand people. All were dancing and singing OM MANI PADME HUNG. Then the monk declared, "My name is Jochung, the Singer of OM MANI PADME HUNG. This is the world of the bardo and hell. All who have connection with me, come follow me. I am going to lead you to the pure land." Suddenly the doors of hell opened spontaneously. The Lords of the Dead fainted, and their weapons fell from their hands. The stream of beings followed the monk. The Lords of the Dead rose in respect and gave this order: "Many of you may leave, but not all." They caught about three hundred from the stream of beings and returned them to their hell cells.

Chokyi had no connection with this monk, so she didn't follow him. She asked the Dharma King, "That monk took away those many men and women with no need of questioning. He liberated those many beings from the strict rules of this court. How did he become so powerful?"

The Dharma King explained, "That monk is called Jochung Ma-we Seng-ge, who sings OM MANI PADME HUNG. He became a monk when he was young. He developed faith in Avalokiteshvara, recited OM MANI

PADME HUNG all the time, and developed compassion for all sentient beings. He observed and promoted fasting rites. Those three hundred people who came with him are those who practiced virtuous deeds and observed fasting with him. Those whom he led away are the people who have faith in him, received teachings from him, saw him, heard him, touched him, made offerings to him, or received blessings from him. Those who were prevented are the ones who had no connection with him or had a negative connection with him."

Next up was an attractive nun. The court's investigation revealed that she had only enjoyed life. She had no faith, gave no charity, and stirred up lots of unvirtuous deeds. She begged to be sent back so she could practice Dharma. She was sent to hell.

Next, a girl with prayer beads in her hand singing OM MANI PADME HUNG approached. Her name was Marza Chodron. She had received teachings and blessings. She kept faith, made offerings, served yogis, and died at the age of thirty-three.

She said, "I was taught by the lamas that whatever good or bad forms and sounds of the external world arise, they are the illusions of the mind. There is no reality. So, all of you whom I see here are the self-appearing forms of my own mind. In truth, there is not a single entity that exists. I don't think that my body exists. Whatever forms or colors appear to my mind, there is nothing to apprehend. So there is nothing to be boiled or burned in the hell realm."

In the mirror they saw even more virtuous deeds than she had listed. But they also noted that she was indirectly involved in some unvirtuous deeds such as killing a fistful of insects. She was also indirectly involved in allowing seven domestic animals to be butchered for her wedding feast. One quarter of the consequences of these killings would go to the parents of the bride and groom, one quarter to herself, one quarter to her husband, and one quarter to the butcher. The Dharma King nevertheless praised her record overall: "By meditating on the nature of the mind, you have realized the nonexistence of things. They all arise as the power of one's own mind. You have trained yourself in the awareness of the nonexistence of delusions. You have trained in the meaning of the indivisibility of mind and the objects that appear to it. That is an absolute virtue. Although you couldn't attain the realization of the absolute truth, as your training wasn't long enough, what realization you did attain is powerful. All the minor evil deeds that you have committed have been purified. Until you realize the nature of the mind, as it is, the pure visions of pure lands will not arise.[2] Now you will take rebirth in Oddiyana* and will train in esoteric trainings for eighty years. Then you will take rebirth in the Blissful Pure Land and attain buddhahood." At that moment, her teacher, Gomchen Kunga Yeshe, arrived. With many who had connections with this teacher, she went away along a white path.

An old man of about seventy arrived, with prayer beads and a prayer wheel in his hands, accompanied by about sixty men and women. They were singing OM MANI PADME HUNG. He proclaimed, "I am Sherab Rinchen, the carver of the mantra OM MANI PADME HUNG on stones. May all who are connected to me come. I have been invited to the pure land of Avalokiteshvara." About four hundred people followed him. But three people were pulled back by the Lords of the Dead.

The Dharma King said, "He has recited OM MANI PADME HUNG almost one hundred million times. He has carved OM MANI PADME HUNG on many stones, which he placed by the roadsides so that people could pay respect to them. He had a wife and three children. The people who were following him were those who had faith in him. He could have liberated many people, but because of the Tibetan attitude that married life is wrong for a lama, many were prevented from having faith in him."

A Glimpse of the Hell Realms

By now, those who arrived at the court with Chokyi had been dispatched up or down after being questioned. With the exception of Chokyi, no one remained out of all those who had arrived earlier. But many new ones kept arriving and were waiting. Chokyi thought, "I don't have any long lists of my virtuous deeds to present. Lying won't work here. What I should I do?" She started to tremble with fear.

At that moment, the Dharma King closed his eyes and started to ponder deeply. Then he instructed the Lords of the Dead, "Let this lady see the World of the Dead. Let her remember all that she sees. Then bring her back here quickly."

A tiger-headed Lord of the Dead set down a black ladder. Climbing down, he asked her to follow him to see the hell realms. When she descended, she found herself on an iron ground burning with flames. This

---

* Oddiyana is an ancient land in northwestern India that was known in Tibetan tradition as a center of esoteric training. It is believed to have been on the border of present-day Pakistan and Afghanistan, around the Swat Valley of Pakistan.

ground was enclosed within a huge burning iron wall and leveled into eight stories. On different floors, Chokyi witnessed beings going through different kinds of sufferings.

Among the hell worlds that Chokyi, Tsophu Dorlo, and other delogs traveled through were the eight hot realms and eight cold realms with secondary hell realms. Beings in those hell realms were suffering different degrees of torment caused by different degrees of negative karmas of physical, vocal, and mental deeds, mainly based on anger or hatred committed in past lives.

On the first level down, numerous beings were thrown on their backs on the burning ground and cut into pieces by various executioners. All the beings regarded each other as enemies and were killing each other with great anger. Whenever those beings fainted, a voice was heard saying, "May you revive." At once they became reanimated and went through the same tortures again. Those beings were the rebirths of people who had hurt their parents and friends with hateful thoughts.

On the second level down, the executioners were throwing many beings on the burning ground. They drew lines on their bodies and cut them into pieces, following the lines with the blades of burning saws. These beings were the rebirths of those who were hunters or butchers or who had poisoned others.

On the third level down, many beings were being tossed into mortars of burning iron and crushed with burning hammers. Many were also being crushed between burning mountains. They were the rebirths of hunters, butchers, killers of domestic animals, and makers of weapons.

On the fourth level down, many beings were being roasted in flames, and one could only hear their screams. They were merchants of poisons and killers of people, horses, and dogs. They were also those who insulted religious persons and made weapons.

On the fifth level down, in a huge burning hall, beings were burned on the inside and outside. All were crying like thunder. They were the rebirths of people who had offended the Three Jewels, held perverted views, stirred up fights, and robbed religious people.

On the sixth level down, beings were being burned in a huge bonfire. From time to time, the executioner would pick them out, crush them with burning hammers, and throw them back into the flame. These were people who denied the truth of causation of good and bad deeds and who killed beings such as fish and snakes with severe cruelty and contempt for karmic consequences.

On the seventh level down, many beings were stewing in molten metal, and the sounds of boiling metal and bellows were as loud as thunder. They had committed many evil deeds such as burning forests that killed many beings and destroying religious monuments.

On the eighth level down, beings were nailed onto the burning ground, and their bodies were cut and inflicted with torture from various devices. As the beings burned, flames were coming out of the holes in their bodies. They were those who had never accumulated any virtuous deeds, had committed the five immeasurable offenses and secondary immeasurable offenses, and had destroyed religious monuments and community resources. They were also those who broke their esoteric vows, held wrong views, and caused faith in esoteric paths and goals to be destroyed.

Chokyi also visited the secondary hell realms called the "four neighboring hells." In those realms, many beings were sinking in a swamp of filth and being eaten by insects. Many had their tongues pulled out and were being plowed by burning plows. Many continuously injured themselves as they climbed up and down mountains covered with forests of sharp burning weapons, or as they walked in fields of razors. These tortures were the results of polluting pure and sacred places, accusing innocent people, being attached to the objects of lust, and improperly enjoying religious properties or the property of parents.

Then Chokyi visited the eight cold hells, where numerous naked beings were freezing and shivering on a ground of ice with blistering winds. Their bodies were cracking in various designs and colors, and they uttered all manner of cries.

Messages to the Living

Finally, Chokyi returned to the court of the Dharma King. He told her, "You are one of those who were brought here by mistake because of a mixup of names and clans. Your body is still safe at home. Although I looked in the mirror and couldn't detect any happiness waiting for you, this time you can go back home. When you return here next time, make sure that you have no reason to feel anxious for not having done Dharma practices. You have seen for yourself the effect of virtuous and evil deeds." Then he sent the following messages to the people of the world of the living:

There are many who are enjoying a perfect human life
But they leave empty-handed without any Dharma
    achievements.
To those heartless people, convey these messages:
Tell them that you yourself have been to the World of the Dead.
Tell them that you did meet the Dharma King.
Tell them that you have seen the sixteen hell realms.
Tell them that the ocean of samsara is vast.
Though the number of male and female beings is infinite,
When they are pursued by karma,
None has anywhere else to go but one place [the court of the
    Lords of the Dead]. . . .
When the results of evil actions come upon you,
All the appearances will arise as enemies.
There won't be anything that is not an opponent.
For example, a flame that came from you will burn you.
This flame didn't come from anywhere else.
The arising of your own perceptions as enemies
Is a greater opponent than any other force.
Who made those frightening weapons?
How did they get them? By whom are they made and to whom are
    they handed?
Who are the parents who nourished
Those hideous executioners of the Lords of the Dead?
The phenomena of hells are [unreal] like your dreams.
You will not realize your mind as the Buddha
Unless you learn to realize the openness nature of all
    appearances.
When you know the ways of liberating your perceptions,
You will not find any hell even if you search for it.
Even if you find it, it will be a pure land of joy.
Brainless people—who are frightened by
Self-created images of their own mind—
Are in fact being terrified by their own shadow.
Though nothing exists, things appear in various forms.
Though things appear, they do not exist in their reality.
That is the nature of the union of appearances and emptiness.
People who have been introduced to such a nature

Should just contemplate that nature to which they have been
    introduced.
Determine that all are self-images.
All is you, not separate from you.
So determine that samsara and nirvana are your own mind.
Recite OM MANI PADME HUNG with diligence.
Haven't you witnessed here the beneficial power of its
    recitation?
Don't forget all these messages.
Tell everyone the story of what you witnessed here.

The Dharma King instructed Chokyi to return home. Then, facing the snowy mountain pass from which she had entered, Chokyi started walking with the thought of returning home. Instantly, she found herself in her home. Her bed was walled off by a blanket. In her bed she saw the dead body of a snake, as she had seen earlier, wrapped in her own clothes.

Chokyi got upset with her family, thinking, "They know that I am scared of snakes. They are keeping the dead body of a snake in my bed wrapped in my clothes." She decided, "Now, scared or not, I will drag this snake out with the clothes and throw it out the door." She closed her eyes, held the clothes with her two hands, and pulled them. It felt as if she had fallen down on her back, but instantly she found herself in her body, as if she had woken from sleep.

Chokyi took a deep breath, and her elder son called her, saying, "Ama! Ama!" She said, "Ah." Her son shouted, "Ama is back. Everybody come here!" All the relatives rushed to her. Chokyi narrated all the events that she had gone through, and everyone cried. Remembering the sufferings of the hell realms, she also cried. Slowly, she recovered her health. Her relatives made some offerings to the lamas and returned to their own homes.

In the autumn, she sponsored a gathering of many people to recite OM MANI PADME HUNG one billion times. She also made offerings to many monasteries.

Chokyi sent her husband and sons with the necessary provisions to travel to a place where they could practice the Dharma. She and her daughter became nuns and traveled to pilgrimage places, fully dedicating their lives to Dharma practice by leaving all mundane activities behind.

Lingza Chokyi concludes her delog story by saying:

I have witnessed the hell realms in person. The choice of happiness or suffering is in our own hands. When the freedom of choice is in your own hand, please don't worry too much about what you want for this life. You must try to do the best for your next life.

The best thing to do is to abandon the interests of this life. Try to recognize the true nature of your own mind. It is amazingly powerful.

The second best thing is to refrain from committing any evil deeds, whether physical, vocal, or mental, and to devote all your efforts to Dharma activities.

At least, offer some of your wealth to the teachers and Dharma communities, and share it with the poor.

WHAT JUDGMENTS AWAIT ME?:
THE EXPERIENCE OF KARMA WANGDZIN

After her brief glimpse of the ultimate nature, as we saw in chapter 3, Karma Wangdzin was floating around like a feather in the air, since she no longer had a gross body to anchor her consciousness. Now her mind was many times clearer than it had been when she was alive.

A thought flickered into Karma's mind: "Am I really dead?" She looked around desperately for her friends but found none. Then, instantly, she forgot the question of whether or not she had died. She felt lonely and thought it was because she had been staying in a hermitage for a long time. So she told herself, "Merely depriving myself of good food, beautiful clothes, and interesting gossip is not necessarily Dharma practice. It is better for me to return home than just stay in the hermitage nursing feelings of sadness." At the mere wish to return home, Karma found herself at Ogtro, her hometown, and not in the hermitage where she had been staying.

Karma's husband, who was Chief of the valley, was not at home, as he had gone to Traphu Monastery along with many others. Those who remained at home were lamenting loudly and crying out to Karma by her given name: "Oh, Lhawang Putri! Oh, Lhawang Putri!"

Karma tried to lift some of them up by their arms, asking, "Did you get a scolding from the Chief?" But no one responded or even looked at her. Then she heard a loud cry coming from outside her home. In the streets people were telling each other, "Lhawang Putri has died!" Many grief-stricken people were saying, "She was so humble and generous." Others were whispering complaints: "She had strong bones and narrow shoulders," meaning an inflexible heart and a jealous mind.

Then she was back in her home. With loud cries her family members were still wailing, "Our lady has gone!" "Pity for the princess!" "Sorrow for the Chief!" She saw the tears of pain shed by her loved ones. They rained on her in the form of egg-size balls of blood and pus. The rain of those tears was accompanied by thunderous noises and kept piercing her skin and breaking her bones. Most of the time, she saw herself dressed as usual, but when she was in a hailstorm, she felt that her body was vulnerable because she was naked.

From an invisible source, Karma heard a voice say: "Go to Traphu Monastery." Merely by wishing, she reached Traphu. Her husband and others were busy arranging a ceremony. Two monks quickly set up an altar with *thangkas* (religious scroll paintings) and many offerings in front of them. She thought, "Oh they are arranging the Seventh-Day Offering," an annual ceremony of the monastery. One after another, many people started to arrive from Ogtro to console her husband and serve him the customary drinks.

Then the manager of the Chief's estate arrived. He had brought Karma's jewelry with him and placed it on the altar. Then he saluted the Chief and pleaded, "Chief, please don't cry. It is true, this is a grave tragedy. It is a time of great pain in your heart. But she wasn't taking any responsibility as the lady of the Pagtro residence. She was even talking of helping many girls in the neighborhood to leave home life to pursue the Dharma. We, the public, would regard a pain in our index finger as more serious than her death. Now we must concentrate on the funeral arrangements."

Shedding a stream of tears, the Chief said, "The sun has set at midday. We lived together for only a very short time, I have no parents. She was the only real friend I had. Now I have lost her too."

Then the Chief instructed, "Until the completion of the forty-nine day ceremony, it is better to preserve her body as it is, without embalming it. She's the kind of person who might return to life, as a delog. Lingza Chokyi, for example, came back with many stories of afterdeath." Karma was crying and thinking, "Am I really dead?"

But the next moment, Karma had resumed believing she was alive. Holding her husband's hand, she kept trying to assure him that she was alive and that there was no basis for him to feel sad about her so-called death. But neither he nor anyone else would even respond to her pleas. She concluded that everyone was angry with her.

Her husband asked an assistant to give a yak-load of tea bricks to someone. But Karma saw that on the way out, the assistant quietly stole some tea bricks and put them into a bag for himself. She was ashamed of his wrongful act for such paltry gain.

Soon the attendants brought a meal for the Chief. Karma expected to eat with him as usual, but no one served her, and even her husband wouldn't bother asking her to have something. She wept, thinking, "Now I cannot even share a little meal." She got upset and thought about her husband: "You are the one who wouldn't let me stay with my loving parents and didn't allow me to go and follow the Dharma, saying, "I will take care of all your needs." But now you are behaving like all your attendants. I have no power even to share a little meal with you. Now I am going back to my hermitage."

Before leaving, she thought of her husband again. "When I was the darling of my parents and had the freedom of going to the Dharma, you lured me with promises of this and that. Now you won't even give me a little share of food and drink. You have removed my jewelry, which was given to me by my parents. Before, you saw me as a goddess. Now you are forcing me to wander around like a stray dog, ignored by everyone. There is nothing in you that I can trust anymore. All my hopes and your promises are like drawings on water. At last I understand the meaning of that old saying, 'Until the noose is tight around their neck, women do not notice any problems.' Now I should warn all the girls who are still unmarried and urge them to leave everything and follow the Dharma as nuns."

Then she screamed to everyone, "Chief and all the attendants, listen to me! My staying here has become an annoyance to all of you. You enjoy the satisfactions of your wealth and privilege. I will satisfy myself with the Dharma. Chief, don't have any regrets!" No one asked her not to leave, but they continued to moan. She left the place.

Up in the valley she saw a group of spirit-beings descending from the upper land of the valley. They were whispering, "There is a ceremony in Gechu Valley. We should go there." Following them, she too reached Kunga Ling Monastery. The dogs that used to be friendly toward Karma were now all barking and rushing at her. She had to hide and wait outside. Then a yogi who was performing an offering of water and *torma* (ritual cake) threw out the offerings. All kinds of beings, like black flies on filth, enjoyed these offerings. The main offerings were enjoyed by the spirits to whom they were actually dedicated. The leftover offering materials were shared by others, to whom the offerings were not necessarily dedicated.

However, many weak and sick spirit-beings left empty-handed. In great desperation, they fell face down on the ground and cried loudly with hunger and thirst. Some of them were crying and holding each other. Karma felt ashamed of herself, as she was in much better shape. Toward those suffering spirit-beings, an unbearable compassion developed in her mind, but she couldn't do anything for them; it would be like the blind helping the blind. She cried very loudly for them. At that instant, she heard a clear voice saying:

First, there is no past accumulation of merits in them.
Second, their sufferings are the results of their own evil deeds.
Third, here a small number of beings are involved.
A feeling of sadness will help no one. So just relax.

Then Karma wished to go to Zagrum to see her parents. Instantly she found herself in Zagrum. Karma's mother was doing circumambulations around a temple as an exercise of her respect and devotion. Karma quickly said to her mother, "Amala, give me something to eat." Her mother didn't say a word and kept doing her circumambulations. Karma thought, "When I used to arrive by horse with gifts carried by porters, she would exclaim, "Oh, my daughter has arrived," and would receive me with great joy and with welcoming *chang* [beer]. Now she, too, is ignoring me. A letter from the Chief complaining about me must have reached her. She must care more for my husband, someone else's son, than for her own daughter."

Clutching at her mother's clothing, Karma pleaded, "Since I married the Chief as arranged by my parents, I thought, 'Whatever happens to me I accept as the result of the lines of my own skull, my own fate.' The Chief had a relationship with a a girl from Shar, but I was the one who was blamed for it and beaten up. I didn't even bother to tell my own parents about this incident. Since I couldn't bear a child, I am not even getting a share of food and drink. Please give me something to eat. Then I will leave for Dharma practice."

Without even glancing at her or saying a word, her mother went to her house. Although her mother didn't ask her in, Karma followed her to their house. In her parents' home, the family got together and enjoyed their lunch. Karma was hungry and sat behind her mother, waiting for her share of food, but again no one bothered to offer her anything. After lunch, the people went out, and Karma did too. Believing that all these

You haven't committed many evil deeds. But many people in this degenerate age face the danger of falling into hell because they are harboring so many negative emotions and committing so many harmful deeds in their human lives.

You will be going back to your body in the World of the Living as a messenger from the World of the Dead. So you must be strong and watch all that happens here carefully. You must remember all that you see and hear without forgetting it. Now let us go over there.

Glimpses of Hell Realms and Messages from the Dead

At the western corner of the vast field, Karma saw a terrifying man with the head of a deer holding a black noose in his hand. With wide, bulging eyes, he was chasing down an elderly woman, who appeared to be wearing jewelry on her head. Karma asked White Tara, "Alas! Who is that deer-headed person? Who is that mysterious woman?"

White Tara said, "Don't be afraid of the deer-headed person. He is one of those manifestations of the deities of the palace of one's own skull.* Deities of various colors, forms, and dimensions appear according to one's own nature. The old woman came from Chenying in Kham province. She was the wife of the town leader and conspired with him in robbing, murdering and hunting. This is her perception of the transitional passage. After this she will be judged and will have to go to the hell realm."

Next Karma encountered a huge iron bridge over a massive river called the Great River of Samsara. At the eastern end of the bridge, there was an unimaginable city, inhabited by people of contrasting lives. Part of the population—among them monks, nuns, and laypeople—was joyful, rich, and beautiful. They dwelled in amazing, decorated mansions. Some spent their time happily singing and dancing. Others devoted their lives to prayer and singing the mantra OM MANI PADME HUNG. Yet others were giving away inexhaustible charity to others. None seemed to have ever been touched by any fear or suffering.

The other part of the population, however, had no place to live or food to eat. They were constantly afflicted by hunger and thirst. Many were cupping their hands over their foreheads, as if searching for something on

---

* Tib. *thopa*, *Thod Pa*, skull or brain.

the far horizon. They were desperately looking for any hopeful sign that their relatives might dedicate some merits to them in funeral ceremonies to improve their future. Now and then the Lords of the Dead would show up to take many of them away.

This was a place where many of the dead would wait before they were taken to the court of the Dharma King for judgment.

Looking at the beings of this place, a Lord of the Dead explained to Karma, "Among these people, many are joyful because they lived a clean life and treated others with respect. Many are singing prayers and enjoying themselves because of the strength of their past spiritual experiences. The Lords of the Dead won't even dare to look at them. Many have inexhaustible wealth and are still receiving and giving, because they gave whatever they had when they were in the World of the Living.

"Others among these people are suffering from hunger and thirst because they didn't serve or respect others or give anything in charity. Instead, they blamed, robbed, and assaulted others in their past existence. They are waiting, some with the gesture of watching, in the hope that their relatives will dedicate some merits for them. Soon they will be taken to the court of the Dharma King, where some will be liberated while others are sent to inferior realms."

Next Karma visited the realm of hungry ghosts. All the beings here were naked. Their stomachs were huge like valleys. Their limbs were thin as straw. Their necks were as narrow as a single hair of a horse's tail. Because of severe thirst, flames were blazing from their mouths. Unbearable hunger pangs were torturing them.

Looking at them, a Lord of the Dead explained to Karma, "These people never felt generosity in their lives. They never offered anything for religious purposes or gave anything to any needy being. They never had a generous thought, only a mentality of boiling desire, burning hatred, an avalanche of pride, the darkness of ignorance, and a storm of jealousy. They obstructed others from making offerings and giving, and they couldn't enjoy food and drink even for themselves—all because of their miserliness."

Karma saw that the Buddha of Compassion was visiting the hungry ghosts. From the hand of the Buddha of Compassion, streams of nectar were flowing to ease their sufferings. But many of them not only were unable to enjoy the stream of nectar, they couldn't even look at the buddha or remain in his presence.

Then, at the gate of a bridge, an attractive young girl was singing and dancing one moment and crying the next. White Tara asked her, "O beautiful woman! What was your birthplace and family? Why are you singing and dancing, and also crying? Where are you going, up or down?"

The girl responded, "Alas, I am from the highlands of Southern Tibet. The name of my town was Neudong. My father was Chogyal Tsering and my mother was Sechung. My name was Dorje Gyalmo. My valley was ransacked by the Mongols, who took me to Mongolia by force. I died of a severe illness. I got here without any chance of seeing my parents again. The Dharma King told me, "Daughter, you are from an excellent family and have a clear mind and no ego. However, you are too attached to your parents and to your possessions. Moreover, you still have some of your life span left to enjoy. So you must go back to take rebirth as a *manmo** in your own valley.""

White Tara again asked her, "Why is your mind so attached?" The girl responded, "After my death, instead of donating my possessions for a good cause, to make merits, people sold them to a strange woman. So, even in the midst of frightening visions of the Lords of the Dead, I kept thinking about this unhappy incident. Because of that attachment, the King of Dharma ordered me to take rebirth as a manmo."

Crying, the girl pleaded with Karma to convey the following message to her parents: "I am Dorje Gyalmo. I am attached to my parents and to my jewelry. Dear parents, please offer all my possessions to a lama to perform feast and purification ceremonies and make hundreds of torma cake offerings. Please serve chang to the village people and let them say prayers. If you could do that, I will gain a human birth instead of taking rebirth as a manmo."

In her account, Karma does not mention traveling to each of the hell realms, but she did see numerous beings suffering inconceivable pain. She was able to receive messages from a few of them for their loved ones in the human world.

Summoned to the Court

Then White Tara led Karma to the palace of the Dharma King of the Lords of the Dead. Five concentric circular walls surrounded this palace. There were four gates at each direction, and eight guards in terrifying

---

* Tib. *sMan Mo,* a class of female spirit-beings.

forms protected each gate. They were armed with frightening weapons and thundering: "Hung! Hung! Phat! Phat! Beat! Beat! Kill! Kill!"

In front of the northern gate, on a huge stage of stone, Karma saw heaps of body parts. They had been cut into pieces by spinning iron wheels of sharp weapons that had landed on them from the sky. They had been crushed into dust by all kinds of implements by the executioners at the order of the Lords of the Dead. With great fear and sadness, Karma collapsed on the ground. White Tara picked her up and said:

> They are reaping the fruits of their own deeds.
> Even if the Buddha himself were to come in person, there is
>   nothing he can do,
> Because they are experiencing the results of their karma.
> Don't you feel so sad.

Karma's heart was tormented with the great pain of regret, thinking, "I didn't do any serious Dharma practice while I was in the world of the living. Now what kinds of questions will the Dharma King of the Lords of the Dead ask me? What kind of judgments await me?

If I get the chance to go back to the human world, I will explain the seriousness of karma to people by telling them exactly what I witnessed, with no sugar coating. I will donate all I possess to everyone without attachment. Leaving all worldly activities behind, I will contemplate the nature of the mind. Without clinging to anyone, I will wander alone from one hermitage to the next. I will visualize my lama in my heart all the time, and I will pray ceaselessly to the Three Jewels. I will not entertain attachment to friends and relatives."

At that moment, Karma heard a loud voice coming from the palace of the Dharma King. A guard approached Karma and White Tara, saying, "This is the signal of your summons to the court of the Dharma King."

Great pain struck Karma's heart as if it were struck by an arrow. She was tormented by great regret for neglecting to perform serious Dharma practice. Weeping, she thought, "However, I have said prayers to the buddhas without a pause. So, buddhas, please look after me with your loving eyes."

Wiping away Karma's tears, White Tara said, "You haven't given any material gifts in charity, nor have you established any solid meditation attainment. But your mind is like a clear mirror, unstained by the effects of evil deeds. You and I have remained inseparable for a long time, because of our mutual karmas and aspirations."

Holding Karma's hand, White Tara led her through the gate. They climbed up a huge stone stairway. Karma was trembling terribly. Then they entered a huge hall. In the center of the hall was the Dharma King of the Lords of the Dead. Karma saw the Dharma King in the form of Guru Rinpoche, Padmasambhava. Seated on a throne supported by four lions, he was dressed, ornamented, and holding implements as Karma had seen in paintings. At the sight of Guru Rinpoche, Karma's body and mind were instantly filled with waves of devotion. The hairs on her body stood up. Tears of joy streamed from her eyes. She wanted to rush forward and prostrate herself before Guru Rinpoche, but she held herself back for fear of the wrathful male and female deities standing around him.

These wrathful deities were in frightening forms, wearing horrifying costumes and brandishing terrifying implements. At the feet of Guru Rinpoche, on his right, was a Lord of the Dead with a human body and the head of an ox. He was holding a mirror in which they were observing the deeds of the beings who were presented before the Dharma King. Next to him was the Tiger-Headed Lord of the Dead, bearing the records of what beings had done. On the left side of Guru Rinpoche was the Snake-Headed Lord of the Dead. He was inspecting all who were present at the court. In front of Guru Rinpoche was the Pig-Headed Lord of the Dead. He was keeping the accounts and schedules. In addition to these, there were many Lords of the Dead with heads of other animals, holding all kinds of implements.

White Tara reminded Karma, "Outwardly, the one who is sitting in the center is the Dharma King of the Lords of the Dead. Inwardly, he is Guru Rinpoche. Outwardly, the one at Guru Rinpoche's right side, watching us with bulging eyes and thundering, "Hung! Hung! Phat! Phat!," is a Lord of the Dead. Inwardly, he is the wrathful form of Manjushri, the Buddha of Wisdom. If you open yourself in prayer to them, you will be freed from danger and fears. All the wrathful male and female Lords of the Dead are peaceful and wrathful buddhas. If you open in prayer to them, you will take rebirth in higher realms. You must remember these crucial points. You haven't committed any serious evil deeds, so don't be depressed. Get up and pay homage to them, and make aspirations for yourself and all mother-beings."

Karma made one prostration as a gesture of respect, but before she could make another prostration or make any aspiration, the Snake-Headed Lord of the Dead interrupted her. He motioned to her to sit down in a corner. As soon as she had done so, in a blustering voice the Dharma King told the Lords of the Dead who were standing in the courtyard of the palace, "A deceased person from the human world is arriving. Bring her here at once." In the courtyard of the palace, numerous representatives holding all kinds of implements rose up with a great roar of HUNG! HUNG! PHAT! PHAT!

At that moment a woman appeared in the courtyard. Faced with this frightening scene, at first she tried to run away, but there was no escape. Then, brandishing the baton of OM MANI PADME HUNG, she sang the Six-Syllable Mantra. As soon as the Lords of the Dead heard the sound of the holy six syllables, they all calmly settled down where they were. The woman was accompanied by a lady in white robes. Her hair was arranged in a a topknot tied with a red silk ribbon. She was holding a rosary of crystal beads. Taking the woman by the arm, the white-robed lady led her into the palace. She had been freed. No Lords of the Dead seemed to have any power to detain or intimidate her. However, when they checked, she had many virtuous deeds to her credit, such as praying to the Buddha of Compassion. However, she also harbored resentment toward unfair bureaucratic systems of the society. For that reason, she would have to take birth first as a bird and only later as a human being.

Then Karma heard a loud voice. She looked toward the direction from which the sound came, and there she saw a monk wearing a hat. He told her, "Now you have understood the effects of karma. You have seen the face of the Dharma King. You have witnessed the threats of the Lords of the Dead. You must bear in mind the certainties of karmic consequences and the instructions given by the Dharma King. Now you must go back to the human world. Your family is about to dispose of your body." Having said that, he disappeared in a breeze.

Then White Tara pleaded with the Dharma King:

O Dharma King, please heed me!
Karma has awakened her mind to the Dharma.
Because of her excellent karmic connections, she is seeing you
    as Guru Rinpoche.
Her body and consciousness separated before her life span was
    exhausted.
Because of her attachments, she suffered these transitional
    experiences.
She reached the Dharma King because of her past aspirations.

She witnessed the fear of the Lords of the Dead, the truth of
  karmic effects.
She has been spending seven human days here, and
Her empty house–like mortal body is perishing [in the human
  world].
So she should be sent back as your messenger to the people of
  Jambu continent.*
Or she should take birth again as a human being.
Or she should be dispatched to the stages of knowledge-holders.
O Dharma King, where should she go? Please give your order.

The Dharma King stared at Karma and was absorbed in thought for a
while. Then, watching the mirror, he checked the details of Karma's past
deeds and said, "In the past, Lingza Chokyi† returned to life because the
Lords of the Dead brought her, having mistaken her name and her clan's
name. Then two girls, Samten of Dartsedo‡ and Yungtrung Wangmo
from Kham, were sent back. Samten of Dartsedo was sent back with
strict instructions that she must must practice Dharma without committing evil deeds. Yungtrung of Kham was sent back so she could practice
Dharma in order to realize the nature of mind."

The Dharma King said, "Now you are going back to the Jambu
continent to inspire people to the Dharma and also to bring messages
from beings of the World of the Dead to their loved ones in the World of
the Living. Because of your past merits and aspirations, you will accomplish great benefits on your return to your body."

The Dharma King gave Karma detailed instructions and prophecies
with the following messages to the people of the Jambu continent:

Tell them that I, the King of Dharma, am here.
Tell them that here we have sophisticated ways
Of finding out whether people have committed evil deeds or
  virtuous deeds.
Tell them that people devoted to the Dharma ascend to higher
  realms.

---

* *Jambu* is an ancient term for the Asian continent.
† Lingza Chokyi's bardo account is summarized in the first section of this chapter.
‡ This must be a reference to Samten Chotso, whose account appears later in this chap-
  ter. Dartsedo is now known as Kanding in Sichuan.

Tell them that people indulging in evil activities descend to hell
    realms.
You, the people of Jambu continent,
Must follow the teachings of Buddha Shakyamuni in general
And especially observe these orders of mine:
Outwardly, I am the Dharma King [of the Lords of the Dead];
Inwardly, I am Avalokiteshvara, the Buddha of Compassion.
Recite OM MANI PADME HUNG, the essence of Avalokiteshvara.
Outwardly, I am the Dharma King;
Inwardly, I am Guru Rinpoche.
Recite OM AH HUNG VAJRA GURU PADMA SIDDHI HUNG.
Outwardly, I am the Dharma King;
Inwardly, I am Buddha Shakyamuni.
Train in the teachings of the Buddha.
Always strengthen your mind in virtuous deeds.
Abandon even the smallest evil deeds immediately.
Imagine your lama at the crown of your head.
Offer great services to all mother-beings.
Noontime has arrived now [at your home].
With pure aspirations, think of your home.

At this, many of the deceased who had been brought before the court
of the Dharma King by the executioners, pleaded with Karma: "Fortunate
one, if you are returning to the human world, please give my message to
my loved ones. Ask them please to perform some pure virtuous deeds and
offer services to the Three Jewels on my behalf. For pacifying the sufferings of the hell realms, there is no more effective prayer than OM MANI
PADME HUNG. So, please recite or request others to recite OM MANI PADME
HUNG, tens of thousands of times. Please carve this mantra on stones and
pile them up. Print it on cloths and hoist them as flags. Print it on pieces
of paper and spin them as prayer wheels."

Karma Returns to Her Body

Then the thought came into Karma's mind, "Now I should go back to
my valley." Instantly, she found herself in Traphu, her home.

At the entrance to her house, she saw the dead body of an old dog. Its
eyes were deeply sunken, and foam was caked around its mouth. Karma
was both frightened and disgusted. First she ran away from it, but then

she thought, "I could get into my house by walking over the body." When she stepped over the dog's body, her mind instantly entered her own body and she was trapped in it. She had been seeing her own dead body as the body of a dead dog.

First she fainted, which felt like the darkness at dusk. After a while, she started slowly to regain consciousness, but she could not move, as there was no strength left in her body. Slowly, her memory became a bit sharper. When she made a small movement, the person who was sitting by her and keeping his eyes on the body witnessed the movement. He excitedly shouted PHAT! three times. She was still preoccupied with the images and feelings of the sufferings of the hell realms, but the sound of the PHAT blew them away. The piece of cloth that covered her face billowed a little bit. The person wondered, "Is a spirit force entering Karma's body and making her a zombie?" He opened the veil and pressed her head many times. Then he pressed her hands, but she didn't have the strength to press his hand or say that she was alive. Then the man checked her chest and found that there was heat at her heart. He called out to Karma's family members: "Come here! Princess has returned!"

Karma's mother arrived, crying. She kept saying, "My daughter, are you back?" People quickly opened the cloth that Karma's body was wrapped in. At that moment, the Chief arrived. He ordered people to move his wife to another location and serve her milk and honey. However, Karma couldn't eat or even sip liquids for a week. People had to pour a little liquid into her mouth. From the next day, little by little, she started to regain strength and recover her complexion.

Later, Karma and her family engaged two transcribers. They planned to write down and divide into two parts all the messages the dead had sent to their loved ones through Karma. In one part, they would include the messages to loved ones in Ü (Central), Tsang (Western), and Lotrag (Southern) provinces of Tibet. In the second part, they would put the messages to the loved ones in Mongolia and Mon provinces. She also planned to travel in person around the country to convey the messages of the Dharma King to the public.

But unfortunately, the mother of Choje'i Trung, a powerful noblewoman, said, "Karma is from a lowly background. She has returned from death in order to snatch people's lives." Others listened to her and said, "She is a demon!" Instead of trusting Karma, people attacked her.

At this, the Chief decided, "It is better to keep the whole thing secret for a while," and so they did.

After some time, Karma went to receive teachings from an important lama called Ponlob Jetrung Rinpoche. He was amazed by Karma's meditation progress and observed, "It is not easy to have such realization even for those who have studied for a long time." At this, an attendant of Karma's inadvertently told the lama, "Of course, it would be easy for her to realize the ultimate nature, as she has returned from the World of the Dead."

The lama replied, "I too have been to the World of the Dead—three times. We should compare notes and see whether our experiences are similar or not. Princess, please tell us your experiences."

Karma started to tell her experiences to the lama. One by one, people who were receiving his teachings came near to listen too. Both the lama and these other people were shedding tears at what they heard. For one whole day, instead of the lama's usual teachings, everyone listened to Karma's narration.

Fully believing Karma's story, the lama said, "Your account is totally trustworthy. In this valley, you are being wasted. You must travel all over the country to serve people. I will provide you with transportation, attendants, and provisions. You must tour the entire country!"

However, as it turned out, Karma mainly stayed with her mother. When she had come before the Dharma King, she had been so scared of the Lords of the Dead that in her haste, she had prayed to attain buddhahood for herself but neglected to pray for the benefit of all sentient beings. In addition, she was too attached to her mother. For these two reasons, Karma did not achieve greatness in her services to others.

No Fear of the Foes: The Experience of Denma Sangye Seng-ge

Denma Sangye Seng-ge's delog account is notable for its ideas about how we can ease our fears and delusions and remember to remain in the meditative state.

After exiting his body, Denma reported, he traveled through the whole universe in an instant. He felt he was seeing all the events of the past, present, and future simultaneously. He seemed to have a body of light and was able to travel by the light of his body. He felt himself being enveloped in the rays of five colored lights. With great ease, he moved with the speed of light, able to reach any place he wished.

Holding on to a beam of light of five colors that appeared in front of him, Denma shouted HIK seven times. He rose up into the sky. He found himself in the ultimate buddha pure land, called the Unexcelled Blissful Celestial World. There he beheld a most exquisite scene with a precious mansion filled with numerous enlightened knowledge-holders. It was a joyful pure land. There Denma was met by a lama as his guide. The lama said:

> Son, you have been pure [of karmic obscurations] for seven lives.
> Fortunate person, don't be distracted. Look at the nature of the absolute awareness.

For a moment Denma had the experience of seeing the five buddha families and their pure lands. That vision was followed by the five buddhas appearing as the Dharma King and the Lords of the Dead.

He kept falling into delusions again and again. For a while he saw the people of his village and wasn't sure whether he was dead or not. He saw a crystal stupa, which in fact was his body covered with frogs. People shedding tears were circumambulating the crystal stupa. As the effect of their grieving and crying, he felt blizzards of blood and pus falling upon him.

Denma saw two sets of circles of spheres (Tib. *thig-le*), five each, each made of a different colored light. One set consisted of five large circles, and the other of five small ones. They were the five primordial wisdoms, the realized true natures of the five emotions.

The next moment, Denma was struggling to learn whether he had really died. Finally, he reached the conclusion that he was dead by seeing the following signs. He was able to move through the eye of a needle and through the tiny holes in a tent. His steps didn't make any footprints in the sand at the riverbank. His body didn't make any reflection in the water, nor did it cast a shadow in sunlight or moonlight. Even though he was starving, no one cared to serve him food. He approached his loved ones and called them by name, but no one responded. When he looked at people's faces, they seemed shaded by a thin, shadowy veil. He saw that his mother kept shedding tears, which was unusual for her character, and she was saying, "Now I wish to die."

Realizing that he had died, with fear and sadness Denma prayed to the Buddha of Compassion. Instantly the Buddha of Compassion appeared in front of him and gave him detailed teachings and blessings.

Denma's mind became distracted by mundane delusions, however, and he encountered further obstructions on his journey. He felt himself pushed by the force of a karmic storm. He heard the roar of angry beasts. But eventually he was able to remember that these things were the manifestation power of emptiness.

Next, he saw white and red lights blocking his path. From behind him came a rain of weapons. When he remembered that they were delusions, they became the mere self-power of his intrinsic awareness.

Next, he found himself following a high, steep, narrow mountain path of red rocks that went on and on, never ending. Below he saw a turbulent river carrying rocks away. He made his way along the mountain path by grasping handfuls of grass now and then. Many people had fallen into the river, and he could hear their cries. Again, when he thought of the emptiness nature of all things, these fearful appearances were pacified.

Next, he felt he was trapped in a land of total darkness filled with beasts. He heard a voice saying, "Don't get distracted! This is the realm of animals." He sang OM MANI PADME HUM. Suddenly, the atmosphere was filled with hosts of buddhas and lamas welcoming him. It seemed as if the whole environment was vibrating with the sound of prayer.

Next, he experienced attachment to his friends and possessions in the world of the living. At that moment, he heard the voice of the Buddha of Compassion: "This is the time of death. No friends or wealth will help you anymore. These are the expressions of the emptiness nature. Look at the emptiness nature without letting your mind be distracted." When he heard this, all Denma's attachments fell away.

Again, he felt he was passing through a narrow, rocky passage filled with turbulent water, flame, and storm. He reached the top of the passage, but because of blizzards he could neither advance nor retreat. He entered a temple where he saw many people, including many known to him while he was alive. Some were happy and enjoying their lives, while others were hungry and suffering. Many were singing, and others were crying. Because some of them had been brought here by mistake from the human world by the messengers of the Lords of the Dead, they had to wait until they had exhausted their human life spans before they could go on to new rebirths. Others had come early because their lives had been cut short due to sudden accidents. Many, too, were still hanging on or were stuck here, instead of going to their next destinations, because of their attachment to their human lives. Rich people were hanging on here because of attachment to their treasures. Lovers were hanging on here because of their attachment to their lovers. Rulers were hanging on here because of their attachment to their law and order. Poor people were hanging on here because of attachment to their huts and begging bowls. Angry people were hanging on here, wishing for revenge against their enemies. Others were waiting here for their relatives and friends in the human world to make merits and dedicate them in death ceremonies, so as to improve the onward journey of the deceased. Those were the people who did not have strong good or bad karmas to push them swiftly to their destination.

Then Denma felt he was reaching the top of the Sandy Mountain Pass of the Dead, which was decorated with heaps of human and animal skulls. He heard vengeful voices coming from all these heads. From there he beheld the vast, frightening Field of the Dead before him. Then he felt he was leaving the World of the Living behind him. He was struck with a great shock and pain, with fear and sadness, as if his heart and lungs had fallen to the ground. Again he heard a voice coming from a great distance, saying, "Look at the true nature without distractions."

Next, Denma felt he was walking through the Colorful Field of the Dead, a field of sand whipped by sandstorms. It was filled with frightening images and sounds of pain. Before him, he saw the path of light of different colors. From behind, he felt he was being pushed forward by a karmic storm. On the right, he saw darkness. On the left, he saw whitish light. Again he heard the voice of the Buddha of Compassion, saying, "This is the Colorful Field of the Dead. The beings here are suffering as the result of stealing and robbing."

Then he felt he was crossing the Dreaded Red River of the Dead, which was rushing with waves of lightning. It had six awesome bridges. Both sides of the river were crowded with beings. They were being commanded by the Lords of the Dead and had all kinds of armaments in their hands. Again he heard the voice of the Buddha of Compassion, saying, "Son, without distraction, meditate on the nature of the mind." Instantly, he flew to the other side of the river like an eagle.

There on the other bank he saw the Ox-Headed Awa, one of the chief assistants to the Dharma King of the Lords of the Dead. He was sitting on a throne of human and animal skulls in the middle of hosts of executioners. They had human bodies and heads of various animals. The entire surroundings were crowded with many beings. Many of them were frightened and crying or being tortured. Others were joyful and moved around by miraculous means.

Finally, Denma reached a palace made of precious materials, set in the midst of an aura of lights in which various deities appeared. He heard music played by hosts of celestial beings. The Dharma King of the Lords of the Dead was sitting on the throne held up by an elephant, a horse, a peacock, and a *shang-shang*.* The Lord had four heads and four arms. He was in Sambhogakaya costume. In his first two hands he was holding a mirror and notes. His two lower hands were in the contemplative gesture holding the Wheel of the Existents. He was surrounded by various Lords of the Dead with human bodies and animal heads.

The Dharma King asked Denma about his life and deeds. Giving a brief account of himself, he sang the song of fearlessness:

> OM MANI PADME HUNG!
> I am a yogi who has fully realized the state of nonduality.
> There is no fear of the foes, the foes of grasping at duality.
> I am a yogi who has realized the boundless ultimate nature.
> There is no fear of the foes, the foes of weapons arising from emptiness.
> I am a yogi who has realized the spontaneously accomplished wisdom.
> There is no fear of the foes, the foes of the Lords of the Dead created by my five emotional poisons.
> I am a yogi who is free from the passion of hope and doubt.
> There is no fear of the foes, the foes of the Lords of the Dead.
> I am a yogi who has realized the true nature.
> There is no fear of the foes, the foes of the illusory appearances of the bardo.

At this, the Ox-Headed Awa struck Denma with his sword. But the sword went through Denma without causing any injury, as if it had tried to pierce the sky. Astonished, all the Lords of the Dead praised him, saying, "Ha! Ha!"

The Dharma King also praised Denma, saying, "This excellent person is telling the truth."

Then Denma traveled through various realms of hell to ease their sufferings and then returned to his body to bring messages to the people of the human world.

---

* Skt. *jivamjiva*, a mythical bird with two heads, according to Sir M. Monier Williams's *Sanskrit-English Dictionary*.

Visits to the Eighteen Hell Realms: The Experience of Tagla Konchog Gyaltsen

When Tagla Konchog Gyaltsen experienced being separated from his mortal body, he saw that the whole atmosphere to the west was covered with reddish clouds. The White Guardian Deity said, "Those are not clouds. That is the storm of the Red Desert Mountain Pass that divides the World of the Living from the World of the Dead. You could cross it easily by your own spiritual power." Tagla invoked the blessing power of buddhas and lamas to cross the pass easily. Instantly, a carpet of white light extended to him from the south. On it he saw the Buddha of Compassion and the wrathful form of Guru Rinpoche with hosts of deities. The Wrathful Guru struck the mountain pass with a giant prayer flag three times, and the pass crumbled from its base.

Again, Tagla saw that the sky was covered with flame. The earth was filled with flowing blood and molten metal. The White Guardian Deity said, "This is the Impassable Brown Massive River of the Dead. Pray to your guardian deities." Tagla invoked the guardian deities and lamas. Suddenly he heard the sound of loud thunder from the south. There he saw the Buddha of Compassion—as bright as a snowy mountain touched by the light of thousands of suns—amid a rainbow light aura with a rain of flowers of various colors. Tagla found himself in a boat of light accompanied by numerous youthful people holding prayer flags and singing OM MANI PADME HUNG. Instantly he joyfully crossed the river with them. Tagla felt that the Buddha of Compassion, Guru Rinpoche, the prayer flags, and the lamas were inseparably one. By witnessing such amazing powers, Tagla's mind and body were filled with boundless devotion.

Again, Tagla was moved onward by the force of his karma, arriving at a vast field cloaked in massive darkness. This darkness was punctuated by flashes of lightning and red sparks. This was the Vast Gray Field of the Dead. As advised by the White Guardian Deity, Tagla performed his prayers, which enabled him to cross the field easily. He observed the arrival of a great ascetic yogi accompanied by hosts of ascetics and monks holding giant prayer flags in their hands, singing OM MANI PADME HUNG. Following them, Tagla crossed the field in an instant.

Then Tagla felt that he was outside the huge, amazing wall of the hell realms. Pema Dechen, Tagla's principal teacher, accompanied by many lamas in the form of monks and ascetics, appeared before him. They were turning prayer wheels with their right hands and holding giant prayer flags with their left. Both the White Guardian Deity and the Dark Demon had disappeared.

Pema Dechen told Tagla, "You must see the hell realms so that you can describe them to people on your return to the World of the Living. It will help people to learn about and believe in the existence of the hell realms, and to be inspired to follow the Dharma. However, you cannot travel by yourself to the hell realms without relying on my power. Pray to the Buddha of Compassion and follow me."

Led by his teacher, Tagla visited the eighteen different hell realms. In each one, numerous beings were tormented by all manner of sufferings. These sufferings were the result of the negative emotions and harmful deeds that they had committed in their lives.

Of the eighteen hells, the first eight are the hot hells:

1. In the reviving hell, on a ground of burning metal, beings incessantly kill each other out of anger, only to revive and suffer the same endlessly.
2. In the black line hell, on burning grounds, executioners draw lines on beings' bodies and saw them into pieces with burning saws, over and over again.
3. In the crushing hell, beings are poured into huge mortars of burning iron and crushed by burning hammers again and again.
4. In the howling hell, beings roast in burning metal houses, screaming and crying endlessly.
5. In the great howling hell, beings who are enclosed within double blazing walls cry continuously with great suffering.
6. In the heating hell, beings are boiled in molten bronze.
7. In the intense heating hell, beings in burning metal houses are pierced with burning tridents and wrapped in burning metal sheets.
8. In the hell of ultimate suffering, beings are burned in a mountain of blazing iron, and molten bronze is poured into their mouths. Only the sound of painful cries is perceptible, for one cannot see the beings themselves amid the burning-red flames.

Then there are the eight cold hells, whose names suggest the horrible ways in which naked beings suffer in them: (1) the hell of blistering cold, (2) the hell of bursting blisters, (3) the hell of chattering teeth, (4) the hell of lamentations, (5) the hell of cries, (6) the hell of *utpala*-like cracks on their bodies,* (7) the hell of lotus-like cracks, (8) the hell of huge lotus-like cracks.

There are also two secondary hells: (1) In the neighboring hells, beings fall into pits of hot embers or swamps of filth, walk through fields of razors or forests of swords, and are pierced by the sharp weapons of the Hill of Iron Trees, and are eaten by vultures and men or women. (2) In the ephemeral hell, beings are born into and trapped in various places and objects, such as rocks, pillars, walls, and even furniture for long periods of times.

In each hell realm, Pema Dechen saw the causes of the sufferings of each being through his omniscient wisdom and would explain them to Tagla. He also explained how long each being had to suffer and what efforts would help them. Until their negative karmas for living in hell are exhausted, the beings who suffer there will not die from their pain, for suffering is part of their life as hell-beings, not the ending of it.

By the power of the Buddha of Compassion and the lama, many beings became able to remember their previous life on earth. Encouraged by Tagla, many sent messages about their most excruciating circumstances to their families and begged their loved ones to do some virtuous deeds in order to change the karmic cycles of both the dead and living.

In his delog account, Tagla has given the names of many people from Eastern Tibet who were suffering in different realms of hell. He describes their suffering and what messages they sent to their loved ones. Sometimes Tagla wouldn't see the people who were giving the messages, but would hear their crying voices calling to him.

For example, a group of hell-beings said, "Kindly give the following messages to our relatives: Please establish connections with true religious people. Please give food and materials to hungry and needy animals and people. Please carve OM MANI PADME HUNG on stones and print it on pieces of cloth and hoist them as prayer flags. Please ransom the lives of animals from the hands of butchers. Please make burned offerings of food (*sur*) and water offerings (*chutor, Ch'u gTor*) for the suffering beings of the

---

* The *utpala* (Skt.) is described in Tibetan literature as a blue flower. According to Sir M. Monier Williams's *Sanskrit-English Dictionary*, it is a blue lotus or water lily. Both delog and Buddhist texts describe the sufferings of the sixth, seventh, and eighth hells in terms of different degrees of cracks or splits in the skin and the bursting of the flesh from those cracks, likening this to different degrees of blossoming of the petals of smaller and larger flowers.

spirit world. Please offer lights to the buddhas and build prayer wheels. Please say OM MANI PADME HUNG, whenever you hear our names or remember us."

Then Tendzin Dargye, another of Tagla's teachers, appeared and said, "Now you should go to the court of the Dharma King of the Lords of the Dead." At that moment, the White Guardian Deity and the Dark Demon reappeared on either side of him, and each took him by one of his arms. They led him through a huge iron gate protected by many frightening animals. Inside, Tagla saw the Dharma King of the Lords of the Dead in a sphere of mountainous flame. He had a dark complexion, with four faces and two hands. With his right hand he brandished a slate. In his left hand he held a black noose. Standing on a fierce-looking buffalo, he was terrifying to look at. Accompanying him were hundreds of thousands of Lords of the Dead, including Ox-Headed Awa, the keeper of the slate; the Snake-Headed Harmful One, the keeper of the scale; and the Monkey-Headed Youth, the keeper of the notes. They were all thundering HUNG! HUNG! PHAT! PHAT!

The White Guardian Deity and the Dark Demon presented Tagla to the Dharma King and instructed him to tell the deeds of his life to the Dharma King. Tagla listed all the virtuous deeds that he had performed. The Dharma King said, "You human beings are skilled in lying. Who knows if you are telling the truth?"

As instructed by the Dharma King, the Ox-Headed Awa checked Tagla's deeds in his mirror, in which the deeds of every being appear clearly. The Snake-Headed Harmful One checked his deeds by weighing them on the scale. The Monkey-Faced Youth checked his deeds by reading the list in his notes. They all supported Tagla's claim.

At that moment, the Dark Demon got up and shouted, "Ha! Ha! I contest your findings." As proof he upended his shoulder bag, which contained pebbles representing Tagla's evil deeds. But only eight dark pebbles fell out. Then, shouting Ha! Ha! the White Guardian Deity defended the findings and produced a mountain of white pebbles out of his shoulder bag as proof of Tagla's virtuous deeds.

At that moment, Tagla saw the Dharma King appearing in the beautiful form of the Buddha of Compassion. The eight chief Lords of the Dead of the court appeared as eight bodhisattvas.

From the right side of the Dharma King, a white carpet of light extended toward the west. The Dharma King said, "By this path of light, you could go to the Blissful Pure Land. But instead, you must return to the human world as my messenger to serve the people." The Dharma King persuaded Tagla to go back to the human world to tell people what he saw in the bardo and convey the messages that people in hell had sent through him. Tagla didn't want to go back because of his old age, but he consented.

Suddenly he saw a white stupa coated with snow and merged into it. This stupa was in fact his own body. Instantly the perception of this world became vivid to him. Slowly, he recovered from the sicknesses of his mortal body and returned to normal.

Tagla served many people by teaching and leading prayers and meditations for years. Then, at the wedding ceremony of a relative of his, when Tagla heard that fifteen hundred animals had been slaughtered for the occasion, with great sadness he suddenly passed away. This time he did not come back.

DISTRACTED INTO DELUSION: THE EXPERIENCE OF DAGPO TRASHI NAMGYAL

The account of Dagpo Trashi Namgyal illustrates vividly how one's mental focus in the bardo changes abruptly and rapidly.

Dagpo performed a phowa meditation for himself and transferred his consciousness through the upper portal of his body. There he saw a blanket-like light unfold. He reached a joyful pure land. In the pure land he saw buddhas, dakinis, and lamas. He enjoyed healing food and drink, sweet music, and joyful dance.

In the pure land, he met a lama who was his guardian deity. The lama asked him questions, and Dagpo responded. But suddenly Dagpo's mind got distracted and he saw an unimaginably high mountain pass with prayer flags on the top. He saw a huge field, and below it a huge dark brown river flowing forcefully. Over the river there were six bridges, and on the other side was a big city.

Again he felt that he was talking with his guardian lama. But his mind became distracted, and he started to see the delusory appearances of hellish sufferings.

He went back to feeling that he was talking with his guardian lama, when his mind suddenly got distracted once again. He started to see the Lords of the Dead conducting many beings to the hell realm.

A number of times, as he was having Dharma discussions, his perceptions would suddenly and uncontrollably change into delusory appearances. His experience demonstrates that we must establish the habit of stability in our mindstream while we are alive.

Finally, Dagpo was in the court of the Dharma King. Pointing to the main figures of the Lords of the Dead, the guardian lama said, "You cannot conceal the evil deeds you have committed. The rules of the Dharma King of the Lords of the Dead are very strict. Among the Lords of the Dead, the Ox-Headed Awa is skilled in counting. The Lion-Headed One is skilled in taking notes. The Monkey-Faced Youth is skilled in reading the mirror. The Tiger-Headed One is skilled at weighing deeds on the scales. The Leopard-Headed One is skilled in reading the notes. The Bear-Headed One is skilled in determining what is a virtuous deed and what is an evil deed. The Brown Bear–Headed One is skilled in weapons. These skilled Lords of the Dead are amazing at distinguishing what is a virtuous and what is not a virtuous deed."

The guardian lama continued, "Son, you must watch the nature of the intrinsic awareness without distractions. All beings have strayed into samsara by becoming distracted from the true nature. For the ignorant beings of samsara, there is no end of suffering. Buddhas have pure perception and see everything as a joyful pure land. Beings have impure perceptions and see things such as the burning iron grounds of the hell realm. Mundane phenomena are one's own mental habits of delusory perception. Those whose perception makes them see everything as pure lands will not encounter the Lords of the Dead, but instead will see buddhas, since in their true nature the Lords of the Dead *are* buddhas."

Then the Dharma King gave instructions to the Bear-Headed Lord of the Dead, saying, "Show this yogi the experiences of hell realms in detail. He should be dispatched back to the World of the Living."

Then the Bear-Headed Lord of the Dead told Dagpo, "Don't let your mind get distracted. Remaining in the state of openness, which is the nature of the intrinsic awareness of your mind, please follow me." The Lord of the Dead took Dagpo around the realms of unimaginable sufferings of hell and other inferior realms. Then he brought Dagpo back to the court.

The Dharma King told Dagpo, "You must understand that all the teachings given in the Vinaya, Abhidharma, and Sutra* are on training the mind. Realize the nature of the mind, the unborn intrinsic awareness.

---

* These are the major divisions of the Buddhist canon, known collectively as the Tripitaka, or three baskets: Vinaya on moral discipline, Abhidharma on metaphysics (or discriminating knowledge), and Sutra on meditation.

Relax evenly in the unceasing expanse. Stay stable by relaxing in the state of what it is."

The Dharma King ordered three Lords of the Dead to take Dagpo back to the World of the Living. The guardian lama explained, "I am an emanation of Avalokiteshvara Buddha." The Ox-Headed Awa said, "I am an emanation of Vajrasattva Buddha." The Monkey-Headed Youth said, "I am an emanation of Ratnasambhava Buddha." The Pig-Headed Rakshasa said, "I am an emanation of the Buddha of Infinite Light." They all said, "Now you return to your own body, which is the mandala of the buddhas."

After six days' travel through the hell realms, Dagpo felt as if he had woken up from sleep. His guardian lama and the Lords of the Dead had disappeared. He found himself in his old meditation cave, where a monk, a nun, and a layperson were looking after his body. He tried to look around but couldn't see anything. It took some time for his body to return to health.

Crossing the Field of the Dead: The Experience of Gyalwa Yungtrung

Yungtrung was a Bonpo, a follower of Bon, the indigenous religion of Tibet. This delog tale shows us that the sincere prayers of any faith will be beneficial at the time of death. Yungtrung had been exposed to Buddhism, so he witnessed Buddhist as well as Bon deities and masters liberating beings in the bardo. Interestingly, like the esoteric Buddhists, Yungtrung also views the court of the Dharma King as part of awakening to the profound religious path and goal. For him, the court wasn't just a place of judgment deciding where one is to take rebirth. If one realizes it as such, it is an inner spiritual awakening of the intrinsic awareness, the true nature of the mind.

After coming out of his body, Yungtrung suddenly felt he was flying like a bird, and he crossed many mountains and valleys. He saw a high mountain pass decorated with a heap of human and animal skeletons. They were all making noises. Suddenly a Divine Lady,[3] who was his guardian deity, appeared before him in a cotton dress and with three peacock feathers on her head. She said, "Ha! Ha! I am not sure that you will see your mother." However, she gave him advice, and accordingly he crossed the pass and found a fork of three roads. A red fork goes to the west and a blue one to the east. A colorful one in the middle goes to the court of the Dharma King, the ground from which you attain liberation or deviate to samsara. Yungtrung took the middle road, which was colorful like a snake. He walked quickly.

The path became so narrow that it was as if the mountains and rocks of the two sides were touching each other. Again, Yungtrung saw two paths as narrow as a hair. A white path was on the right side and a dark path on the left. Many people were trying to rush along these paths, and many were falling.

Yungtrung took the white path, but soon it was totally blocked. Then a Bon lama dressed as a layperson with long hair arrived from the other side, leading about a hundred people to liberation. The lama told Yungtrung, "The white path is the way for those who are working for the benefit of sentient beings. The dark one is for beings in general, and it leads to the place where the Dharma King resides."

Then Yungtrung found himself at the door of a cave. It had one small hole, which only his fist could get through. All the paths led to this cave, and there was no other way out. He thought, "Now I don't have any physical body. Consciousness can get through anything." He repeated loudly the same message three times to the crowd. Suddenly he found himself on the other side of the rock door.

He was standing in a huge gray field, from which he could see neither mountain nor valley. He thought, "This field is limitless, but crossing it is not impossible, as I am emptiness." Instantly he found himself at the other edge of the field.

There, three frightening, turbulent rivers were merging. A red river was coming from the east. A dark river was flowing from the south. A brown river met them from the north. There was only one long, narrow bridge over this huge merged river. Near the bridge, many men and women were crying because they had to cross the river but were unable to. With compassion, he told them, "You all pray with me. I will make a prayer for you." They all listened to him with signs of respect. With strong devotion, Yungtrung prayed to masters of both the Bon and Buddhist lineages:

Hri! I pray to the great master Tranpa Namkha
I pray to master Tshewang Rigdzin.
I pray to master Padmasambhava.
I pray to Montul Tenpa Wangyal.

I pray to the gracious Root Lama.*
Please lead the consciousnesses of the dead to liberation.
Bless them and make their fears of the bardo vanish.
Bless us to accomplish the mind-transferring practice of phowa.
Bless us to achieve blissful fruits of the path of liberation.

And he contemplated in the meditative state free from concepts. As a result of his meditations, all who were present took rebirth in happy realms.

At that point his guardian deity appeared again. He saw a huge translucent castle, as high as if it were touching the sky. He asked the Lady, "What is the name of this mansion? Who lives in it?" She said, "This is the great union of appearance and emptiness, the castle of the Lords of the Dead. The Dharma King of the Dead resides in it. At this moment, the Dharma King has a peaceful demeanor. It is best that we go see him quickly."

Yungtrung heard awesome sounds filling sky and earth. At first he was frightened by them, but then he told himself, "All sounds are the natural sounds of the intrinsic awareness. Lights are the lights of the intrinsic awareness. Rays are the natural rays of the intrinsic awareness. There is nothing to be afraid of." With renewed confidence, he moved on.

In the giant Castle of the Dead there was a huge throne made of precious materials. It was held up by eight different powerful animals. Seated on it was a frightening giant man of reddish complexion, huge as Mount Sumeru. He was semipeaceful and semiwrathful, with three eyes and four fangs. He had reddish hair floating around his head like a burning flame. He was wearing robes of fur and a crown of skeletons and had rosaries of skeletons as well. In his right hand he held a scepter with the mark of a *svastika*,† and in his left hand a full moon–like mirror, in which he could see all the phenomena of the world. He was roaring a HUNG sound that made the three worlds tremble. Yungtrung was convinced that this giant was the Dharma King of the Dead.

Yungtrung made three prostrations and said, "O Dharma King of the Dead, I am Latri Lama Gyalwa Yungtrung of Kham. Where is my mother, named Adron?"

---

* The root lama is one's main Dharma teacher.
† The *svastika* (Skt.; Tib. *yungtrung, gYung Drung*) has been an esoteric symbol of change-less strength in both the Hindu and Buddhist religions for many centuries.

Instead of answering directly, the Dharma King said, "Ha! Ha! You are here to liberate the mother-beings of the three realms who have descended down here because of their misdeeds. Now, with your power, you must liberate all who are connected with you. If you cannot, I will be ashamed of you."

At that moment, Yungtrung saw an old Bonpo man arrive at the court. He was with a person of white complexion attired in white robes and a person of dark complexion attired in dark robes. The white one defended the old man, presenting a bag full of white pebbles to represent his good deeds. The dark one presented a bag full of dark pebbles and argued against him. Then, as the Dharma King ordered, the Monkey-Headed and Lion-Headed Lords of the Dead weighed the old man's deeds. His virtuous deeds came out a little heavier. The Monkey-Headed Lord checked the mirror and saw only lights. Then the Dharma King told the man, "You have done many great virtuous practices. But more important, you have maintained pure perception and respect for your lama. Therefore, you may go to Shambhala."*

Numerous people began to pass through the judgments of the Dharma King. Lamas kept coming and liberating many of them.

Yungtrung visited many places and recited prayers. Many sufferings of the hell realms just disappeared when he shouted a PHAT! while absorbed in contemplation in the state in which there is no grasping.

After touring the hell realms, he returned to the castle. The Dharma King ordered the Monkey-Headed Lord of the Dead to lead him away. He did not find his mother.

On the way back, he met two lamas who were stuck under a bridge. When they were in the human realm, one of them had performed an exorcism for the wrong purpose, and the other had indulged in funds meant for religious purposes. But because they had faith in Buddhism, Yungtrung prayed to the buddhas and Buddhist-lineage lamas with strong devotion and performed the meditation on phowa. As a result, both lamas were liberated from that place.

Then Yungtrung returned across the bridge, crossed the Field of the

---

* Shambhala is a legendary kingdom ruled by the law of esoteric virtues. It is believed to exist in the Himalayas, visible only to highly accomplished spiritual beings. In many esoteric Buddhist teachings, the spiritual qualities of one's own body and mind are explained in terms of the details of the Shambhala cosmos.

Dead, and walked along the narrow path of the dead and the pass of the dead. He reached home as the sun was rising over the tops of the mountains.

Yungtrung subsequently had a second delog experience, in which he traversed the path into the bardo by means of the meditative power of contemplation on the union of awareness and emptiness, just as he had done during his first delog journey. This time he toured different places in the human and demigods' realms.

Suddenly a beautiful dakini appeared before him. Yungtrung prayed to her to take him to his mother. The dakini made no reply but turned into an eagle and flew through the sky. Realizing that he didn't have a gross body, Yungtrung also transformed into an eagle, simply by wishing, and flew higher and higher, following the dakini. Then, to the north of Mount Sumeru, they landed in a land of flowers. There, in a tent of flowers, he saw a sage.

The dakini said, "Come here." There was a flower, less tall than the others, which had just opened. In it were three babies. Pointing to one of them, the dakini said, "He is your mother. Can you recognize him?" The baby recognized Yungtrung and said, "Apho, why did you come here?" His mother, in her new, male rebirth, didn't remember her previous home or family, but she remembered her son. Then, as advised by the dakini, they went to the sage. The dakini then asked the sage to give teachings to Yungtrung's mother in her new rebirth, The sage accepted the request.

The dakini then took Yungtrung to see the realm of the gods. After giving prophecies, she flew away to Oddiyana. Yungtrung found himself back in his body, in his own residence.

PURIFIED BY STREAMS OF NECTAR: THE EXPERIENCE OF SAMTEN CHOTSO

Samten Chotso first toured the hell realms with the help of Yeshe Tsogyal, the consort of Guru Rinpoche. Usually, delogs go first to the court of the Dharma King, but Samten and some others visited the hell realm first. Eventually Samten reached the court of the Dharma King. The White Guardian Deity and the Dark Demon argued for and against her. The Lords checked the mirror. They found that she had killed many birds and insects and had sworn a lot. So she was instantly tortured by being whipped on a burning field and having molten metal poured on her. She remembered Guru Rinpoche and prayed to him. As a result, her White Guardian Deity arrived to take her to the Dharma King. Although she thought her experience had lasted a year, the Dharma King told her it had only lasted the time it takes to drink a cup of tea.

Then the Dharma King asked the Lords of the Dead to check the scale, and Samten's meritorious deeds proved to be much heavier than her unvirtuous deeds. Finally the Dharma King ordered two Lords of the Dead to take her to the human world. He advised Samten to perform Dharma practices and to help people. Then he added, "From now on, there is no need for you to come here. You may go the Blissful Pure Land."

On the way, Samten saw Mother Yeshe Tsogyal, who inquired about her journey. On the way back, she showed Samten the five buddha pure lands made of five colored lights in the four directions and above.

Samten asked Yeshe Tsogyal to lead her to the Blissful Pure Land. Riding a lion, Yeshe Tsogyal led Samten astride a white mule. They reached the top of a mountain in the western direction. From there they saw the Blissful Pure Land clearly. With great joy, Samten made three prostrations. The mule and the lion disappeared. Suddenly the land where they were became a soft and gentle ground. At every step she took, a flower grew. She bathed in a shower of nectar and drank the nectar as it streamed down. All her impurities and evil karmas were purified. Her body became white as if made of conch. She crossed a valley with each step. Finally she reached an amazingly beautiful pure land with beautiful trees, fruits, flowers, precious materials, and ornaments. Bodhisattvas in the form of birds were singing. Whatever Samten wished for appeared spontaneously.

In three steps, Samten crossed three layers of walls. She came before the Buddha of Infinite Light, who was sitting at the foot of an amazingly luxuriant giant tree. At the right side of the Buddha of Infinite Light was Avalokiteshvara, and at his left side Vajrapani. Each was in the midst of one hundred million bodhisattvas and monks. Various male and female buddhas and bodhisattvas were everywhere, amid oceans of their disciples. There were also all kinds of deities, including Guru Rinpoche, in wrathful forms. She also saw countless lamas of various lineages.

This delog does not tell how she returned to her body.

Don't Be Discouraged: The Experience of Changchub Seng-ge

Changchub wished to go home, and suddenly he found himself in his parents' home. He went around to the neighbors and asked for food and asked questions, but no one would answer him or even look at him. He thought everyone must be upset with him.

A young girl was carrying water. He asked for some water, but she wouldn't say a word. When he tried to help himself to some water from her pot, it slipped from her hand and broke into pieces. He held the tail of a horse, and the horse just fell down. A woman was spinning thread and wouldn't answer him. when he tried to touch the wool, it blew away in a storm and she had to run after it. That made Changchub worry more, because he recalled a folk saying: "Spirits, though invisible, can cause things to move."

Then he thought: "Now I should go to the monastery." On the way, a barking dog ran after him. A woman scolded the dog, saying, "Damn dog, you must be barking at demons," as it is believed that dogs and cats can see spirits. Thinking she was calling him a demon, Changchub retorted, "Show me your god that is not a demon!" She didn't hear him. Then he reached the monastery. He saw a dead body in his quarters. It was being guarded by two huge, fearsome hunting dogs. Changchub was very scared. The thought occurred to him, "I might be dead!"

At that moment, he found himself on the other side of a huge mountain. He was in a land of darkness, pushed from behind by a karmic storm. Lords of the Dead were shouting like thousands of thunderclaps. A burning iron ground scorched his feet. An infinite number of beings with bad karmas were crowding all around.

In great fear, Changchub prayed to Avalokiteshvara. Instantly, he saw an eight-year-old boy with a white complexion, attired in silk and adorned with jeweled ornaments. He was sitting on a lotus, sun, and moon throne. Bestowing blessings, he assured Changchub that the two of them were connected throughout many lives. This was Changchub's guardian deity, so he prayed to him.

Changchub toured many hell realms. Then he reached the abode of the Dharma King of the Lords of the Dead. In a huge palace, the Dharma King was seated on lotus, moon, and sun cushions on a throne of precious materials, held up by eight animals and birds. His upper body was ornamented with white silk and precious jewels. His lower body was attired in a tiger skin with a black snake for a belt. The rays emanating from his body were so bright that they were unbearable to look at. The Dharma King's eyes were blood-red. He held a flame and water in his hand. To his right there was a clear mirror, and to his left was a slate. He was surrounded by about a thousand Lords of the Dead. They all resembled the Dharma King. Before him were gathered an infinite number of beings, as many as the grains of sand by a river, and an infinite number of Lords of the Dead were deciding their fate.

The Dharma King sent Changchub to see the various realms of hungry ghosts, animals, human beings, and demigods. Afterward, through Changchub, the Dharma King sent messages to the beings of the World of the Living, saying, "Trust in the Three Jewels, develop enlightened attitudes, make offerings, receive teachings and transmissions, and especially recite OM MANI PADME HUNG, which is the essence of Dharma."

Changchub asked the Dharma King, "Do all human beings have to see you when they die?" The Dharma King replied, "There is no one in the human world who will not meet me, with the exception of two kinds of people. People who have been committed to the Dharma from their birth will go to the Blissful Pure Land as soon as their minds are separated from their bodies. They will have no need to see me. Those who have committed grave misdeeds from their birth will go straight down to hell. They will have no chance to see me."

Again Changchub asked, "Is there any virtuous deed that will not benefit, or is there any evil deed that will not harm?" The Dharma King answered, "Yes, even if you spent wealth for virtuous projects, if you have taken it from vajra masters or your parents by deception, from ascetics by force, or from any others as taxes, then it will not count as a virtue. Opposing enemies of masters and of the Dharma will not count as an evil deed. If, with the intention of protecting the weak or vulnerable, you oppose harmful beasts, poisonous snakes, thieves, murderers, and other beings who hurt others, that is not unvirtuous. Then the Dharma King said, "Now there is no need for you to come to see me again. You will perform great services for sentient beings, and you will attain buddhahood."

And so Changchub returned to the human world. He reached the hut where he had been doing his meditation retreat before his delog experience. In his house he saw the dead body of a dog. A fly had landed in the mouth of the dog and was reciting OM MANI PADME HUNG. Then a pigeon landed on the roof and asked him, "Pity, did you have a hard time?" And a swallow asked, "Son, have you arrived?"

Changchub saw that a piece of his clothing was near the dead dog. When the thought of removing the clothing came to him, suddenly his mind became trapped in the dead body of the dog, which was in fact his own body. He wanted to get up but couldn't. His body was as cold as a stone in water. He was so unhappy that he felt pain in his heart. Then he had a vision of Avalokiteshvara, who consoled him, saying, "My son, don't be discouraged. You have obtained precious human life. You have returned to your meditation retreat hut." Then slowly Changchub came back to consciousness.

HELL IS THE UNEXCELLED PURE LAND:
THE EXPERIENCE OF TSOPHU DORLO

This delog account is a work of deep meaning, beautifully written in the original Tibetan.

Tsophu Dorlo felt that his body was naked, but he still possessed all his sense faculties just as when he was alive. He started his journey along the long, narrow, gray path of the bardo. He kept moving rapidly, propelled by the force of his karmic winds, and had no freedom to remain motionless. The dark atmosphere, without sunlight or moonlight, was filled with storms, floods, and blizzards, and resounded with thunderous shouts of "Kill! Kill! Beat! Beat!"

Many beings had come there from the human world and were tormented by fear, confusion, hunger, and thirst. Among them there was a lama, Chotrag Zangpo, whom Dorlo knew. He asked him, "Lama, what are you doing here?" The lama answered, "I am here to liberate some people with whom I have karmic connections." He liberated many through the power of Avalokiteshvara, the Buddha of Compassion.

Dorlo prayed to the Buddha of Compassion for his suffering fellow-travelers. Instantly, Avalokiteshvara appeared before him with a joyful, smiling face and said, "You must spin the great wheel that turns samsara upside down. You must lead the beings of the bardo to pure lands." So, singing OM MANI PADME HUNG, Dorlo gave teachings to the beings and said aspiration prayers.* Instantly he felt that the world of the bardo had emptied. But then, in an instant, it was all filled up again by newcomers.

Next Dorlo reached the Vast Gray Field of the Dead, which was a field of hot sand. This was a place of six uncertainties: beings had no certainty of where to go or stay, where to get shelter, what to do, what to eat, and with whom to keep company; and they were uncertain of their feelings, because everything kept changing all the time.

Since Dorlo didn't have any physical channel, his energies were exposed and he had no control over his consciousness. So his mind ran like a wild horse. As there was no inner sun or moon of physical red and white essences, he didn't feel any light of an outer sun and moon either, and everything was filled with darkness. The lights of his body's five winds arose like the dawn. Unbearable rays kept flashing, as if planets and stars were landing on the earth. In such an atmosphere of darkness and light, his mental habits projected forms of frightening, dangerous monsters.

Out of many beings, Dorlo saw a lama who was suffering. Dorlo prayed and turned his prayer wheel, but because the lama had no trust in him, Dorlo couldn't help him.

Then Dorlo reached the Sandy Mountain Pass between the Dead and the Living. He saw two roads. One was a dark road for those who had committed grave evil deeds. People on this path were just sliding down like rocks straight to the burning iron grounds of the hell realm. The other road was white, for those who had accumulated virtuous deeds. By this road people go to the court of the Dharma King for judgment. From there they might go to pure lands through the paths of lights of five colors.

Dorlo saw that Zhagsar Trashi, whom he had known in the past, was suffering tremendously. Trashi begged Dorlo for prayers, so Dorlo recited them and spun his prayer wheel. Although Trashi had committed evil deeds, because he had faith in Dorlo and had past connections with him, he was liberated from that place.

Then Dorlo reached the Impassable Massive Brown River of the Dead. It was a huge river of boiling molten iron filled with all kinds of vicious beings—the reflections of one's habitual karmic makeup.

Spanning the river was the Iron Bridge of the Dead. Some people who had performed virtuous deeds saw it as a wide bridge, easily crossed, and they hardly noticed anything menacing below in the river. But a great

---

* Aspiration prayers entail reciting or chanting texts for achieving various wishes.

rush of people who were guilty of unvirtuous deeds experienced the bridge as so narrow that it seemed as if made of only a few straws. They were being chased across by the Lords of the Dead. Many were falling into the river and suffering by being burned and bitten by the vicious creatures there. Dorlo said prayers and spun his prayer wheel, and this action of his liberated many beings.

Then Dorlo went to the hell realm. It was a land of burning iron ground where the sounds of cries and shouting were heard amid the tall flames. It was an unbearable place to behold. Turning his prayer wheel, Dorlo made prayers and aspirations. He proclaimed his teachings:

Recognize your delusory perceptions [as they are].
The hell realm is the Unexcelled Pure Land.
The Dharma King is the body of universal truth [dharmakaya].
His retinue, the Lords of the Dead, are the peaceful and wrathful
    deities.
May you attain the true nature, as it is.

Three times he sang OM MANI PADME HUNG. Suddenly the hell realm was filled with rainbow lights. All the beings experienced feelings of peace and joy.

Then about a hundred thousand executioners headed by the Lords of the Dead and the White Guardian Deity arrived to welcome Dorlo with music and offerings. Dorlo entered the court of the Dharma King, followed by about a hundred thousand deceased beings. The Dharma King exclaimed, "How wonderful that you are here! If you can recognize me, I am the body of universal truth, the dharmakaya. If you cannot recognize me, I am the Dharma King of the Lords of the Dead, who decides who has performed virtuous deeds and who has committed unvirtuous deeds. Beings with hatred go to the hell realm, those with attachments to the hungry ghost realm, those with ignorance to the animal realm, those with jealousy to the demigod realm, and those with arrogance to the god realm. Beings whose virtuous deeds are mixed with these five afflicting emotions go to the human realm. Those who perform pure virtuous deeds have no need to suffer in the bardo or in the hell realm. They will go straight to pure lands such as the Blissful Pure Land as soon as they die, as an eagle flies through the sky."

The Dharma King issued his orders to the Lords of the Dead, saying, "I see on the slate that the time of death has arrived for hundreds of thousands of beings. So look to see whether they have done virtuous or unvirtuous deeds. View their deeds in the all-appearing mirror. Consult the book that shows the details. Weigh their deeds by the scale that is fair. Listen to the sound of the victorious drum. And don't make any mistake.

The executioners requested the Dharma King to look into the matter by himself, because the details of the karma of these beings is hard to determine. At this, the Dharma King ordered the White Guardian Deity and the Dark Demon to carefully represent the case of each being.

The White Guardian Deity pleaded for those people who followed Dorlo. He assembled a mountain of pebbles to represent the virtuous deeds accumulated by each of them. Then the Dark Demon argued against them and piled up a mountain of dark pebbles to represent the misdeeds committed by them. Based on those findings, the Dharma King sent the ones with virtuous deeds to pure lands or to the human world, and the ones with unvirtuous deeds to inferior realms.

Then the Dharma King instructed Ox-Headed Awa to take Dorlo to see both the hot hell and cold hell realms. Dorlo traveled through all the eight hot hells. In many places he prayed to the Buddha of Compassion, chanted OM MANI PADME HUNG, and meditated on "exchanging oneself with others,"* and in this manner he liberated many beings. Dorlo met many beings from the human world; some he knew and some he didn't, but they all sent messages to their families, begging them to do some Dharma activities and dedicate the merits in their names.

Many lamas and buddhas were traveling in the hell realms and liberating by giving teachings and blessings.

Then Dorlo returned to the Dharma King, who ordered him to return to the human world. He said, "Please describe the sufferings of the hell realms to people. Please practice virtuous deeds and renounce unvirtuous deeds. Give teachings. You will benefit many greatly. In your next life, you will go to a celestial pure land and benefit many more."

Now Dorlo felt that he was returning to the human world along a path of light with music and incense everywhere as the White Guardian Deity's send-off.

For a while Dorlo fell into a faint. He had a vision of Guru Rinpoche,

---

* Tib. *dag shen jewa, bDag gZhan brJe Ba*. Exchanging oneself with others is a meditation practice in which you give your happiness to others and take others' suffering upon yourself through the power of compassion. In recent years, this practice has become popular among Western Buddhists using the particular meditation of *tonglen* (giving and taking).

who performed a long-life empowerment for Dorlo and gave inspiring prophecies. Finally Dorlo woke up and found himself in his human body amid human surroundings.

FORM INSEPARABLE FROM WISDOM: THE EXPERIENCE OF DAWA DROLMA

Dawa Drolma traveled to a number of pure lands and hell realms. In this summary I give more attention to her experiences in the pure land of Guru Rinpoche,[4] since the hell realms have been described amply in other delog accounts.

The Manifested Pure Land of Guru Rinpoche

Dawa Drolma felt that she moved through the sky, soaring like a vulture. She found herself in the manifested pure land of Guru Rinpoche, the buddha in the form of a realized master. There was a boundlessly vast field. In the center, she saw a giant red rock mountain in the shape of a heart. That mountain was surrounded by many sharp swordlike mountains, all shining with a reddish color. The sky was adorned with a canopy of five-colored rainbow light. All kinds of beautiful birds were singing and playing joyfully. The land was covered with flowers of all kinds and colors. The whole atmosphere was filled with an amazingly sweet fragrance that overwhelmed all her senses. There was also a blue mountain, as if made of sapphire. These were not vague appearances, but vivid images with real presence.

White Tara was Dawa Drolma's guardian deity. Dawa Drolma prayed to Guru Rinpoche by repeating the Vajra Seven-Line Prayer and meditated on Guru Yoga.

She performed prostrations and offered mandalas to the pure land.

In the middle of the mountain, she saw the inconceivable palace of Guru Rinpoche called the Lotus of Light. The palace was the enlightened wisdom of Guru Rinpoche himself, spontaneously appearing in the form of a luminous mansion of light. It was in the form of a most opulent structure made of five precious materials with an abundance of rich designs and decorations. Each detail signified and taught a particular wisdom and quality of buddhahood. This pure land was filled with enlightened masters, dakas, and dakinis.

At the eastern gate of the palace, four dakinis helped Dawa Drolma to put on a new dress, colorful and shining like a rainbow. After entering the spectacular gate of crystal, she climbed a long flight of stairs. Then, in a huge chamber, she joined lamas and dakinis in performing a great feast ceremony. She recited purification prayers with them. Then a dakini with a blue complexion escorted her to a spacious mansion, the main palace among many in this boundless compound, where she participated in a ritual purification by bathing with many others.

Dawa Drolma was shown around this amazing palace and also taken to other palaces within the same complex. At these different places she was welcomed and blessed by masters in radiant celestial forms, radiating overwhelming spiritual power. Some of them were her own teachers who had died, but others were important masters of the distant past, such as Yeshe Tsogyal, Princess Mandarava, Legyi Wangmo-che, Khyentse Wangpo, and many dakinis. She paid respect to them and prayed with heartfelt devotion.

At the Feet of Guru Rinpoche

Accompanied by White Tara, Dawa Drolma entered another inconceivably beautiful palace, made as if of red crystal. It was an immeasurable mansion so vast and lofty that its dimensions were beyond any imagination. It was profusely decorated with rich ornaments and filled with an inexhaustible abundance of wealth and unimaginable heaps of feast offerings.

Finally, in the middle of a great hall, Dawa Drolma saw an enormous throne—higher, it seemed to her, than a three-story building. The throne was emanating rays of light in all directions. On that throne she beheld the amazing presence of Guru Rinpoche, Padmasambhava, the embodiment of the wisdom, compassion, and power of all the enlightened ones. Around the throne, she saw an infinite number of dakinis and masters in various forms, with different complexions, clothing, postures, and gestures, and surrounded by different strains of music. Upon seeing Guru Rinpoche, all her concepts spontaneously ceased. She attained certainty in the oneness with an ineffable, inconceivable, and inexpressible state. For a while she rested in a state that was both joy and loneliness.

Then Dawa Drolma drew closer to the throne and touched her forehead to the feet of Guru Rinpoche. The Guru blessed her by touching her head with his hand and said the Vajra Seven-Line Prayer.

As Dawa Drolma toured the pure land, numerous masters gave her benedictions and teachings. She also met a great lama named Dechen Dorje, who was her own late uncle. He had taken rebirth in Guru Rinpoche's pure land. He imparted teachings, prophecies, and blessings to her, and advised her to return to the human realm.

Then Dawa Drolma was taken to a charming room furnished with a bed, pillows, and bolsters, with an attendant standing by. She slept for a while. After waking, she went to see Guru Rinpoche again and said the Vajra Seven-Line Prayer and made aspiration prayers. Guru Rinpoche bestowed upon her empowerments and blessings. With great compassion, he said, "Now, with awareness of the sufferings of the six mundane realms, you must return to the human world. Tell people what you saw and entreat them to pursue virtue."

Dawa Drolma took leave of the presence of Guru Rinpoche with a heavy heart and a stream of tears. On her way out, at many different palaces and gates, she bade farewell to the masters and dakinis and received their blessings.

Wise Words for the Human World

Then White Tara led Dawa Drolma to the hell realms. Dawa Drolma journeyed through the experiences of the bardo. She saw the Dharma King of the Lords of the Dead in wrathful and terrifying form in his Court of Judgment. During her visit to the hell realms, she helped many suffering beings by teaching, praying, and singing the mantra of Guru Rinpoche, OM AH HUNG VAJRA GURU PADMA SIDDHI HUNG. She also saw the results of the karmic effects and the severity of sufferings of the hell realms with her naked eyes, so she would be able to teach more effectively on her return to the world of the living. She also brought many messages from the dead to their loved ones in the world of the living.

White Tara then took Dawa Drolma to visit Potala, the pure land of Avalokiteshvara, and Yulo Kopa, the pure land of Tara, before returning to the human world.

When Dawa Drolma was visiting the pure land of Tara, she suddenly felt that Dharmapala Tseringma was calling her three times, saying, "Dawa Drolma! Come to the human world!" Then the thought arose: "My uncle Rinpoche, my parents, and all my loved ones are in Throm Valley. I must go back!" With White Tara, she returned in an instant.

At home, Dawa Drolma's teacher, Tromge Trungpa, opened the door of the room where her body lay and performed a long-life ceremony for her. Soon, Dawa Drolma's mindstream returned to her body. She described her reentry in the following way:

She felt numbness in her body and hardly any clarity in her sense faculties. She was absorbed in devotion to the enlightened ones, joy in the memories of the pure lands, and a sense of sorrow for the sufferings of the hell realms. From such a mixed state, she regained her full consciousness, as if she were slowly waking up from a deep sleep. Her uncle Trungpa was standing in front of her, holding a long-life ceremonial arrow and looking at her with concern in his bloodshot eyes. She didn't dare say a word, as she felt a little embarrassed. Lamas performed a purification ceremony. Crying, her friends kept asking, "Are you tired?" "Are you hungry?" "Are you thirsty?" She wasn't feeling any hunger or thirst, but she couldn't convince them. Finally, they all enjoyed the celebration of an offering feast.

Dawa Drolma gives advice to all on averting rebirth in the hell realms and to ensuring rebirth in the pure lands. The following is a summary of her message for the people of the human realm:

- ' Purify through meditation the evil deeds that you have committed. Refrain from indulging in them anymore.
- ' To generate merits, recite the scriptures, make copies of them, and pay respects and make offerings to sacred objects such as images.
- ' Perform the rites of various deities and recite their mantras.
- ' Perform feast offerings.
- ' Rescue others from harm, and ransom the lives of animals that are intended for butchering.
- ' Hoist prayer flags, carve mantras on stones, spin prayer wheels, and observe fasting rites. Generate and maintain devotion to the Buddha and the Dharma.
- ' Develop compassion for all beings.
- ' Especially, observe and perfect the three pure perceptions: seeing everything as a buddha pure land, hearing all sounds as sacred, and experiencing all feelings (physical, mental, and emotional experiences) as buddha-wisdom, ultimate peace, joy, and omniscience.
- ' Finally, dedicate all the merits of your virtuous deeds for specific individuals as well as for all beings.

Dawa Drolma spent the rest of her life teaching Dharma based on her delog experiences and totally devoting her life to the service of others.

She would say to people who were complaining, "No matter how difficult your life is in this human realm, there is no way of comparing it to the sufferings of the hell realms."

Dawa Drolma went on pilgrimage to Central Tibet, where she conceived her first son, Chagdud Rinpoche, who escaped to India and then moved to the West. He taught and established a number of Buddhist centers in the United States and in Brazil. Then she had a daughter, Thrinle Wangmo. In 1941, at the age of thirty-two, she died soon after giving birth to another son, who also died. People witnessed many miracles at the time of her death and cremation. She and her delog accounts inspired the hearts of many people in many parts of Eastern Tibet to believe in the law of karma and rebirth. That in turn awakened a kinder nature in many, stimulating a culture of caring for one another.

LET EVERYONE BE LIBERATED: THE EXPERIENCE OF SHUGSEB JETSUN LOCHEN

Shugseb Jetsun Lochen beautifully describes her visit to the pure land of Guru Rinpoche and teaches that the hell realms are mere delusory perceptions of the mind.

Journey with the One-Eyed Dakini

Jetsun's mind had left her body. Suddenly, a very attractive dakini with a turquoise complexion, beautiful eyebrows, and loosely hanging hair appeared before her inner vision. This dakini had only one eye in the center of her forehead. She asked Jetsun, "Daughter, would you like to go to the Glorious Copper-Colored Mountain, the manifested pure land of Guru Rinpoche?" Jetsun responded, "Yes!"

Holding the dakini's hand, Jetsun swiftly floated with her through the air over many lands. They crossed a vast field and passed a huge river. Then they traversed a land with tall trees that seemed to touch the sky. Finally, they reached the top of a high pass. All the geographical features they had passed over were the landmarks of the bardo. Then the dakini said, "Look!"

In the far distance, Jetsun saw an enormous and extraordinarily beautiful continent, reddish in color. An amazing sensation of powerful energy with heat filled her body. The dakini told her:

O fortunate lady, look over there.
That body of land is the supreme Ngayab continent.
It is the land that was blessed by the buddhas of the three times.
In the ancient times, that is where the heart of a demonic person
    [ego] was tamed.
By the blessing power of Vajravarahi,*
Amazing secret teachings are flourishing there.
Merely by seeing, hearing, and thinking of that land,
It is said, people will attain enlightenment.
So, if you actually get there, there is no question.
Even if you merely look at it with devotional eyes,
You will attain the experience of the pure land.
So bow down to it with devotional mind.

Strong devotion arose in Jetsun. She prostrated herself to the Glorious Mountain many times. There she saw a magnificent giant palace in the design of a mandala made of luminous precious materials. It was so huge and high that it seemed to be touching the heavens. Around the palace she saw numerous dakas and dakinis making offerings of inconceivable wealth and joy. This palace was also surrounded by vast gardens filled with all kinds of wish-fulfilling trees, colorful flowers, and beautiful lakes.

The top part of the palace was the pure land of dharmakaya, the state of ultimate openness. The middle part was the pure land of sambhogakaya, land of everlasting prosperity. The lower part of the palace was the pure land of nirmanakaya, a manifested pure land that can be enjoyed by the eyes of ordinary devotees. Merely by seeing this palace, Jetsun experienced the natural state of her own enlightened mind.

Entering the Glorious Mountain

At that moment, the dakini said, "Now we will go there." As they moved toward the Glorious Mountain, Jetsun felt the presence of a large crowd of people watching them. In a moment, they arrived at a most impressive gate made of precious materials. The dakini knocked at the door of the gate. A woman of reddish complexion with a forceful manner came out and demanded, "Who are you?" The dakini answered,

---

* A female buddha.

This woman came from Tibet, the land of Dharma.
She is a mind-manifestation of the Radiant Blue-Light Dakini.
She came to see the Great Master, the embodiment of all the
  knowledge-holders.
But she has been confused by the traces of her karmic defilement.
Please guide her so she will not face any obstructions on her
  journey.

The reddish woman replied, addressing Jetsun:

I am merely an action dakini of the feasts.
Without asking the Ladies inside,
Taking you in immediately is not proper for me.
Daughter, please wait there for a moment.

The woman turned and went back inside, followed by the dakini. Soon,
five very beautiful women emerged with vases in their hands. They
washed Jetsun with cleansing nectar. Then they led her to the inner gate.
Instantly her body was overwhelmed with a feeling of bliss.

At the elaborately decorated gate of the palace, Jetsun was met by a
dakini who was noble and beautiful-looking with a slight trace of wrath-
fulness. Instantly, Jetsun's mind merged into meditative absorption. She
experienced the contemplative state of the tenth bodhisattva stage. Jetsun made sevenfold devotional prayers to the dakini. This dakini led Jetsun up sixteen steps of a crystal stairway. There Jetsun found herself
inside the palace. It was a boundlessly spacious space. From it, one could
see all the phenomenal existents, without any obscuration or hindrance.

In front of Jetsun, there was a curtain of white silk with gold designs.
As the curtain opened, she saw the very presence of Guru Rinpoche in
royal posture on a lotus seat upon a precious throne. He had a white complexion with reddish hue, and projected great peace, total openness, and
wrathful power. On his head he wore a lotus-like hat decorated with images of the sun, the moon, and eagle feathers. He was attired in three
Dharma robes with a brocade gown over them. His right hand held a
vajra scepter, and his left hand held a skull cup with a long-life vase in it.
His radiance was greater than a hundred thousand suns. She felt she
could never have enough of looking at him.

Around Guru Rinpoche Jetsun saw vividly an enormous crowd of all
the great masters of the past from India and Tibet.

With his loving eyes, Guru Rinpoche gazed at Jetsun. Every hair of her body stood up. Her face was bathed in tears of boundless joy and irrepressible devotion. She prostrated herself before the Guru many times and prayed on behalf of all mother-beings. Guru Rinpoche gave many prophecies and offered these words of teaching to her:

> O Manifestation of Radiant Blue-Light Dakini, listen to me.
> This is the supreme land, the Glorious Copper-Colored Mountain.
> Excepting the men and women of good karma,
> Ordinary people are incapable of enjoying it.
> This is the supreme pure land of mine, the Great Master.
> Among the adepts and masters who are here,
> There is no one who has not attained the high stages of
>   accomplishment.
> Whoever sees this kind of pure land
> Will never deviate from the path of enlightenment.
> So generate devotion and feel happy.
> Now, without taking too long, you must return to Tibet.
> Be the leader who teaches about karmic causality.
> Be the master who demonstrates the Mahayana teachings.
> Be the crown jewel of all the dakinis.
> Be the heart essence, the holder of my teachings.
> Revive the traditions of the earlier masters.
> Whoever sees your face or hears your words
> Will attain enlightenment. These are the words of
>   Padmasambhava.
> O knowledge-holders who are assembled here,
> Please bestow the blessings of your minds upon her.

Blessings of the Great Master

At that moment beams of light of various colors, white, red, yellow, and blue, emanated from the hearts of all the assembled adepts and merged into Guru Rinpoche's heart. Led by Guru Rinpoche, all the adepts sang together the Vajra Guru Mantra: OM AH HUNG VAJRA GURU PADMA SIDDHI HUNG. That sound filled the whole atmosphere. Then, putting his hand on Jetsun's head, Guru Rinpoche said:

> May your body, speech, and mind
> Be blessed with my body, speech, and mind!

Instantly, Jetsun felt a tingling sensation all over her body, and she began shaking. She sang prayers to Guru Rinpoche with various sweet melodies, and made aspirations for the happiness of all mother-beings. Then, with a heavy heart at leaving, she said:

> O Ocean-Born Great Master,
> The embodiment of all the buddhas;
> The knowledge-holder adepts of India and Tibet,
> Who are discoursing upon the teachings of the nine vehicles;*
>
> The ocean of dakinis, the mothers,
> Who are enjoying the glory of bliss and joy
> In the Glorious Copper-Colored Mountain Palace,
> Where the fortunate ones are assembled!
>
> I am a beggar called Lochen
> Who came wandering alone from the suffering land of Tibet.
> Alas, it must be the result of my past misdeeds
> That I have to return to Tibet.
> O Great Ones who are assembled here!
> Do you see my pain?
> All the sufferings endured by the beings of the six realms and the
>   three worlds,
> May they all come upon me, to be borne for them.

At that moment, the dakini who had met Jetsun at the door came to her. Blessing Jetsun with a long-life arrow, she said:

> O fortunate girl, listen to me.
> I am the Radiant Blue-Light Dakini.
> You and I are inseparable,
> Like the moon and the reflection of the moon in water.
> Please do not feel sad at going back;
> Thanks to the kind blessings of Guru Rinpoche,
> You will benefit an inconceivable number of beings.

---

* The nine vehicles (Skt. *yana*) include the entire teachings of Buddhism. According to the Nyingma school of Tibetan Buddhism, they are the three vehicles of sutra (Shravakayana, Pratyekabuddhayana, and Mahayana); the three vehicles of outer tantras (Kriyatantra, Charytantra, and Yogatantra), and the three vehicles of inner tantras (Mahayoga, Anuyoga, and Atiyoga [Dzogchen]).

Touching the feet of Guru Rinpoche with her head, Jetsun received the four empowerments from him. She also received blessings from other adepts. The Radiant Blue-Light Dakini led her to the gate, giving blessings and prophecies. There, once again, Jetsun was met by the one-eyed dakini. With her, Jetsun left on her return journey.

Compassion in the Realms of Suffering Beings

In a moment, Jetsun reached the realm of the gods. There the men and women were indulging in the entertainments of music, dancing, and other sensual enjoyments. The beings in the demigod realm were tormented by fighting with each other. The beings of the animal realm were being enslaved and consuming each other. The hungry ghosts were in a state of severe hunger and thirst.

Then Jetsun crossed a vast field and climbed a high mountain pass. From the top of the pass she saw the dreadful and painful hell realm, and her mind sank and was filled with great sorrow. She thought, "I should go there and plead with the Dharma King of the Lords of the Dead to release those suffering beings." Hell-beings were undergoing torments by unbearable torture for countless years. They were being burned on flaming red iron fields. They were being cut into pieces, crushed into dust, baked in burning cells, pierced by burning instruments, and scalded by burning liquid iron poured down their throats. Because of their karmic conditions, they would never die, but would return to consciousness again and again until the karmic effects of their hell life were exhausted.

With a tearful face, sorrowful mind, and compassionate heart, Jetsun prayed. Instantly, a dakini with the Buddha of Compassion above her head appeared and gave spiritual instructions to Jetsun. Accordingly, Jetsun prayed from the depth of her heart. She felt that the degree of sufferings of the beings was reduced. All the suffering beings were staring at Jetsun, and some of them were even able to take refuge in the Three Jewels. Jetsun sang to them the following teachings:

> Now, if you want to attain liberation from these sufferings,
> See your master, in whom you have faith,
> As the embodiment of all the ultimate refuges: the Buddha,
>   Dharma, and Sangha.
> Pray to him or her with a mind of strong devotion.

Develop remorse for evil deeds that you have committed in
the past.
Promise not to commit such deeds again.
Wish to take the sufferings of others upon yourself.
See the hell guards as the Buddha of Compassion.
Think of the hell realm as the pure land of the Buddha of
Compassion.
Hear the noises of beating and killing as the sounds of OM MANI
PADME HUNG.
The nature of suffering is emptiness [in its] essence.
The natural power [of the mind] is present spontaneously and
ceaselessly.
All appearances arise from the power of emptiness and are liber-
ated into emptiness.
The arising [of things] and their liberation are not successive but
simultaneous.

OM: Visualize your body as the open luminous body of the Buddha
of Compassion.
MA: In it imagine the central channel with four qualities.
NI: In it the mind is in the form of a ball of five colored lights.
PAD: With the power of vase-breathing,
ME: Into the heart of the Buddha of Infinite Light,
HUNG: Shoot [the ball of light, your mind] and unite as one, and
HRI: merge by repeating PHAT five times.

This is the training on phowa.
It liberates the consciousness of beings, even those with evil deeds,
by force.

Today I am performing phowa for the beings of the hell realm.
By the kindness of the lamas and dakinis,
May all of you be liberated from the inferior realms and attain
buddhahood.

At this, many beings died and left the hell realms.

The Power of Her Own Intrinsic Awareness

A desire to see the Dharma King of the Lords of the Dead came to Jetsun's mind. Instantly she felt that a beam of light had emanated from her

head. At the other end of the light, she saw a huge, terrifying iron fortress. In the fortress, on the throne of a corpse, sun, moon, and lotus, was the Great Dharma King. He had a wrathful form, wore a wrathful costume, and had a dark purplish complexion. He was in the midst of a blazing storm of fire and flowing streams of blood. He held a slate and a mirror in his hands and was roaring a wrathful sound: A-RA-LI! He was surrounded by a mass of retinues of Lords of the Dead.

At that moment Jetsun felt that the dakini, who had been with her till now, merged into her heart and that the Buddha of Compassion had dissolved into her head.

She paid respect to the Dharma King and his retinues, and they all seemed to wobble. Then she said prayers, and they all seemed to be repeating the same prayers after her. When she closed her eyes in devotional concentration, they all seemed to be imitating her. At this she realized that all these appearances were the mere manifesting power of her own mind's intrinsic awareness.

The Dharma King questioned Jetsun, and the deputies checked her past deeds in the mirror, in the notes, and with the scale. Finding that she had only good deeds, they directed that she be sent to the path of liberation.

Jetsun said to them, "How can I go alone, leaving all mother-beings behind in these inferior realms? Please let everyone be liberated." The Dharma King replied:

> Don't you know that hell is a mere reflection of your own mental
>   characteristics?
> I did not create the iron burning grounds and the blazing flames
>   of hell.
> They are productions of the anger and attachments of your own
>   mind.
> Each of the sufferings in the hell realms
> Is created by its own unliberated mental emotion, such as
>   anger.
> For a liberated mind, hell is the pure land of Great Joy.
> We ourselves are the peaceful and wrathful buddhas.
> Suffering is "the liberation at arising."
> On your return to the world,
> Give this message to people: "The karmic laws do not deceive."
> You, Jetsun, have witnessed them yourself.

Jetsun visualized herself as the Buddha of Compassion with a hundred peaceful and wrathful deities within him. Then, saying OM MANI PADME HUNG, she remained in contemplation on the meaning of total openness. As a result, many beings were liberated from the hell realm

Soon Jetsun returned to her body and regained her strength. During the delog experience, her mother and friends kept vigil by her body around the clock. Sometimes they experienced the fragrance of incense, sometimes the smell of a dead body, sometimes a very sweet smell, and sometimes the odor of filth. These smells were the indication of the particular place that Jetsun was visiting at that time.

NOTHING TO ACCEPT OR REJECT: THE EXPERIENCE OF DO KHYENTSE YESHE DORJE

Do Khyentse (1800–1866),[5] born in Golok province of Eastern Tibet, is known as one of the greatest masters and miraculous adepts of the Nyingma school of Tibetan Buddhism. The travels to pure lands by great adepts such as Do Khyentse are usually categorized in Tibetan Buddhist literature as pure visions or enlightened activities, not as delog experiences. Also, Do Khyentse only mentions, but gives no details of, his travel to mundane world systems such as hell realms, which is very important for delog literature in order to inspire people. So his report of traveling to pure lands cannot really be classified as a delog account.

Nevertheless, I am including Do Khyentse's travel to the pure lands because his account illustrates the theme of visiting other life systems after leaving one's body behind, and it also gives details of the manifested pure land of Guru Rinpoche.

In his youth, as a hermit, Do Khyentse wandered in areas of Amdo in Northeastern Tibet as instructed by his main teacher, the first Do-drupchen Rinpoche. Suddenly he got sick with chicken pox, which in those days was fatal. As a result, he expired and remained dead for fifteen days. Since he had exhibited unusual mystical power from his childhood, his followers didn't touch his body, hoping that he would return to life.

The Illusory Body Is Devoured

Do Khyentse felt that he was accompanied by his sister Dakini Losal Drolma (1802–1861), who was also a great adept, and two other women and a yogi. Together, they traveled to many parts of the world, from the hell realms to the celestial lands. Although Do Khyentse felt he had companions, his friends didn't share the same experience. For example, his sister was studying with Dodrupchen at that time.

Crossing many continents, they went toward the Glorious Copper-Colored Mountain, the pure land of Guru Rinpoche. On the way, they met various beings at different places. Although he couldn't understand their languages, he was able to communicate with them all through the power of intrinsic awareness of his mind.

At the beginning of an enormous bridge, his party was met by ten wrathful deities. The deities performed a rite of dispelling harmful traces. Travelers were still carrying with them harmful traces from their human habits, even though they were realized masters who had been separated from their bodies.

After going through the outer and inner gates, they were met by a great adept holding a vase filled with nectar. The adept purified them by washing their impurities with the stream of nectar from the vase.

Then they entered a palace with inconceivable manifestations of prosperity. Inside, they saw Guru Rinpoche in wrathful form with such overwhelming power that Do Khyentse fainted away in great fear for a while. When he regained consciousness, he witnessed all the deities enjoying a human body as a feast. It seemed to him that the body they were enjoying was his own.

At that moment, two wrathful dakinis approached his sister, who was sitting beside him. They skinned her and arranged her flesh, bones, and organs as a heap of offerings. A wrathful deity appeared from the sky and blessed her body. Then the dakinis offered her heart to the chief deity. Other deities devoured various parts of her body without leaving anything behind. Do Khyentse felt an unbearable love and sadness at the disappearance of his sister. Generally, resistance against giving or losing our physical body, born of our habits of attachment, is strong. To get rid of that habit of attachment is a powerful spiritual feat.

Receiving Empowerments

Then they climbed up a great crystal stairway. Do Khyentse felt as if they were floating up like pieces of paper in the wind, not having gross bodies anymore, since those bodies had been devoured by the deities on the way. They entered an astonishingly beautiful and joyful palace. The beauty of the structure, the richness of the details, and the exalted sounds of Dharma were just as described in the aspiration prayers of the Glorious Copper-Colored Mountain.

In the center of the palace, Guru Rinpoche was sitting on a precious throne, radiating rays of light in all directions. Both earth and sky were filled with clouds of enlightened ones in male and female forms. Do Khyentse wished to receive a blessing from Guru Rinpoche by touching him, but it occurred to him that he couldn't do this, as he no longer had a body.

Then a dakini with a white complexion holding a skull in her hand approached Do Khyentse. She explained, "Guru Rinpoche is the embodiment of all the buddhas of the three times. His manifestations appear in every realm of the universe, like one moon with reflections in numerous vessels of water. Like a reflection in a mirror, you too are manifested by Guru Rinpoche and delegated to Tibet to serve human and nonhuman beings and to discover and preserve the mystical hidden teachings. Since you were obscured by womb defilement of your illusory body, your body was consumed by the deities as a feast. Now you have the body of light with the essence of wisdom. You must receive the four empowerments from Guru Rinpoche and sow the seed of the four stages of knowledge-holders."

All who were present in the palace then performed ritual ceremonies for seven days. Guru Rinpoche presided over the ceremony as the vajra master. King Trisong Detsen acted as the assistant vajra master, Guru Chowang as the chanting master, Nyima Trakpa as the master of rites, Duddul Dorje and Karma Lingpa as the masters of discipline, and Rigdzin Goddem as the master of the bestowal of blessings. There were numerous knowledge-holders, dakas, and dakinis in attendance. At the end of the ceremony, Do Khyentse received the four empowerments, which purified his womb defilements. Do Khyentse was also entrusted with a casket that contained a hidden mystical teaching (*terma*). At the end, Guru Rinpoche gave the following teachings:

> When you realize that all the appearances are emptiness,
> There is little need of living in solitude.
>
> When the falsehood of phenomenal appearances has collapsed, and
> The unmodified innate nature is realized—

Without discrimination even of subtle dualities, or
Attachment even to the contaminated virtues—
Maintain the truly secure state of primordial purity.

When you realize all appearances as dreams,
Enjoy all sensual objects as mere illusions.
In delusory samsara, there is nothing to accept or reject.
Remain performing the vast bodhisattva activities.

Realize the perceptions of the day as the luminosity of
    dharmakaya.
Realize the perceptions of the night as the power of
    sambhogakaya.
Unite the son and mother—the intrinsic awareness and ultimate
    sphere.
Progress through the ten stages and five paths* with the speed of
    the sun and moon.

When you perfect the unchanging great bliss,
You are in the state of oneness with me.
Not moving, not describing, and not modifying
Are the final modes for liberation—be aware of all this.

Guru Rinpoche laughed three times, so loudly that Do Khyentse felt
that the whole continent shook with his laughter. After receiving instructions and blessings from Guru Rinpoche, Khyentse and his companions took their leave. Then the dakini with the white complexion came
forward again and said:

Like the sun and its rays,
You, the manifestation, and Guru Rinpoche, the source of the
    manifestation, are inseparable.
But because of interdependent causation,
At present, you are appearing as the chief and the retinue.
In future, you will unite as water with water again.

Then a wrathful deity with wide-open eyes told Do Khyentse:

---

* Through training, one progresses through the ten stages of the bodhisattva and the
five paths (accumulation of merits, joining, realization, meditation, and beyond training, which is buddhahood) to attain enlightenment.

Without being attached to places or sensual objects
Accomplish all the works that are assigned to you.
My protection of you is unswerving.
May you attain buddhahood that tames the three worlds.

Return to Earth

Do Khyentse and his companions came out of the gate. Then they traveled to the pure lands of the Buddha of Infinite Light, Avalokitesh-vara, and Tara. Finally, they returned to the earth. First, still in his mental body, Do Khyentse went to his root teacher, the first Dodrupchen Rinpoche, at Yarlung Pemako, a ravine in Ser Valley. He received more teachings and empowerments from Dodrupchen.

Then he went back to his body. He saw a red woman—who was protecting his body—come out of his body and disappear into the air. He felt he was touching his body, and instantly he was in his physical form. For a long time, he had to struggle to see, speak, and move. Then, with great effort, he was able to move his limbs a little bit, and his waiting disciples rushed to his aid. A Chinese doctor gave him some medicine, and he slowly was cured of chicken pox and weakness within about a month.

According to oral accounts, Do Khyentse traveled to various world systems on a number of occasions. Sometimes he would go to pure lands and see buddhas and masters. Sometimes he would go to hidden lands or realms of various beings on earth to serve them. Sometimes he traveled in his body, by disappearing and reappearing, and at other times he left his body behind, as described earlier.

6

~~~~~~~~~

Rebirth
The Ineluctable Karmic Cycle

Whatever karmic habits, positive or negative,
We have planted in our mental stream in the past
Will cause us to take rebirths,
With happy or unhappy qualities accordingly.

MANY PEOPLE HAVE a hard time believing that there will be any rebirth when the present life is over. How do we know that rebirth is possible?

Although modern science may not be able to produce definite proof to answer this question, we should not dismiss the testimony of traditional authorities in the field of spiritual practice and experience, who have investigated the truths of existence. Rebirth or reincarnation is a major pillar of several Eastern belief systems, and some mystical Jewish schools also accept that rebirths occur in a continuous wheel of life. Many great Buddhist masters have actually been able to remember and describe their past existences. The Buddha himself told hundreds of stories of his own past lives, in a well-known collection called the *Jataka Tales.* He also identified the past lives of other people.

Even ordinary men and women—of different countries, ethnicities, and religions—have spontaneously remembered their identities in past lives, the families they came from, and the towns in which they lived. Especially striking are the numerous instances of young children who have spoken in vivid detail of their past identity, even though in their present young lifetime they could never have visited their former birthplace or met anyone from there. The most famous study of children's past-life memories was made by Ian Stevenson, M.D., who documented thousands of cases in South Asia and the Middle East over forty years, in an effort to research the subject in a scientific manner. In Tibet, there have been countless examples of dying persons predicting the names of their future parents and hometown, as well as children who remember details of their previous lifetime.

In the Tibetan Buddhist tradition, there are thousands of senior monks or priests with the title of Tulku (Tib. *tulku, sPrul sku;* Skt. *nirmanakaya,* manifested body). It is believed that a tulku is either the manifestation of a fully enlightened buddha or the rebirth of a highly accomplished meditator. At the time of death, lamas will sometimes instruct their disciples where his or her tulku rebirth will take place. In some cases, the tulkus, when they start speaking as young children, will tell who they were in their past lives and what they wish or need to do. However, the most commonly accepted formula for recognizing a tulku in Tibet, after checking many indications, is formal recognition by another highly respected lama. Nevertheless, there are people who have wrongly been identified as tulkus by the influence of ambitious parents or other selfish interests, or just by sheer mistake.

A number of tulkus have remembered their past lives or exhibited qualities of their past incarnation. For example, my teacher, the fourth Dodrupchen Rinpoche, at the ages of three and four, amazed many people by continually telling them the place where the third Dodrupchen had lived, reciting prayers that he had not been taught, reciting unknown verses from memory, and exhibiting miracles. He also gave the description of the Pure Land of Guru Padmasambhava as he had seen it.[1]

Even in America there is increasing acceptance of reincarnation. A Gallup Poll conducted a few years ago reported that twenty-five percent of Americans said that they believe in "the rebirth of the soul in a new body after death." The mainstream, exoteric Western religions, however, reject the idea of reincarnation. Despite this, they generally agree with Buddhism on two important points: if you have been selfless and served others with loving-kindness, a happier condition awaits you after death—and if you have committed hateful acts and harmed other beings, you will face unpleasant consequences.

No matter what we have done up until this present moment, most religions hold out the hope of improving our future situation. Whatever name or description the various traditions use for this potential change—such as repentance, forgiveness, conversion, redemption, salvation, or liberation—it generally means that through our own intentions and efforts, combined with reliance on a sacred source of blessings, the way is open for us to uplift ourselves and others to a happier, more spiritually conscious life.

LIBERATION OR REBIRTH?

According to Buddhism, everyone inevitably takes rebirth after death, unless they transcend the cycle of birth and death by attaining enlightenment through meditation. Once you have attained fully enlightened buddhahood, you will never again be reborn in any of the mundane worlds, since you will no longer be subject to the karmic cycle that causes rebirths. You will remain in the everlasting union of buddha-wisdom and buddha pure land, the ultimate body (dharmakaya) and enjoyment body (sambhogakaya) of buddhahood. It is the utmost peaceful, supremely joyful, and omniscient state. Thereafter, others will be able to see your manifested body (nirmanakaya), which will appear on earth in various forms, visible to those who are mentally and karmically open toward you. This manifestation as a fully enlightened being is not due to any karmic causality, but rather arises from your compassionate aspirations to serve the beings in samsara.

Attaining enlightenment in this lifetime (or during one of the three other phases in the journey of our cyclical existence) is the accomplishment of advanced masters of meditation. If you are an ordinary being—not a highly accomplished master, and not enlightened or fully enlightened—then after death you are bound to take rebirth according to your own karmic consequences. Once again you will begin another passage of life, the phase we have discussed in chapter 1. In this chapter we will look at why and how we take rebirth, whether in a pure land or in one of the six realms: the realms of gods, demigods, human beings, animals, hungry ghosts, and hell-beings.

Even if you are not a highly accomplished master and are under the control of karma, if you have accumulated the positive karma of virtuous or meritorious deeds, you will take rebirth in a pure land or in a human realm endowed with precious qualities. In this way, you will be able to provide beneficial service to others. Gradually, the ultimate goal of enlightenment might also be reached.

If you take rebirth in a pure land, it will be a *manifested* pure land. This is not the same as the *ultimate* pure land of buddhahood. You take rebirth in a pure land because of your positive karmas. You will still have a dualistic mind, enjoying positive emotions and joyful sensations. But after taking rebirth in a pure land, you will never waver from your journey toward the goal of enlightenment. The attainment of buddhahood will be certain. (We will look at some descriptions of the Blissful Pure Land in the next chapter, "The Buddha of Infinite Light and His Blissful Pure Land.")

If you take rebirth in one of the six realms, you will be trapped in a particular physical body (human or otherwise), environmental influence, and social culture. Then, as long as you are alive in that body, you can still make karmic improvements in order to have a better present or future life. However, it will be almost impossible to attain the ultimate state of everlasting oneness, which is the quality of buddha-bodies in absolute buddhahood. For one who is ready, such a total transformation will be easier after death, when one is unencumbered by this gross physical body.

THE CAUSES OF REBIRTH

Rebirth does not take place without cause. The causes of birth in the six realms are the six afflicting emotions: arrogance, jealousy, desire, ignorance, greed, and hatred. These afflicting emotions in turn are rooted in the dualistic concepts of the mind. Dualistic concepts arise as soon as our mind grasps at the "self" of any mental object, perceiving mental objects as truly existing entities.

Having tightly grasped at the "self," we form the habit of differentiating between this and that, instead of perceiving oneness. This habit of discrimination arouses the afflicting emotions of liking and disliking, wanting and not wanting, attachment and hatred. Then we put those emotions into vocal and physical expression. Repeated patterns of positive mental and physical actions cause happiness and result in rebirth in high realms and in pure lands. Negative mental and physical actions cause sufferings and result in rebirths in the lower realms.

I have mentioned that if you are a highly accomplished master, you may attain liberation from the cycle of rebirth by becoming enlightened.

Figure 1. The Wheel of Life lies in the clutches of the Lord of Death, conveying life's transience.

The inner circle shows the three negative emotions that give rise to unenlightened birth. The pig stands for ignorance, the snake for hatred, and the chicken for greed.

The second circle illustrates the karmic laws governing birth. Negative karma is represented by a monster dragging frightened beings down. Positive karma is symbolized by a divine figure welcoming joyful beings up.

When you perfect the realization of the wisdom of openness—the basic emptiness that is our nature—then your concept of grasping at "self" will be liberated, marking the end of suffering and karmic causation, which means that no more rebirths will occur. With the attainment of this realization, you can become the source of effortless benefits for many others.

However, most of us perceive and grasp mental objects as truly existing entities, and we reinforce this grasping with the energy of either positive or negative emotions. Moreover, we tend to express our emotions, not just as thoughts and feelings, but also in the more active form of words and deeds. These mental, vocal, and physical actions create karma, the life-determining habitual patterns in our mindstream. That karma in turn causes our rebirth, either in a pure land or in one of the six worldly realms.

Note that all dualistic concepts and emotions—even positive ones such as caring, compassion, and wishing others well—are accompanied by grasping at "self." So although positive emotions are good, they still fall short of perfection, which is the primordial wisdom beyond dualistic thinking and emotional sensations. Grasping at positive qualities is nonetheless a stepping-stone to perfection, helping us eventually to loosen the grip of grasping at "self" and to experience sensations of peace and joy. So, transforming from negative to positive, and then from positive to perfection, is the ideal way to move toward buddhahood, or full perfection.

The third circle depicts the five realms of birth: (1) human, (2) hungry ghost, (3) hell, (4) animal, and (5) god and demigod.

The outer ring shows the twelve links of dependent origination: (1) The unenlightened state (ignorance) is symbolized by a blind person; (2) creation of karma, by a potter; (3) consciousness, by a monkey looking out a window; (4) name and form, by a person rowing a boat; (5) sense faculties, by a prosperous house; (6) contact, by a couple in embrace; (7) feeling, by an arrow piercing a man's eye; (8) craving, by a drunkard; (9) clinging, by a monkey plucking fruits; (10) becoming, by a pregnant woman; (11) birth, by the delivery of a baby; (12) aging and death, by a corpse.

At the top right, the Buddha points to the teachings on liberation, in a box on the upper left. They read:

Exhort [yourself to virtue] and abandon [evil].
Enter the buddha-dharma.
Like an elephant in a swamp,
Destroy all the Lord of Death's forces.

Drawing based on a traditional Tibetan block print, from *King Udrayana and the Wheel of Life* by Sermey Geshe Lobsang Tharchin (Howell, N.J.: Mahayana Sutra and Tantra Press, 1989), p. 160.

The Six Realms of Worldly Existence

The six worldly realms are collectively termed samsara, or cyclical existence. They are depicted in Buddhist iconography in the image known as the Wheel of Life (see figure 1 on page 172). Samsara has three lower realms and three higher realms.

The three lower realms are the worlds of great sufferings:

1. In the *hell realms*, beings suffer from the never-ceasing heat of burning flames and molten metal or the cold of freezing snow and ice.
2. In the *hungry ghost realm*, beings suffer from ever-tormenting hunger and thirst.
3. In the *animal realm*, beings suffer from fear, dullness, and servitude.

These beings will not die from their pain, even if they are being burned by the flames of the hell realm, unless the karma that caused their rebirth is exhausted.

The three higher realms are worlds of many kinds of happiness, yet they also involve endless suffering.

4. In the *realm of the demigods*, beings enjoy material prosperity, but they suffer from their constant warring and fighting.
5. In the *realm of the gods*, beings enjoy great happiness and prosperity, but these enjoyments are merely ever-changing sensual pleasures, and they also suffer. They live long lives compared with human life spans, but because of their lack of awareness, they feel as if it has all ended in a short time. The god realm is part of our mortal mundane world, not a paradise or kingdom like that of the gods of Western mythology. As soon as their karma in the god realm is exhausted, these beings will suffer by dying and being reborn in lower realms, where they are subject to their karmic consequences.
6. In our *human realm*, even if we are fortunate to enjoy great intellectual abilities, material abundance, and positive experiences, we nonetheless suffer from the chain of birth, sickness, old age, and death. We suffer by losing what we want, being forced to accept what we don't want, not getting what we desire, and having to protect what we have.

Six Emotions: The Seeds of Rebirth
in the Six Realms

Which one of these six worldly realms could be waiting for you as the place of your next rebirth? It depends on what predominant emotion you have been programming into your mind's karmic software. Is it a negative emotion such as hatred, greed, ignorance, desire, jealousy, and pride? Or is it a positive emotion such as kindness, generosity, knowledge of right and wrong, contentment, joy, and humility? The habitual emotional pattern that you have programmed in your mind will react in the form of rebirth in the corresponding birthplace of the six realms or the pure lands.

According to many texts,[2] karmas imprinted predominantly with the emotion of hatred and expressed through violent physical and vocal actions will lead to the suffering of burning and freezing, and they will also react in the form of rebirth in the hell realm.

In chapter 1, we spoke of the four parts of an action that are necessary in forming a fully constituted karma: the object (or basis), the intention, the execution, and the completion. In the example of the karma of hatred, the presence of a person or thing that you hate is the object. Having the motivation of hating the object is the intention. The mental act of hating the person is the execution. Experiencing the feeling of hatred is the completion. Whatever action you are executing, if that action has all four elements, it becomes a fully constituted karma, which will unavoidably result in future consequences.

There are many people who appear to be born angry and afflicted with the feeling of hatred toward almost everyone. Then whatever they say or do becomes an outburst of that anger, which stirs up suffering and violence in their own lives and in the lives of all who are associated with them. If that is the nature of your present life—whether you admit it or not—you will have no peace and joy in your life, only the experience of pain, fear, and misery. Although you are now in a human body, living in the human realm, your experience will be just as hellish as if you were a hell-being in the lower realms.

You might be acting as if you are strong, brave, and heroic, but in reality this façade is merely a device to cover up your insecure, vulnerable, and injured ego. As soon as you die, because of the mental habits of hatred that you have harbored throughout your life, your mental experiences and phenomenal appearances will arise in your consciousness as the hell realm. In reality, no powerful judge will be condemning or punishing you—it will all be mere reactions of the karmic patterns engraved in your mindstream by your own afflicting emotions.

In the delog accounts of the bardo that were summarized in chapter 5, we saw some very vivid and frightening examples of the sufferings of hell. Here we must remind ourselves that all the sights, sounds, and feelings of the bardo and the various realms are nothing but reflections of the experiencer's own mental complexities, like appearances in a dream. They are the mere symptoms of the positive and negative emotions that one has programmed into the mindstream by grasping at "self," perceiving the objects as real. Shantideva says:

> All the fears and inconceivable sufferings
> Came from the mind.
> Thus taught the One Who Saw the Truth [Buddha].
> Who specifically manufactured the instruments of the hell realms?
> Who constructed all those burning iron grounds?
> Where did those flames come from?
> "All of them are [mere reflections of] your unvirtuous
> mind,"
> The Buddha has said.[3]

As in the case of hatred, karmic patterns engraved predominantly by the other afflicting emotions, expressed through vocal and physical actions, are the cause of corresponding sufferings and rebirth in other lower realms. In summary:

- The emotion of hatred or anger causes the sufferings of burning and freezing, and rebirth in the hell realms.
- The emotion of greed or miserliness causes the sufferings of hunger and thirst, and rebirth in the hungry ghost realm.[4]
- The emotion of ignorance or confusion causes the sufferings of dullness and fear, and rebirth in the animal realm.
- The emotion of desire or attachment causes the sufferings of birth, old age, sickness, and death, and rebirth in the human realm.
- The emotion of jealousy causes the sufferings of war and fighting, and rebirth in the realm of the demigods.
- The emotion of arrogance or pride causes the sufferings of distractions and fear of dying, and rebirth in the realm of the gods.

Higher degrees of attachment, jealousy, and arrogance become greed. Thus, the six afflicting emotions can be condensed into three poisonous emotions—hatred, greed, and ignorance—which cause suffering and rebirth in the three inferior realms. As Nagarjuna writes:

> Greed leads you to the hungry ghost realm.
> Hatred leads you to the hell realm.
> Ignorance mostly leads you to the animal realm.[5]

It is not only the character of the emotion alone, but its degree that will determine the cause of rebirth in a particular realm. According to Gampopa, whatever negative deed you have committed:

' If you have committed the misdeed with hatred, if you have repeated it numerous times, and if you have committed it against a highly sacred object or individual, then the consequence of that karma will be rebirth in the hell realm.[6]

' If you have committed the misdeed with greed, have repeated it many times, and have committed it against an average sacred object or individual, then the consequence will be rebirth in the hungry ghost realm.

' If you have committed the misdeed with ignorance, repeated it only a few times, and have committed it against a lesser sacred object or individual, it will cause your rebirth in the animal realm.

The gravity of the karmic consequences also depends on whether you have put your afflicting emotions into action by expressing them in unvirtuous words and deeds; especially how much these unvirtuous expressions of yours have hurt others; and whether they have caused other people in turn to commit unvirtuous deeds.

Among numerous karmic consequences, which one will you reap first? First, you will experience the result of the karma that is most intense among them all. That will be followed by the karma created at the time of death. So whatever you do at the time of death will make a great impact on the next steps of your future life. After that you will face the result of the karma in which you are most experienced, and lastly the one committed most recently.[7]

Since karmic causation is rooted in your mind, the good news is that you can avoid the experience of negative rebirths, such as the hell realm, if you change the habitual patterns of your mind.

Choosing Your Next Rebirth Could Be in Your Hands

In the later part of your passage through the bardo, you might face a great deal of fear, loneliness, and pain. The emotional pressure of finding a new birthplace will be so great that you may not be very concerned about the quality of the place where you end up. At that juncture, you must be extra vigilant, because the opportunity to block the wrong birthplace and choose the right one could be in your hands. For this purpose, you must learn to recognize the signs of the birthplaces. We have already discussed some of these signs in chapter 4, "The Bardo," in the section headed "Hints of the Rebirth Awaiting Us" (see page 90).

If powerful positive or negative karma is pushing you, you may have no opportunity to choose a birthplace, since you may be totally controlled by a karmic drive—in effect, the choice will be made automatically, without your conscious intention. But if your karmic forces are not so powerful, every effort that you make will maximize your chance to acquire a positive birthplace. To succeed in this, an understanding of the methods of blocking the wrong birth doors and choosing the right one could be crucial.

In chapter 9, "Ritual Services for the Dying and the Dead," we will look at meditative rituals for avoiding birth in the six realms and especially in the three lower realms. Here, I will simply summarize the teachings on blocking the signs of the wrong birthplaces and choosing the signs of the right ones.

Blocking the Wrong Birthplaces [8]

If you are a highly accomplished meditator—one who has realized and perfected the enlightened nature of the mind—you must remain in that realized state without wavering. If you do, instead of taking rebirth, you could attain buddhahood.

If you do not have such realization or have not perfected it, but if you have accumulated pure merits and have devotion to any particular buddha and pure land, then you should generate devotion to that buddha and pure land, and make strong aspirations for taking rebirth in that particular pure land. Such aspiration could rescue you from the cycle of rebirth in the six realms and lead to rebirth in your intended pure land.

For example, if in your lifetime you have cultivated the habit of devotion to the Buddha of Infinite Light—by trusting in him as a body of unconditional love, omniscient wisdom, and invincible power—and if, at the time of death or in the bardo, you can awaken your devotional memory of him and his pure land, then your perceptions will arise instantly as the presence of the Buddha of Infinite Light and his Blissful Pure Land.

But how will you build up this kind of habit of intense devotion and trust? It is done gradually by thinking about the buddha, the pure land, and their merits again and again, as well as by singing or chanting their prayers as often as possible. At first this practice might seem strange, but it will soon become familiar and eventually will become part of your very life and breath. Then, after death, all your perceptions will arise in the form of buddha-images of love, peace, and wisdom and a pure land of joy and beauty. (For details on these practices, see appendix A.)

You may not have any karma for taking rebirth in a pure land, yet you might have created karmas such as love, generosity, knowledge of what is right, detachment, rejoicing, and humility, especially by expressing them in the service of others. If so, you might have the choice of taking rebirth in one of the high realms with positive endowments. So you must remember the signs of the particular birthplace and choose it.

For example, if you are seeing the signs of the god realm but are aspiring to take rebirth in the human realm, you must block the soft white light, which is the birthplace sign of the god realm, and instead think of and choose the blue light by going toward it.

While you are wandering in the bardo, you must not think about your loved ones and your possessions back home, as these thoughts will only divert you away from your right path. You must focus your mind on your chosen birthplace.

As we saw in chapter 4, the door to your rebirth in one of the six realms may appear as a pale light. A pale white light indicates the god and human realms. A yellow light generally stands for the demigod and animal realms. Alternatively, the animal realm may instead be indicated by a blood color, and the demigod realm by a snowstorm or rainstorm color. A smoky light suggests the hungry ghost realm, and a light that resembles a piece of log or floating black wool indicates the hell realm.[9] You might even see your own body turning into light of the color representing your future birth.

Some teachings enumerate five ways to block entrance into the wrong birth doors:[10]

1. When you are seeing the lights that are the signs of future birth-places, you might also see a couple making love, especially if you are headed for a human birth. The couple represents your potential parents. If that happens, don't go to them or get involved in attachment or jealousy toward them. See them as your guru consorts—the embodiment of your guru in male and female form. Alternatively, you might see them as Padmasambhava in union with his spiritual consort, Yeshe Tsogyal, or as any pair of buddha consorts. Mentally pay your respects to them and make offerings to them. With intense devotion, develop a strong intention to receive teachings and blessings from them.

2. If that does not block the birth door, then see the couple as deity consorts, such as the Buddha of Infinite Light or the Buddha of Compassion in male and female form. Pay your respects and make offerings to them. Strongly feel that you are receiving blessings from them.

3. If that does not block the birth door, then reverse the attachment and hatred. Generally, if you are going into a male rebirth, you will experience attachment toward the female member of the couple making love, and jealousy or hatred toward the male. If you are going into a female rebirth, you will feel attachment toward the male and jealousy or hatred toward the female. Also, owing to your past habits, you may think you are seeing a human couple, but in fact you may be being pulled toward male and female birds. If so, you would take birth as a baby bird. So, at this point, you must make a strong commitment: "I will never allow my mind to entertain attachment and hatred."

4. If that does not block the birth door, then with strong conviction see all the experiences that you are having as unreal, like illusions. Such conviction will dissolve your mind's grasping at the experiences as real, and that will block the birthplace.

5. If that does not block it, then just see everything as luminous absorption. Think: "Phenomena are my own mind. Mind is emptiness," and then contemplate in the natural state without any modification. Let your mind remain in its natural state, nakedly, like water pouring into water, all waters becoming indivisibly one.

Jigme Lingpa advises: "When the beings of the bardo see a couple having sexual intercourse, they rush to them like flies to garbage. The particular being who has the karma of taking birth will be drawn into the womb, with no possibilities of avoiding it. At that time, you must make good aspirations, go for refuge in the enlightened ones, or formulate wishes to choose a favorable womb. That could help you find a precious human birth."[11]

Choosing the Right Birthplace[12]

If you are determined to take birth in a pure land, you must generate the feeling of revulsion toward birth in the six realms. Do not get attached to your loved ones or your possessions. Make strong aspirations, and have confidence in your ability to reach a pure land of your choice, such as the Blissful Pure Land, by thinking: "I will be miraculously born from a lotus at the feet of the Buddha of Infinite Light in the Blissful Pure Land."

If taking rebirth in a pure land is not possible for you, then you might see your birthplace in one of the six realms. However, you may see a vision of your birthplace, not as it really is, but instead in a symbolic form such as the following:[13]

- ' Pleasant multistoried houses are said to be the birthplace sign of the god realm.
- ' A forest, a ring of fire, or rain can be the sign of the demigod realm.
- ' Aimlessly chattering people or houses that are ordinary, precious, or pleasant are signs of a precious human birth.
- ' Caves, huts, and fog are signs of the animal realm.
- ' Dry river beds or dark dusty places are signs of the hungry ghost realm.
- ' Red houses or dark land, a dark pit, or a dark path signifies the hell realm.[14] (However, some authors say that those with gravely negative karmas may go to the hell realms without any bardo experiences of lights or images.)

When you see such appearances, you may be eager to take refuge in any of these places, since you will not have had shelter for so long. You might want to hide in any of them, as you may feel frightened and exhausted by the scenes of threatening illusions of the Lords of Death. But now is the time to try to be alert, because you must not go toward any signs of the lower realms. You must try to choose the human realm or the realm of the gods, if birth in a pure land is not possible.

It might be hard for you to recognize the right birthplace. You could be seeing a positive birthplace as a negative one or a negative birthplace as positive because of the deceptive illusions displayed by your own karmic obscurations. So it could be important to use the following techniques.

If you have had training in meditation on any wrathful buddha, such as Vajrapani, the Buddha of Power, you should instantly visualize yourself in the form of the deity. His body is gigantic, majestic, and overwhelming. His voice is frightening and earth-shattering. His mind is loving, omniscient, and peaceful. If you visualize Vajrapani, you might witness the dissolution of the Lords of the Dead—the frightening mental fabrications that were hunting you down. That will give you the opportunity to employ the minor clairvoyance that many beings possess in the bardo to find the real qualities of the birthplaces and choose the right one in peace.

You must also develop this strong intention: "I will be reborn in a family of sincere and virtuous practitioners." I will take rebirth as a person who has the capacity to serve all sentient beings."

In addition, while entering the womb, bless it as a palace of the deities. See that this palace is filled with numerous divinities, such as the Buddha of Compassion, and pray to them. Then enter the womb, thinking that you are being initiated by the deities. Alternatively, with devotion see the male and female in union as your spiritual master consorts.

When any sign of rebirth appears to you, even if it seems to be a positive birthplace, it is crucial not to get into the state of mind of attachment to it. Even if it appears to be a negative birthplace, don't get into the state of mind of hating it. Enter the best possible birthplace, or womb, with great equanimity, free from the emotions of rejecting or accepting.

Unless you have been an experienced meditator, it will probably be hard to alter your usual habits of discrimination in order to discern a desirable birthplace when you are in the bardo. However, you can try to follow these practices:

- Don't forget that you are in the bardo, the transitional passage.
- Remember to walk keeping your head pointing upward.
- Pray by continuously saying the names of the buddhas. Take refuge in them.
- Take refuge in the Three Jewels—the Buddha, the Dharma, and the Sangha.
- Pray to the Compassionate Ones, such as the Buddha of Infinite Light and your own spiritual masters.

- Let go of attachments to your loved ones and possessions, as they will only divert you from your right path.
- Enter the path of the blue light of the human realm or the white light of the god realm.

If you have little likelihood of liberation but hope to be reborn in the human or god realm, you may be assisted in your aspiration by helpers while you are dying or after your death. They can continue to repeat the above instructions to you. Having a helper to remind you of these practices may make it easier for you to remember them when you enter the bardo. Even after you have died, your consciousness might be lingering in the World of the Living for a while. Therefore, instructions addressed to you by a living helper may still reach you and benefit you. We must try all the best possible methods to enable us to think and act effectively in the bardo.

In this book, we are giving special attention to taking rebirth in a pure and peaceful world after death. For a Buddhist, that might be the Blissful Pure Land of the Buddha of Infinite Light (although any other buddha pure land may be chosen). We now turn, in chapter 7, to a closer look at this Buddha and his Blissful Pure Land as the source of blessings, the object of contemplation and devotion, and a place to which we may aspire to be reborn. Since remembering and praying to the Buddha of Infinite Light and making merits enable us to take rebirth in his Blissful Pure Land, a realm of great peace and joy, it will be helpful to review the description of him and his pure land given in the sutras by the historical Buddha, Shakyamuni.

7

The Buddha of Infinite Light and His Blissful Pure Land

A mind replete with faith in the Buddha of Infinite Light
Is assured rebirth in the sublime Blissful Pure Land.
A mind awakened with buddha-qualities
Is in union with the Blissful Pure Land, wherever it is.

B UDDHIST COSMOLOGY encompasses an unimaginably vast number of world systems beyond our earthly home. Outside of the mundane world, the six realms of samsara, there exist innumerable pure lands extending in all ten directions of the universe (the eight points of the compass, the zenith, and the nadir). These purified paradises are the dwelling places of advanced beings, including celestial buddhas and great bodhisattvas.

Among the countless pure lands, several are especially important, including those of Vairochana, Vajrasattva, Tara, Avalokiteshvara, Maitreya, and Guru Padmasambhava. The best known is Sukhavati, the Blissful Pure Land, which lies in the western direction, beyond numerous universes. This ideal world is the abode of the Buddha of Infinite Light, who presides over an untold number of seekers of enlightenment, ascetics, and other disciples. Because the light of his body fills all the buddha pure lands without hindrance, his name is Amitabha in Sanskrit, meaning Infinite Light.[1]

Amitabha is the focus of a devotional tradition known as Pure Land Buddhism that became very popular in China, Korea, and Japan. In Tibet, the Blissful Pure Land is a favorite object of prayer and meditation, especially in rituals for the dead. In the sutras, the historical Buddha, Shakyamuni, assures devotees that this is the easiest pure land for taking rebirth and the most joyful and powerful place for advancing toward enlightenment. Whoever takes rebirth in the Blissful Pure Land will attain full enlightenment, at least in one lifetime, because of the qualities of this pure land, the blessings of the Buddha of Infinite Light, and their own merits.

Sources of the Pure Land Tradition

Several Buddhist scriptures are the sources of the tradition of buddha pure lands. Both sutras (common teachings) and tantras (esoteric teachings) contain the names and descriptions of various pure lands, but Shakyamuni Buddha gave the greatest attention to describing the Blissful Pure Land of Amitabha Buddha, in vivid and beautiful detail.[2]

Of particular importance are two Mahayana sutras known as the Larger *Sukhavati-vyuha Sutra* and the Smaller *Sukhavati-vyuha Sutra*. These teachings are the discourses of the Buddha to his close followers. He taught the larger sutra on Vulture's Peak (Mount Gridhakuta) near the town of Rajagriha (in modern-day Rajgir, Bihar State, India) to Ananda and Ajita and a huge assembly of other disciples. He taught the smaller sutra in the Jeta Grove (in Shravasti in modern-day Uttar Pradesh State, India) to Shariputra and a great assembly of disciples.

These two sutras have appeared in many translations, including Chinese (since the third century c.e.), and Korean and Japanese (since the seventh century). The great Tibetan translator Yeshe De rendered them from Sanskrit into Tibetan in the ninth century. This chapter is based mainly on the Tibetan versions as well as some other texts and commentaries.[3]

The Three Aspects of the Pure Land

As we noted earlier, the Buddha of Infinite Light and his Blissful Pure Land as described in this book belong to the "manifested form," one of three aspects or bodies of buddhahood.

The first is the ultimate body (dharmakaya), which is the formless, pure nature of buddhahood, identical with reality itself. It is the absolute state of total openness and emptiness, free from dimensions, characteristics, and limitations.

The second is the enjoyment body (samboghakaya), which is the state of nonduality and oneness. This is the pure land with form body, pure and inseparable from the buddha-wisdom itself. It is all-pervading, everlasting, never-changing, and ever joyful.

The ultimate pure land and the enjoyment pure land can be seen only by those who are enlightened.

The third aspect of buddhahood is the manifested body (nirmanakaya). This is the physical form in which Shakyamuni Buddha and other buddhas have manifested in our human world. The manifested pure land is the relative form that can be perceived by ordinary or mundane beings like us if we have accumulated meritorious deeds. If we are reborn in one of the joyful, peaceful manifested pure lands, we will advance our spiritual attainment and reach the absolute pure land.

As I have emphasized a number of times, the perceptions and experiences we have at different stages of life, especially at the time of death, are a result of the mental habits that we have generated and ingrained in our mindstream in the past. If our minds have been inflamed and turned into a burning rod of anger, hatred, and negative perceptions, then appearances and experiences of this life and especially of our future lives will arise for us in the form of a hellish world. If our minds have been occupied by peaceful, joyful, and caring thoughts and actions, and if we have been enjoying positive perceptions, such as the forms and feelings of the Blissful Pure Land, then the world that will arise as the place where we take birth will be a positive world of peace and joy, such as the Blissful Pure Land.

The main focus of the trainings described in this book is to take rebirth in the manifested form of the Blissful Pure Land. It is easier to take rebirth there than in any other pure land because of the powerful vows made by the Buddha of Infinite Light to bring all beings to his Blissful Pure Land and help them attain enlightenment.

THE POWER OF THE BUDDHA'S VOWS

The Larger *Sukhavati-vyuha Sutra* tells the story of how the Blissful Pure Land came about. Infinite eons ago, a monk called Dharmakara—who was destined to become Amitabha Buddha—generated the enlightened attitude (Skt. *bodhichitta*) and made a vow before his teacher, the buddha Lokeshvara, that he would serve all beings. At that time, Dharmakara also made special vows of aspiration to create his own unique pure land with a number of uncommon qualities. When he attained buddhahood, his vows resulted in the universe of the Blissful Pure Land.

According to the Tibetan translation of the sutra, Dharmakara made fifty-one vows or promises to lead beings to his new pure land.[4] The following five give us an idea of the nature of these vows and his pure land.

In his first vow, Dharmakara pledged not to attain buddhahood if any beings born into his pure land should endure the sufferings of the demigod, animal, hungry ghost, or hell realms. So, for example, from the moment a hell-being takes rebirth in the Blissful Pure Land, all his suffering as a hell-being will stop and he will become a happy being of the pure land. (Recall that the distinction between a being of the lower realms and a pure land being is how they see and feel the mental objects that arise in consciousness.)

In his second vow, he promised not to attain buddhahood unless all the beings born in his pure land would never again have to endure rebirth in any lower realms.

In his fourth vow, he promised not to attain buddhahood if the beings born into his pure land would have characteristics other than those of the human and god realms. He wanted his pure land to be totally pure, but also to have positive qualities similar to those of the human and god realms.

In his nineteenth vow, he promised not to attain buddhahood until all who wished to take rebirth in his pure land, and who practiced his name-prayer and dedicated the merits for it, actually did take rebirth in the pure land: "May this be so even if the person has repeated the thought of taking rebirth in my pure land only ten times, so long as he or she has not committed any of the 'five immeasurable offenses' or renounced the Dharma." These conditions are not up to the buddha's choice; if beings are not open to liberation, the buddha cannot force it upon them.

In the thirtieth vow, he promised not to attain buddhahood until the beings of his future pure land would be not only free from suffering, but also endowed with spiritual qualities such as boundless wisdom and confidence.

Amitabha's compassionate vows are indeed powerful. But by themselves they do not grant us birth in the pure land. We must do our part, we must be sure not to block our chances by committing the five immeasurable offenses or renouncing the Dharma, and we must open the way to the pure land with the "four causes" of taking rebirth in the Blissful Pure Land (see appendix A).

THE POWER OF THE BUDDHA'S NAME

Amitabha has vowed to lead all who repeat his name to his pure land. His name becomes a window through which we can view the Buddha of Infinite Light and his Blissful Pure Land.

Mahayana Buddhism teaches us to realize everything as the forms, sounds, and experiences of enlightenment. But to reach this goal, we need to enter through a specific gateway—whether it is an image of a buddha, a feeling of peace, or a sound with positive quality. One such gateway is the name of Amitabha, which he himself blessed to help us reach him and to enable him to reach us.

The name of Amitabha is his very presence, wisdom, compassion, and power. The moment we become conscious of his name, he is in us and with us. So if we concentrate on and unite with his name one-pointedly and with devotion, we begin to enjoy an ocean of enlightening qualities. Devotion and trust in the buddha will flower naturally. Soon we find that there is no room for negative mentalities and afflicting emotions like anger, lust, ignorance, and jealousy. As we become vessels filled with the buddha's blessing powers, we serve others spontaneously. Whatever we see, hear, and feel arises as his presence. Rebirth in the Blissful Pure Land is a natural next step. And the attainment of buddhahood, our final destination, is within reach.

If the blessed name becomes our thoughts and breathing with devotion and celebration, then even while we are perceiving ordinary images, sounds, or feelings—whether we are living, dying, or in the bardo—we will always be connected with the buddha, through his name.

It is especially powerful if you can say the name or name-prayer in the original language (Sanskrit) or in a language that has been blessed by numerous enlightened ones, such as Sanskrit and Tibetan. But if praying in your own language is more inspiring for you, it will be wiser to use your language, because the important thing is to open the mind with devotion and develop trust.

We should say the blessed name of the Buddha of Infinite Light as many times as possible. Appendix A explains how to use the name.

What Is the Pure Land Like?

The manifested body of the Blissful Pure Land appears in many ways similar to the highest qualities of the human and god realms.[5] So, for example, beings born there will take on forms like those of human beings and gods.

Although this manifested pure land appears as the object of dualistic concepts and emotions, it nonetheless blossoms with openness and positive qualities. It is a celestial land, situated in the sky (not in the ocean or on earth) and filled with precious substances. It functions within a hierarchical order of teachers and disciples. All beings who are born into this pure land are disciples, and among these disciples are bodhisattvas who in turn serve as teachers to others.

The Blissful Pure Land resembles the human and god realms in having dimensional structures, distinctions of size and distance, and a relative time zone. However, it is not subject to human sufferings such as the pains of birth, old age, sickness, and death, nor to the sufferings of the gods, such as death and falling to lower realms. Explaining why it is called the Blissful Pure Land, Shakyamuni Buddha said: "In the Blissful Pure Land, there is no suffering in the bodies of beings. There is no suffering in their minds. There are immeasurable causes of happiness. That is why this is called the Blissful Pure Land."[6]

The terrain of the Blissful Pure Land is soft and even, like the palm of a youthful hand. It is boundless, young, fresh, tender, and comforting to the touch, with no thorns, pebbles, rocks, or slopes. It is quiet, peaceful, joyful, and immaculate. It is made of seven precious materials[7] and adorned with golden designs without any trace of harshness, grossness, roughness, filth, dullness, or decay. It is bright and colorful, emitting rays of light. In this very pure land, other immeasurable buddha pure lands appear like reflections in the face of a clear mirror. One can see these reflected pure lands just as if one were watching other continents on a TV in the living room.

This pure land has no dark or ordinary mountains, but it is adorned with many kinds of smooth mountains of precious gems with high and low peaks. Here and there, the mountains are adorned with heaps of precious gems, mines of precious treasures, caves of precious jewels, and huts made of exquisite vines.

Exquisite trees in colorful designs adorn the landscape. There are trees made of one, two, or three precious substances. Many others are made of seven precious substances: the roots are made of gold, the trunks of silver, the branches of lapis lazuli, the leaves of crystal, the petals of carnelian, the flowers of mother-of-pearl, and the fruits of rubies. These trees are soft and comforting to the touch, spreading sweet fragrances in all directions. Soothing sounds are carried by the currents of the wind.

This pure land is adorned with chains of wide and deep lakes, ponds, and rivers where many beings are at play with great ease. Comfortable steps of precious gems lead you to the ponds and lakes filled with uncontaminated water. The ground is made of precious jewels covered with golden sand. The ponds are filled with water with eight healthful qualities: it is clear, cool, light, tasteful, soft, pure, healthful for the throat, and healthful for the stomach. Heavenly lotuses emitting a celestial aroma float upon the waters. The temperature of the water changes according to your wish. Rivers flow with the sounds of hundreds of thousands of symphonies that are incomparable even to any celestial music. The banks of the lakes and rivers are filled with richly scented groves. The rivers vibrate profound and vast Dharma teachings at your bidding.

Infinite celestial birds manifested by the buddha[8] inhabit the pure land. Like the mountains, flowers, and other features of the land, the birds are all manifestations of the buddha and are the buddha himself. As such, they are a source of peace, joy, wisdom, and enlightenment, not sources of confusion, grasping, greed, or hatred. Just as a person in an ordinary realm hears ordinary birdsong, in this pure land you will hear the birds singing the blissful sounds of the Dharma. However, if you prefer silence, what you will hear is solely the sound of silence.

All the flowers are made of precious substances in various colors. They are as big as a half, one, or ten *yojana* (a yojana equals four thousand fathoms). From each flower arises an infinite number of rays of golden light. On each ray of light, infinite numbers of buddhas appear. Appearances of the buddhas fill immeasurable world systems, proclaiming the roar of teachings to the ears of all beings who are open to them.

Disciples in the pure land do not rely on gross food. But if they wish, any delicacies they desire will appear before them and please them without their needing to eat them. Likewise, whatever they want—incense, perfume, parasols, banners, musical instruments, clothes, or ornaments—will appear before them as they wish. But these things will not appear for those who do not wish for them.

For those who want mansions, there will appear multistoried, multidomed mansions made of precious materials, filled with priceless seats, beds, celestial ornaments, and amazing decorations. Each mansion is filled with thousands of celestial beings providing limitless music and pleasing entertainment. Disciples travel through the sky together with their divine mansions, gardens, forests, rivers, and ponds.

Every morning, noon, afternoon, dusk, midnight, and dawn, breezes from the four directions visit everyone. They bring the rain of scented flowers from the trees and cover the earth with blossoms as soft as silk. When you are touched by the scented breezes, you feel as blissful as if you are in meditative absorption. Soon all the older flowers on the ground will disappear, replaced by fresh ones.

Now and then, scented showers bring a sprinkling of celestial flowers and ornaments, accompanied by music and dances performed by celestial beings.

In the pure land, all forms, sounds, and feelings are images, sounds, and experiences of the Dharma. This does not mean that the forms become buddha-images or the sounds become words of the Buddhist scriptures; but rather that all are the source or presence of peace, joy, and enlightenment.

In the center of this abundant pure land is the Tree of Enlightenment. Its height is six hundred thousand yojana. It is adorned with ravishing leaves, flowers, and fruits, and decorated with precious gems and golden garlands. As they are touched by the wind, they emit enchanting sounds heard in numerous world systems. All who hear, see, or smell the Tree of Enlightenment—or who taste its fruits, touch its lights, or think of it mentally—will be freed from wavering concepts and afflicting emotions.

The size and form of the Tree of Enlightenment are described here according to the way ordinary people might see it, but in reality it is inconceivable. At the foot of the tree is a huge lotus seat. This is the seat of the Buddha of Infinite Light, from which he teaches and liberates all.[9]

The Buddha of Infinite Light and His Disciples

Just as the King of Mountains towers over all lesser peaks, so does Amitabha surpass all with his majestic presence. His body is pure and immaculate,[10] adorned with the thirty-two signs and eighty marks of excellent beings. His body is pure and boundless like the sky. It blazes with inconceivable light, illuminating an infinite number of pure lands of the ten directions. His lights are the virtues, realizations, and wisdoms. This radiance, beautiful and pristine like crystalline light, ignites the body and mind of whomever it touches with bliss, wisdom, and supreme joy. Thus he is known as the Buddha of Infinite Light. Because his life span is immeasurable, he is also known as the Buddha of Infinite Life.

His speech brings forth constant melodies of Dharma. His enlightened mind is an ocean of vast, deep peace and wisdom. He knows all knowable subjects through his omniscient wisdom without limit. His mind is filled with love and compassion for all who suffer, like that of a mother for her only child. With great confidence, he delights the minds of all and fulfills their needs with the continuous flow of his inexhaustible ambrosia-like teachings. With ardent dedication he shares with everyone the nectar-like supreme attainment that he has realized. Like a chief herdsman, he travels slowly but steadily, leading an assembly of disciples as vast as the ocean.

In his pure land, the Buddha of Infinite Light presides over an inconceivably infinite number of disciples. They include both seekers of enlightenment for themselves (Skt. *shravaka* and *pratyeka-buddha*) and seekers of enlightenment for others (Skt. *bodhisattva*). Primary among the latter are eight bodhisattvas: Avalokiteshvara, Mahasthamaprapta, Manjushri, Kshitigarbha, Sarvanivaranaviskambini, Akashagarbha, Maitreya, and Samantabhadra. They all possess the fivefold extraordinary knowledge, as follows. (1) They possess the miraculous ability to travel in a moment through numerous world systems to teach others. Every morning these disciples travel to infinite numbers of other pure lands to see and pay respect to the buddhas there and to hear their teachings, before returning to the Blissful Pure Land. (2) They have the ability to remember events from eons past, for the purpose of learning and teaching. (3) Their celestial eyes are capable of looking into numerous world systems in order to spot beings whom the bodhisattva can serve. (4) Their celestial ears are able to hear the teachings of numerous buddhas as well as the prayers of numerous beings. (5) They have knowledge of the mental states of beings in numerous lands in order to serve them appropriately.[11] Through these miraculous powers, the bodhisattvas provide joy and benefits for untold numbers of beings in many world systems.

Not all the beings who are born into the Blissful Pure Land possess such powers as these. This is because they have had doubts about taking rebirth in the pure land or lacked full faith in the power of the Buddha of Infinite Light and his vows.

Other beings who take birth in this pure land may remain in the womb of a lotus for five hundred years and do not even see the buddha during that time. They will enjoy peace and happiness in the immaculate flower, but because they are involved in doubts, the flower remains closed and they do not see the pure land and the buddha.

Not all the disciples in this pure land are bodhisattvas of the tenth, or highest, stage, who seek enlightenment for others; but for all of the disciples, this will be their last life before attaining buddhahood, for everyone here will gain enlightenment—unless they choose differently—thanks to the power of the Buddha's vow.[12]

None of the disciples leads a householder's way of life, with spouse and family, as all are free from attachments to sensual objects. There is no one who deviates from the right mental, emotional, and physical disciplines, for such a way of life is integral to the pure land. Beings in the Blissful Pure Land are mentally, emotionally, and physically much more refined than the beings of any mundane realm. They are even beyond male and female classifications. However, according to the sutras and the Blissful Pure Land teachings, although there are no ordinary women or men among the beings who have taken rebirth in the pure land, there are feminine and masculine divinities manifested by the Buddha of Infinite Light to serve beings.

There is no womb birth, as all are born by miraculous birth in vast, precious, sweet-scented, colorful flowers. No one produces urine, excrement, or mucus, as the beings here do not possess a gross body or eat earthly food.*

---

* According to Abhidharma texts (see NG 183a/2 and CND 30/18), at the beginning of our age, eons ago, human beings on this earth were not distinguished as male and female. They did not have sexual intercourse, and everyone was born through miraculous means. People had no need to eat gross food, nor did they rely on the light of the sun and moon, for they were illuminated by the light of their own radiant bodies. They flew through the sky like birds, though they had no wings. Gradually, over time, human beings started to enjoy earthly substances and then to experience gross emotions. This caused them to lose their power of flying and their radiance. Soon they started to be distinguished as males and females and to have womb births.

The Buddha said:

In the pure land of the Buddha of Infinite Light,
Since all enjoy the food of meditative absorption,
There is not even the name of [ordinary] food.[13]

Everyone enjoys a pure complexion like refined gold. The bodies of all the disciples in the pure land are strong and powerful, displaying the thirty-two signs of excellent beings. The wisdom-lights of their bodies illuminate the entire atmosphere. The Buddha said:

In the pure land of the Buddha of Infinite Light,
The wisdom-lights of the noble ones are always emanating.
There is no darkness,
And no difference between day and night.[14]

Their minds are peaceful, as they are filled with confidence and wisdom. They are joyful, because whatever they enjoy, they enjoy naturally without grasping at, craving for, or being afflicted with it. Even those who have not yet transcended suffering and the causes of suffering nonetheless remain in constant joy, owing to the power of the pure land. No one is subject to sickness or old age. The life span is infinite because of the force of merits. As soon as they take rebirth in the pure land, all the experiences of suffering will cease, for there is no sense of suffering in the pure land.

REBIRTH IN THE BLISSFUL PURE LAND

These descriptions of the Blissful Pure Land are merely partial glimpses of its unimaginably rich qualities. In reality, even celestial eyes cannot see all of these qualities, which are infinite, and even buddhas cannot explain them all, for words are inadequate.

According to the sutras, the vow of the Buddha of Infinite Light is so powerful that if you remember him, you will not only be reborn in his pure land, but you will see him in person in your lifetime and also in dreams or visions. At the time of your death, the Buddha of Infinite Light will appear before you amid his oceans of disciples. Especially if you remember the buddha of Infinite Light in the bardo, that memory will cause you to take rebirth in his pure land. That is because in the bardo, it is easier to change your situation.[15]

To take rebirth in the pure land, you need not have achieved any high meditative realization. Because of the power of the vow of the buddha, what you need is to practice the four causes to open your mind and make it receptive to such a possibility. The only condition is that you must not have committed any of the five immeasurable offenses or renounced the Dharma. Shakyamuni Buddha taught the four causes thus:

> O Ananda, there are people who [1] think of the details of the Buddha [of Infinite Light and his pure land] again and again. [2] They create many, immeasurable merits. [3] They develop the mind of enlightenment [bodhichitta]. [4] They dedicate their merits and make aspirations to take rebirth in the Blissful Pure Land. When they die . . . they will take rebirth in the universe of the Blissful Pure Land.[16]

By cultivating devotion and remembrance of the Buddha of Infinite Light, we assure our rebirth in his wondrous Blissful Pure Land, a universe of everlasting peace and sublime joy, and become a source of serenity and contentment to others. This amazing opportunity is the promise of the Buddha of Infinite Light to each of us. The truth of this promise was proclaimed by the historical Buddha himself. It has been the proven path traveled by Buddhist sages and devotees through the ages.

Some Buddhists who regard themselves as "nontheistic" might assume that the Blissful Pure Land is only for devotees with a more theistic approach. Consider, however, the example of Nagarjuna. He was the most important proponent of the emptiness doctrine of Mahayana Buddhism, a nontheistic school that denies the extremes of existence, nonexistence, both existence and nonexistence, and neither existence nor nonexistence. Yet the historical Buddha himself prophesied that "a monk named Naga[rjuna] . . . will take rebirth in the Blissful Pure Land when he leaves his body."[17] So if the most important master of Buddhism's greatest nontheistic school was to be born in the pure land, any follower of Buddhism, whether theistic or not, could aspire to be reborn there.

To facilitate rebirth in the pure land, it is important for the dying to have a support system both in and around them. The next chapter tells how helpers can provide that support.

8

How to Help the Dying and the Dead

For a mind flitting alone in the bardo like a piece of cotton in
the wind,
To find comfort in the strong hands of people of peace and
wisdom
Is the chance to soar to the pure land without trembling in fear
or crying in sadness.
What amazing solace to be saved from wandering aimlessly
through the unknown!

WHEN SOMEONE IS DYING, we have the opportunity to offer invaluable spiritual assistance. Lamas, trained lay helpers, and fellow practitioners can offer prayers, meditations, and ceremonies aimed at guiding the dying and dead on their afterdeath journey. There are also many simple but meaningful things that caregivers, relatives, and friends can do to help.

MAINTAINING POSITIVE THOUGHTS AND BEHAVIOR

How we conduct ourselves around a dying person or following a death can make a significant difference in that person's experience of this crucial transition. While someone is dying or dead, and for days after the death, it is important for survivors to try to refrain from thoughts and feelings of either attachment or antagonism toward the dead person.

Even if it is not possible to prevent these thoughts and attitudes from arising, we should avoid expressing them in word or deed. We should try not to mourn, cry, or lament. It is important also not to "dig up the dirt" about the deceased, to gossip about their weaknesses or the bad actions they may have engaged in, or even to think such thoughts in our minds. The delog accounts in chapter 5 revealed how mourning and weeping by survivors can cause the dead to experience darkness, blizzards, frightening sounds, and painful feelings as they journey through the bardo. Loved ones of the departed should try to maintain a peaceful and calm state of mind and atmosphere as much as possible. We should celebrate, rejoice, pay respect, and eulogize the person for their achievements. Never should we think along such lines as "Now that this person has died, I will become rich," or "At last, with this person gone, I'm free."

The minds of the recently deceased could be wandering around for hours, days, or even weeks after separating from their body. They even possess some ability to read the minds of the living. If they detect that people are thinking and behaving negatively toward them, that will become a powerful factor in stirring up negative emotions, and this in turn could become the cause of a painful future existence for them.

So, at least for a period from a few days to a couple of weeks after the death of the person, we as survivors should try to preserve positive thoughts and memories about the dead and behave accordingly.

Feelings of sadness at the death of a loved one are natural. But although you will be sad, you should not aggravate the sadness; rather, try to minimize or purify it. The first thing is to try not to see the feeling of sadness as negative and begin an emotional struggle. Instead, you could think, "Yes, I am sad, but it is out of my love and appreciation for my loved one. How wonderful to have such a beautiful memory and affection." As soon as you label it as positive and turn it into an object of joy, the whole painful quality of the sadness will turn into a joyful healing energy. Sometimes, you might need to remind yourself, "If I harbor sad feelings along with the thoughts and images of my loved one, it will affect them negatively, as taught in the teachings and told in the delog stories, so I must stop it." Such understanding and commitment will help to arrest the continuity of sad feelings.

It is important to remember that the death of the loved one is not the end of that person. Life will continue. If they had been suffering sickness or old age, this is a good chance for them to end the suffering and enjoy health and a better life. Especially, if any part of your loved one's life was positive, you must remember it, focus your mind on that part of their time on earth, and rejoice in it. That will generate healing energies for you and spiritual support for the loved one.

The most effective practice, instead of dwelling on sadness and letting it consume your life, is to focus your mind on prayers, meditations, and the enjoyment of blessings from your "source of blessings."

Performing Prayers and Rituals

Whatever prayers or meditations the survivors and especially the helpers choose to do for the deceased, they should first meditate and experience for themselves the inspiration and benefits flowing from their source of blessings. Then they should share them with the dying or dead. If you have not experienced such feelings yourself, there will be very little to share with the dying or dead.

In deciding what prayer, meditation, or ceremony to perform, it will always be important to choose ones with which both the helper and the deceased person are connected or familiar.

Unless the dying or dead person is a fully accomplished adept, it is very important to rely on the power of the source of blessings. Your source of blessings might be a buddha such as the Buddha of Infinite Light, a buddha pure land such as the Blissful Pure Land, a bodhisattva, a saint, a sage, or your own spiritual masters.

The helper must see, feel, and believe that the source of blessings is a fount of omniscient wisdom, unconditional love, and boundless power. If you can envision it in such a way, then the source of blessings will actually be there before you as such, thanks to the power of your own pure perception.

Making Merits

The most valuable service you can perform for the dead and dying is to make merits and dedicate them as the cause of happiness and enlightenment for the deceased person.

Buddhism teaches that to attain buddhahood, you must gather two accumulations: merits and wisdom. Through positive thoughts, emotions, and deeds performed with a dualistic mind, we accumulate merits or good karmas. Through the realization of the ultimate nature, free from dualistic concepts and emotions, we accumulate wisdom that transcends karmic causation. To have a peaceful and joyful life or rebirth, we must accumulate merits. To attain buddhahood, we must realize wisdom.

The numerous ways of making merits include the following:

' Cultivate thoughts and actions of generosity, moral discipline, patience, diligence, and contemplation.

' Apply these thoughts and dedications in numerous positive activities, including the recitation of prayers, the practice of meditations, serving others, nursing the sick, and saving lives.

' Generate trust in and devotion to the source of blessings, compassion for all sentient beings, and contemplation on any positive mental object, whether it is an image (such as a buddha-image), a holy person, a sacred sound, a feeling (devotion, compassion, peace, joy), blessings, pure lands, and so on.

' Observe precepts, purify misdeeds (whether through meditations and ceremonies or through any positive thoughts and deeds that will purify the negative karmas you have committed), give teachings, make offerings to deities, give gifts to the needy, make donations to charities, offer asylum, sponsor religious ceremonies, sponsor or create religious objects (such as statues, paintings, temples, and monuments), and build roads* and shelters.

You can also accumulate merits by performing religious rites in front of or amid sacred forms, sounds, and experiences of the source of blessings. That will open your mind and life to spiritual qualities such as the blossoming of your mind with positive perception and your emotions with devotion, celebration, and boundless joy.

After making merits, one of the most powerful services you can offer for the dead is the dedication of all the merits of your virtuous deeds as the cause of peace and joy of the specific person or for all beings. There are enormous books of dedicational prayers among Buddhist texts. While saying such prayers, one thinks of dedicating the merits to all beings (especially to the dead for their peace and joy), without expecting anything in return.

---

* In places like Tibet where access is difficult, simple roads are helpful for sustaining people's lives. Thus, like any deed that is beneficial for others or any act generated by a positive intention, road-building creates merits or positive karmas that result in peace and joy.

It is good if you yourself are able to perform any of the meritorious deeds mentioned on behalf of the dead; but it will also be meritorious if you simply inspire others to perform them or if you sponsor the performance of merit-making rituals by lamas or laypeople.

Buddhist Rituals for Non-Buddhists

As we know, there are people who are open to Buddhist views even though they are not formally Buddhists themselves. There are also people who appreciate Buddhism in general but do not find it easy to accept Buddhist imagery or complex views of death and afterdeath. Then there are others who are totally closed to Buddhism or even opposed to it or its ideas about death.

In traditional Tibet, the whole population consisted of devout Buddhists, so of course such questions never arose. But now that Buddhism flourishes in the West, it has become an issue. Should we offer assistance in the Buddhist manner even to those deceased persons who would probably reject it if they were alive?

Some teachers reply that beings who are wandering in the bardo are in great need of help. They will be looking for any source of peaceful and joyful images, sounds, and feelings as their support. At the juncture of death, they will be eagerly seeking anything that provides shelter and relief. So they will welcome prayers, meditations, and merits, and such services will help them greatly, even if they did not appreciate Buddhism while they were alive.

Other teachers think that if the dying person had thoughts of dislike for Buddhism or resistance to Buddhist images and concepts while they were alive, they might be carrying the same tendencies into the bardo, since habits of mind are not easy to get rid of. If that is so, then in the minds of such people, Buddhist services performed for their sake might cause resentment or even anger, which will only harm them.

In my view, it is certainly safe and beneficial to visualize or create a peaceful, joyful feeling and atmosphere around any dying or dead person. You can relax in contemplation of that atmosphere, thinking and feeling that you (the helper), the dying person, and the atmosphere have all merged with the feeling of peace and joy. As the helper, you can also imagine seeing positive images and hearing soothing sounds or words; allow these impressions to create a secure atmosphere of peace and joy.

Then relax in it with openness mind. These practices are based on the true essence of Buddhism and possess universal positive qualities, without any specific Buddhist character or Asian culture.

In addition, it is very important to perform any form of merit making as having a universal character and to dedicate the merits to the dead as a way of planting the seed of a peaceful and happy journey and rebirth.

UNIVERSAL MEDITATION FOR ALL

Even if the dying or dead person is not a Buddhist or not even open to Buddhism, the following formulas will be beneficial, safe, and respectful. Helpers can use them all or tailor any part of them that will suit the need of the particular dying person. They are based on Buddhist principles but have universal qualities and appeal.

- In the sky above, imagine that you are seeing the source of blessings in the form of beings of light. These beings of great beauty, unconditional love, boundless joy, amazing peace, profound power, and total openness are sending light rays of warmth and joy in all directions with love.
- See that beams of blessing lights are radiating from the source of blessings. These blessing lights are filling the whole atmosphere with a feeling of great peace and joy that dispels all the darkness of confusion, sadness, and fear.
- Hear the singing sound of celebratory words, sounds, or prayers filling the atmosphere like a symphony. Feel the boundless joy, amazing peace, and total openness created by the vibrations of sound.
- Think and feel that the deceased person is seeing the beautiful blessing lights, hearing the soothing sounds, and feeling the boundless love, peace, and openness, the qualities of the blessing light.
- Finally, feel that you and the deceased person are merged in an indivisible state, in the womb of the boundless light of total peace and joy. Rest and relax in it for as long as you can. Do this again and again.
- Now and then, express strong aspirations by thinking or saying, "May [name of the deceased] be with the blessing lights and enjoy peace and joy in the bardo and in all his or her future lives."

How to Help the Dying and the Dead 201

Instructions for Buddhists and Those Open to Buddhism

In addition to prayers and meditations, helpers may offer words of instruction to Buddhists and to those who are open to Buddhist teachings.

With feelings of devotion to the source of blessings and compassion for the dying person, offer the words of instruction aloud or in your mind. Say all or some parts of the following words of instruction. You may tailor them so that they are appropriate for the dying person.

You might start the words of instruction with a powerful, but a simple line of prayer, such as OM AMITABHA HRI, the mantra of the Buddha of Infinite Light, or OM MANI PADME HUNG (pronounced *hoong*), the mantra of the Buddha of Compassion.* Alternatively, choose any prayer that you and the dying person are familiar with.

> OM AMITABHA HRI! "John" [gently call the dying person by his or her name], please relax and listen to me with a calm mind. "John," you are dead and you are in the bardo, the transitional passage. It is very important for you to realize and accept that you are dead. Please listen to me! Now you must be serious about what you need to think and do. You are at the crossroads of choosing a joyful or a painful future.
>
> With a clear mind and total attention, please remember your meditation and stay with that meditative experience. Please remember your kind spiritual teacher(s) and all the sources of blessings. If you remember them, they will be with you. Think that they are all looking at you with wisdom eyes and loving hearts. Please keep thinking about them, again and again. They will accompany you to secure a peaceful journey and a joyful rebirth.
>
> Today you are at the most crucial juncture of your life. Your future depends on how your mind will react today. In brief, please remember the meditation experiences that you have, the sources of blessing to which you have devotion, and the Dharma teacher(s) with whom you are close, again and again!
>
> OM AMITABHA HRI! "John," in your journey through the bardo, you might see wrathful images, ugly forms, or frightening situa-

---

* For the meaning of these mantras, see pages 242 and 161.

tions. But you must remember that those appearances are not real. They are mere creations and reflections of your own mind and its habits, like hallucinations and mirages. Do not get attached to them, grasp at them, be frightened by them, or fight with them.

Please remember that all the images are images of light in their true qualities. They are peaceful, joyful, and open in their true nature. In their true nature and quality they are the presence of the sources of blessings and your Dharma teacher(s).

When you see any image, beautiful or ugly, if you designate it as the image of light and peace, it will become an image of light and peace. If you hear any sound, if you designate it as the sound of peace, it will become so. In the bardo, if you think in the right way, you can change and transform any situation with great ease, because everything is a mere reflection and reaction of your own mind. Please remember again and again that the unpleasant appearances are unreal, like dreams, and that they are all peaceful in their nature!

OM AMITABHA HRI! "John," in the bardo, the transitional passage, you might see or remember your possessions, your friends, and your loved ones. You might hear people calling you and crying for you. If you do, you must remember that you are now dead. You have been separated from them. Those people who are calling you out of attachment and to whom you are emotionally attached cannot offer you any help, as these images and sounds are just reflections of your own sadness, fear, and confusion. None will be able to come with you, nor can you stay with them. If you are attached to them, because of your attachment they will become obstructions to your path toward peace and liberation. That will only bind you to the world of pain and suffering. So do not get attached to them, go toward them, grasp at them, be frightened by them, or fight with them.

Please see them as reflected images, in which there is no substance. Hear them as the sound of echoes, in which there is no reality. Then your mind's attachments and fears will disappear like mist before sunlight.

Please, you must remember the experiences of your meditation and the presence of the sources of blessings with you and in you. If your mind can see and feel the sources of blessings and the meditation experiences, then they will all become sources of great peace and joy—the path of liberation for you.

So, instead of friends or foes, please remember your meditations and the sources of blessings, again and again.

OM AMITABHA HRI! "John," in the bardo, you might hear thunderous sounds and frightening words. If you do, you must remember that these thunderous sounds and frightening words are merely appearances contrived by your mind. These are sounds fabricated by your own mind like hallucinations and echoes. Please do not get frightened by them, grasp at them, become attached to them, or fight with them.

Please hear the sounds as the sound of the waves of love, peace, and inspiration. Please remember the sounds as the waves of your devotion to the sources of blessings. Also remember the sounds as the waves of love and compassion coming to you from the source of blessings, again and again!"

OM AMITABHA HRI! "John," in the bardo, the transitional passage, you might feel unpleasant sensations of fear and loneliness. If you do, you must remember that these are mere feelings created by your own mind. They are not real; your mind has just fabricated them like a nightmare. Do not get attached to them, grasp at them, be frightened by them, or fight with them.

Please think to yourself that these feelings are unreal. They are like ripples in a pond. Let them go; don't hold on to them. If you let them go, they will dissolve like bubbles. Then you will enjoy the true nature of your mind, which is peaceful, joyful, clear, and omniscient.

Again, please remember the presence of the sources of blessings with you and in you. Remember the feelings of your meditations. Enjoy the feelings of peace and joy that you are experiencing in their presence. Please remain in the feeling of openness, the natural state of your mind—again and again!

MEDITATIONS FOR BUDDHISTS AND OTHER MEDITATORS

If the dying or dead person is a Buddhist or a meditator, and if you, the helper, have trained in meditation, then you may use the liturgies given in the "Simple Buddhist Death Rituals" in appendixes A and B. Or you could use the simple meditations below, adapting any part of them if necessary to suit the situation.

Remember that it is always essential for the helpers to offer their spiritual assistance to the dying and dead according to the state of meditative experience that the deceased person and the helpers actually do enjoy.

Meditation for Highly Trained Helpers

If you, the helper, are better trained in meditation than the dying or dead person, or if both of you enjoy equal training, then you must be active in doing meditation, saying prayers, and performing ceremonies. Also, you must give the dying person all the necessary instructions on dying and passing through the bardo, but in the right proportion. That is, the instructions should not be too numerous or too profound. If you give too many, the dying person may not have the energy, time, and capacity to get any benefit from them (even when still alive). So you have to consider how much you should say and about what. You should impart something pithy and inspiring that is the right thing for this person to hear, so that they will understand and remember it on the long afterdeath journey. Here you have an opportunity to lead the dying through the process of dying and the bardo and to help them reach the peaceful and joyful shore, just as if you were carrying a sick person across a torrent.

You may offer the whole or any part of the following instructions to the dying or dead person. The instructions should be in clear, simple, and heartfelt words. The dying or dead person may or may not be conscious or present to perform the meditations or prayers along with you, so you might end up doing them alone. However, you should think that the dying or dead person is listening to you and praying and meditating with you. Offer the following instructions to her or him aloud or in your mind:

> In the sky in front of you, visualize the amazingly beautiful and vast pure land such as the Blissful Pure Land. In the middle of it, see the presence of a source of blessings such as the Buddha of Infinite Light [or any other buddha, saint, or sage that is appropriate] accompanied by an infinite number of other enlightened ones, such as bodhisattvas, arhats, and spiritual masters. See them as fully enlightened ones who radiate unconditional love, omniscient wisdom, boundless peace, total joy, and invincible power.
>
> The sources of blessings are here to protect you, take care of you, and support you in your journey of the bardo. They are here to lead you to the Blissful Pure Land.

Feel boundless peace and joy in their presence. Feel the warmth of their presence. Feel secure in their presence. Feel the fulfillment of all your needs in their presence. Believe with confidence that from now on you are protected and guided by an ocean of enlightened ones.

Sing prayers or mantras, thinking of and feeling the sounds of the prayers as the waves of invocation to the sources of blessings for their help and blessing. Also think and feel that the sounds of prayers are the waves of your devotional energy to the sources of blessings.

You may hear sounds in general and the sounds of prayers as the waves of love, wisdom, and power from the sources of blessings. Feel the sounds as the vibration of your own joyful heart or mind, devotional prayers, universal love, omniscient wisdom, boundless power, and the peace of openness.

See that infinite beams of blessing light of great peace and joy are coming toward you from the source of blessing. These blessing lights are filling your body and mind and the entire atmosphere around you. They are lights of unconditional love, omniscient wisdom, invincible power, total warmth, boundless joy, and universal peace.

Whatever images you see, sounds you hear, or feelings you experience, you must see, hear, feel, and believe that they are the pure images, soothing voices, and the enlightened wisdom of the source of blessings.

Finally, relax in the awareness of innate peace and the blessings of the sources of blessings. Feel as if all has become one.

Instruction for Helpers of Dying Meditators

If the meditative experiences of the dying person are higher than yours as the helper, then you should meditate, say prayers, and perform ceremonies, but mostly quietly or at a distance, until the dying meditator's dying process has been completed. You should let the dying meditator sail to the other shore by offering only passive support, quietly.

In this case, the most important point is to focus on letting the dying person go their own way at their own speed. Avoid making any sounds or movements around them. Also, as long as the dying process is not completed, the body of the meditator should not be touched. Sounds, touching, or an ordinary person's careless and ignorant suggestions could distract the person from the meditative path of their crucial journey.

So until the dying process of the person is completed, the meditations, prayers, and ceremonies should generally be performed silently or at a distance. When the death process is completed, prayers and death rituals may be performed loudly, both in the presence and in the absence of the body.

In Helping Others, We Help Ourselves

Offering support to the dying and the dead is a great opportunity for learning and training in the journeys of living and dying. When we witness someone dying, we receive a vivid demonstration of the impermanent nature and the meaningless struggle of samsaric existence. It is a powerful tool for inspiring oneself to pure spiritual practice.

However, if we don't take such powerful situations as learning experiences, even though we may witness dying and death all the time, we will soon become numb to the experience. Then we may become insensitive, like a piece of rock, so that nothing can inspire or make any impact on us.

For helpers, serving others at their most extreme hour of need is not just a great opportunity to learn, but also a powerful way of making merits. Moreover, the dying person makes merits as well, by being the cause of the helpers' merit making. In this way, both the helper and the one who is helped benefit. So we must be mindful and skillful, taking the deaths of others as both a teaching and an occasion for spiritual practice. If we allow ourselves to experience the dying and dead just as they are, in their true nature, there will be no reason for us to feel any anger, attachment, or jealousy toward anyone. There will thus be no negative feelings to cause suffering, fear, or confusion. We may then spontaneously enjoy the awareness of selflessness in our hearts, the awareness of the freedom from grasping at "self." This can lead us to the realization of the ultimate peace and joy.

Some Important Observances

Let us reiterate that it is important for family members, helpers, and caregivers at the bedside of a dying person to remain peaceful, calm, and respectful. For days, if possible, no one should say or even think anything that normally would disturb the person. The minds of the dead could be floating around or visiting the homes of loved ones and friends, and if they hear or see anything that is unpleasant, unfair, or rude, it will disturb their mind. If their mind becomes angry, sad, or frightened, that might push the person into a painful journey and a rebirth in a realm of much suffering.

' The people surrounding the dying person or the dead body should be friends, especially spiritual friends. It is important not to allow anyone to be there who is of unhealthy mind or toward whom the deceased person harbors animosity.

' Do not touch the lower parts of the body until the dying process has been fully completed. When there is no heat at the heart and no pulse, the consciousness of the dying person has left the physical body, and the dying process has been completed.

' While the person is in the dying process, do not sit near their lower body or in the direction where their feet are pointing. Nor should you ever place any religious objects around the lower body or where the feet are pointed. According to the teachings, if you allow the attention of the dying person to be drawn to the lower body, their consciousness might exit through one of the lower portals at the time of death. The lower portals could become the doors to rebirth in inferior realms. So it is wise to help the person draw his or her attention upward. This may be done by lightly touching the top of the head (if it is not an offensive thing to do in your culture), sitting beside your loved one at the side of their head (by the shoulder), and especially placing religious objects or altars behind the head, and chanting prayers above or toward the head rather than the feet.

' For a few days after the death, keep the person's belongings in the exact way that they normally like to have them. In this way you will avoid disturbing their consciousness if it should linger near the body for a time.

' It is very important not to let the dead person, their body, or even the memory of them become the object of attachment, anger, and dislike or irritation in the mind of any person, including family, friends, and neighbors. If the person becomes a source of negative thoughts and emotions or a contributor to the creation of negative cycles of karmas, they will suffer from ill effects.

᾽ If you have any blessed substances that are edible, drinkable, or wearable, give them to the dying person to eat, drink, or put on while they are still conscious. In the Tibetan Buddhist tradition there are blessed substances (Tib. *dudtsi, bDud rTsi*; Skt. *amrita*, nectar or ambrosia) in the form of powders or pills made from herbs mixed with blessed materials and consecrated for days with ceremonial prayers and meditation. Such substances are believed to help one to attain liberation if they are tasted, smelled, or touched with faith and belief. Tibetans also use sacred diagrams consisting of buddha-images and mantras printed on paper, consecrated with prayers and meditations. These are folded into a small size and kept on the body while the dying person is still alive, and then cremated with the body after death. Such diagrams, worn with faith and belief, are also said to help the deceased attain liberation.

᾽ Additionally, helpers may place blessed substances in the mouth of the deceased, or spray or place them on the body after death. Although consciousness has separated from the body, the body remains as the main symbol of the person's karmic connection with the mortal world. Treating the body spiritually—by purifying it, teaching it, and blessing it—will therefore help the deceased directly (if their consciousness is nearby and open to the benefits) or indirectly. In Tibet, the body is kept for days while helpers continue performing purification ceremonies using the corpse as the representative of the deceased. (If the body cannot be kept, an effigy is used instead.)

᾽ In traditional Tibetan Buddhist culture, the body is kept for days or weeks (up to forty-nine days in some cases) while the lamas perform continuous prayers and ceremonies (as we will discuss in the next chapter, "Ritual Services for the Dying and the Dead"). However, if the body is disposed of after a day or so, it doesn't seem to make a huge impact on the deceased person's watchful mind. Although the mind of the dead person is clearer and sharper than it was when they were alive, there are some things that they cannot see, or that they see in a different form. Their own bodies, it seems, are in this category. (For example, in the delog accounts, Denma saw his body as a crystal stupa, Chokyi saw hers as a snake, and Changchub saw his as the corpse of a dog.) However, if the body can be kept for a couple of days or so, it may be helpful, as the living organisms within the body, such as bacteria, and the energies of the life forces will have a chance to die naturally. It is especially important not to dispose of the body if there is any heat at the heart. If there is, the consciousness of the person is still with the body. If keeping the body for days stirs up negative emotions in the minds of others and creates turmoil or controversy among relatives or in the neighborhood, then it will cause negative karmic effects rather than any benefit for the dead. If that is so, it might be wiser to dispose of the body as soon as possible. The determining criterion is not a question of individual rights or preferences, but rather of what is good and beneficial for the deceased and for yourself as the survivor.

The most important thing is to maintain a calm, peaceful mind and atmosphere, in order to promote greater peace and joy. Peace and joy bring more peace and joy—that is the law of karma, the natural principle of causation.

9

Ritual Services for the Dying and the Dead

The path of serene meditation and devotional prayer
Envisioned by the wisdom-minds of the enlightened ones,
Traversed by an ocean of masters and devotees alike,
Is the ever-secure road to the pure land or a realm of
   happiness.

C EREMONIAL SERVICES for the dying and the dead are a common feature of the world's religions. They usually serve a dual purpose: for grieving survivors they provide help in the process of bidding goodbye to their loved ones, while for the deceased they offer support and assistance in the afterdeath journey, through prayers and symbolic rituals. The Buddhist services and rituals that I outline in this chapter also benefit both the deceased and the survivors. Their main aim is not necessarily to help the deceased attain enlightenment or transcend the samsaric world. Instead, they are primarily intended to diminish or heal negative concepts and emotions, which are the sole causes of suffering, fear, and rebirth in lower realms. Buddhist death rituals are also an aid in accomplishing meritorious deeds for the deceased, through the power of positive concepts and emotions, which are direct sources of peace, joy, and rebirth in happy realms (such as the human and god realms) or in manifested pure lands.

The Tradition of Death Rituals

Tibetan Buddhist death rituals are performed by lamas and laypersons in various ways depending on the school of Buddhism and the geographical region of Tibet. The death rituals outlined in this chapter are based on the tradition of the Nyingma school practiced in Golok province of Eastern Tibet, where I was born and trained.

The death ritual is usually conducted by a lama, a senior ordained or initiated religious teacher, equivalent to a minister or other clergy in Western culture. If the lama is well trained, the performance of the death ritual will be very effective. A person who is a lama merely in name or designation does not possess any more power than anyone else. Nevertheless, anyone can practice the rituals mentioned in this book, if they have some training in meditations and prayers.

In certain parts and in some traditions of Tibet, death rituals are quite simple. Lamas and/or lay helpers recite prayers, make offerings, and give donations of money, food, ornaments, or animals to monasteries or nunneries, personally to monks and nuns, or the poor. The body is cremated or fed to vultures as an offering to the buddhas and deities. (Although buddhas and deities don't eat, this practice is a meditation and ceremonial exercise that trains our minds to have positive perceptions, seeing all as pure, and to cultivate generosity, devotion, and letting go.) One of the important religious ceremonies entails many repetitions of aspiration prayers such as "The King of Aspiration Prayers, the Aspiration for Excellent Deeds,"[1] along with abundant offerings of lamps, incense, flowers, and donations.

In other parts of Tibet, death ceremonies are more elaborate. Many lamas are invited to the home of the deceased to perform liturgical rites for weeks before the death and then for seven weeks or so after the death. The length and elaborateness of the ceremonies depend on the resources of the family of the deceased. To sponsor the death ritual, most families will spend at least the entire share of the family property belonging to the deceased.

Religious Services for the Dying

It is crucial that we practice the Dharma while still alive, because that will ground us in our spiritual path and instill confidence in it. Then we will be ready to apply our meditative experiences to our death when the day arrives. The third Dodrupchen Rinpoche writes:

> At the actual time of death, it might be very hard to gather any mental ability to start a meditation. So you must choose a meditation in advance and marry your mind with it, as much as you can. Meditation could be the remembrance of a buddha, the feeling of compassion, the energy of devotion, or the realization of emptiness.
>
> Also, think again and again, "At the time of death, I will not let myself be involved in any negative thoughts." In order to achieve meditative clarity and peace in your mind, it is important to meditate again and again, well before the arrival of death. Then, when the time of death arrives, you will be able to die with the right mental qualities.[2]

Any virtuous deed that you perform, whether mental or physical in nature—while you are alive and especially while you are on your deathbed—will greatly benefit your future life. Rites such as purification, merit making, empowerments, and dedication are important to practice before death, but also after death.

Purification

In order to make your present life, your future afterdeath journey, and your rebirth free from difficulties and obstacles, it is extremely important to purify your negative karmic effects from the past. All the ills of your life and future lives are the products of negative karmic causality. Only by purifying those afflicting karmic causes can you improve your life. It is comparable to restoring your physical health by purifying your system of toxins. Through purification, you nullify your misdeeds and their effects.

Any of a variety of positive actions or exercises can be effective as the means of purification. Purification practices include meditations on the buddhas and prayers for the benefit of all mother-beings. They may entail saying prayers and practicing any meditations for purification from the depth of your heart. Parts of the death rituals are also designed to accomplish purification.

Among the special Buddhist practices designed especially for purification is the "Confession before the Thirty-five Buddhas of Purification" (Tib. *tung shag, lTung bShags*) and the prayers and meditations of

Vajrasattva Buddha. The latter practice involves four "powers." The first is the power of the source of purification, Vajrasattva. As you visualize Vajrasattva Buddha above you in the sky, you trust in him as the embodiment of the enlightened nature and the qualities of all the enlightened ones appearing as the source of purification. The second is the power of repentance. If you feel great remorse for misdeeds that you have committed in the past, your purification will be from the depth of your heart. The third is the power of commitment. It means making a strong commitment not to repeat any misdeed in the future. The fourth is the power of purification itself. Saying prayers—such as OM VAJRASATTVA HUNG (or HUM), "O Vajrasattva, please bestow your blessings")—you see, feel, and believe that a stream of blessing nectar issues from the body of Vajrasattva, washing away all the filth of your negative deeds of body and mind, without leaving even a trace behind. In the same way, you can purify the deceased person or other beings. Training your mind by such a process of purification with positive and purifying images, deep feelings, and strong conviction will help to purify the effects of your negative karmas at their foundation.

Although such practices are especially effective for purification, any good deed is a means of purification, especially if you intend or dedicate the merits for such a purpose. Some further examples of purifying practices are saving lives and lovingly protecting others from danger; giving any gift to the needy or for religious projects with a generous heart; sponsoring projects for social welfare or religious services with a pure attitude; and building shelters or religious monuments with the intention to benefit others.

We can also help to purify misdeeds committed by others. If we say prayers, do meditations, or perform practices particularly for purifying others or dedicate the merits for purification of the misdeeds of others, we may be able to accomplish this. But how effective will our efforts be? If the person's evil deeds are strong, our limited efforts may not make much of a dent. If the person has no openness toward us, through trust or even just an attitude of liking; if they and we do not share any strong karmic connection as the channel for such help; or if our prayers are weak or impure, then our purification practices may not be very effective. Nonetheless, they will still be of some help. If the person's misdeeds are "washable" ones, if they have trust in us or at least like us and what we do, if we are connected karmically to them, and if our practices are strong, we will certainly be able to purify the person's misdeeds. If an accomplished master performs special prayers, meditations, and ceremonies, even if the person has committed strong evil deeds, all could be purified and the person led to liberation, because of the power of the masters and the purity of the meditation. So there is no one simple answer, and all depends on many causations and conditions, as in every facet of life. Even if we cannot purify someone totally, even a little bit of cleansing will help a great deal at the juncture of death. Also, if a dying person is inspiring us to perform purifications for them with great devotion to the buddha, we will be making a great deal of merit, and that in turn will cause merits to be made for the one who inspired it all. Repeating again, if we make merits, those merits strengthen our positive qualities and weaken or purify our negative qualities.

Merit Making

In order to enjoy a peaceful and happy life and rebirths, it is essential to accumulate merits and cultivate positive qualities. Whatever happiness and peace you are enjoying today is the direct result of your meritorious behavior in the past. To further improve your future life, you must continue to make more merits by performing virtuous deeds. Just as you gain physical well-being by providing your body with proper nourishment and exercise, so you must care for your spiritual health by making merits.

Any positive deeds or service will work as the means of merit making. You could accumulate merits by saying prayers and doing meditations. You could make merits by serving the poor, making offerings for religious projects, saving and ransoming lives (as by buying and freeing domestic animals), building and clearing roads, building and repairing temples and religious monuments, and sponsoring or performing prayers and meditations with love, respect, and devotion.

Empowerments

Empowerments or initiations are highly effective as the means of purification of the ill effects of misdeeds, reenforcement of past virtuous deeds, reminders of past spiritual experiences and attainments, showing the path to liberation or pure lands, introduction to the buddhas and pure lands, bestowal of the blessings of the buddhas, and awakening the primordial wisdom, or buddhahood, of the recipient. Empowerments such as the "Liberation from the [Six] Realms" (Tib. *ne dren, gNas 'Dren*) may be performed for those who are in the process of dying. Such rites purify the dying person's negative karmic seeds that would otherwise cause rebirth in the suffering realms. They will help to accumulate merits, the cause of rebirth in happy realms. They will swiftly bring the blessings of the buddhas to awaken the mind to enlightenment or to rebirth in a pure land.

Understandably, it will be very important that the leader and/or performers of the death ceremonies be accomplished in meditation or at least well trained in these particular ceremonies. Also, if there is a positive spiritual relationship between the performer and the deceased, the benefits will be most effective. At the very least, there should be a harmonious connection between them.

If elaborate rituals such as empowerments are not feasible, any prayer or meditation performed with love for all mother-beings and for the dying person, or with devotion to the buddhas, will be highly beneficial, especially if it is conducted by an accomplished meditator. An appropriate service might consist of reciting prayers, reciting the names of the buddhas and bodhisattvas, repeating mantras, or performing any simple ceremony. Numerous litugical texts and prayers are available in Tibetan; I provide a very short ceremony of the Blissful Pure Land later, in appendix A. In addition, the performance of phowa by an accomplished master is an especially beneficial practice, both during the dying process and after death. A short phowa text with explanation is provided in appendix B.

Dedication and Aspiration Prayers

After doing anything virtuous such as praying, it is important to dedicate the merits and make aspirations. Dedicating merits multiplies their power exponentially. The greater the scope of the dedication, the greater the power. So dedicate merits, not just to the deceased but also to *all* mother-beings, as the cause of their happiness and enlightenment. Then enormous merits will redound to them.

Next make aspirations. This is a way to invest merits for a particular goal and further magnify them. Using your dedicated merits as the seed, make aspirations that all mother-beings may enjoy the fruits of happiness and rebirth in the pure land.

Beings in the bardo in particular need us to dedicate merits and make aspirations for them. If we repeatedly dedicate whatever merits we and the dead person accumulated—no matter how meager—to that person and all mother-beings for their rebirth in the pure land, we can be sure that the merits will cause that result.

You could also chant and meditate on various prayers of dedication and aspirations, such as the *Bhadracharya-pranidhanaraja Sutra* (Sutra of the King of Aspiration of Excellent Deeds).[3] This Mahayana text, which is part of the *Buddhavatamsaka Sutra* (Sutra of the Garland of Buddhas), teaches us how to dedicate merits and make aspirations as Samantabhadra did. The dying person may additionally be given blessed substances to taste, such as nectar (Tib. *dudtsi, bDud rTsi*), and remnants of sacred or blessed ceremonial objects, or these items might be placed on the person's body. Members of the Nyingma tradition attach particular significance to placing a blessed esoteric diagram of sacred syllables written in the ancient Indian or Tibetan script, known as "Liberation by Touching" (Tib. *tag trol, bTags Grol*), and other sacred syllables at the heart or other parts of the body.

RELIGIOUS SERVICES AT THE TIME OF DEATH

At the time of death, any religious services—prayers and meditations that provide a peaceful, loving, and blessed atmosphere—are very beneficial. The following rituals are some of the significant services that Tibetan lamas offer.

Instructions for Ordinary People

The best time to receive instructions, advice, or teachings is while we are still alive, so that we can hear and understand what the instructor is saying. Instructors must give teachings to which our mind is open and that we can digest. If a dying person resists accepting the approach of death, it may not be wise to give any instruction at that time. Instead, it might be better to talk about general teachings or teachings on healing. That will not scare the person, but will provide some feeling of peace and awareness.

If the dying person is ready to hear about their own death, they should be reminded about their meditations and the sources of blessings. Instructors should let them know what to expect in the passages of dying, ultimate nature, and the bardo, and how to handle these experiences.

Dodrupchen Rinpoche summarizes the important things for the dying to focus on at the time of death:

> You must think of the following again and again. Think that death, which now has arrived for you, happens to all. Let go of all your attachment to loved ones, to possessions and to power. In front of the Enlightened Ones, confess and purify all the misdeeds that you have committed in this lifetime or in past lives—both known and unknown. Make promises to yourself and to the Enlightened Ones that you will never commit such misdeeds again. Thereby, elevate your mind with a feeling of joy in which there is no anxiety. Remember all the virtuous deeds that you have done in the past and rejoice because of them again and again, without any arrogance or egotism.[4]

And he adds:

> Dedicate the merits and make aspirations, again and again, thinking and saying, "Throughout my successive lives, may I be able to practice the essence of the path of enlightenment. May I be guided by virtuous teachers. May I be endowed with faith, diligence, knowledge, and mindfulness. May I never be affected by unvirtuous friends and afflicting emotions."[5]

It is very important to have virtuous thoughts at the time of death. Dodrupchen says:

> In the sutras, Buddha Shakyamuni told many stories to illustrate why someone had become his disciple or why someone in particular had become one of his gifted disciples. In many instances, the main cause he gave was that these people had made virtuous aspirations when they were dying. So, what wishes you make at the time of death will have a great impact on your rebirth.[6]

As mentioned above, the important meditation rituals called phowa may be performed both before and after death (see page 265).

It will be beneficial at death if you can remember your own spiritual teachers in whom you have faith, their teachings, and the deities and spir-

with great joy and generosity. Such mental offerings will create a great amount of merit, too.

Buddhists believe that even if you make a small contribution to a great goal, your merits can become as vast as the merits of the goal itself—like drops of water that fall into the ocean and will not dry up until the ocean does. Also, if you form a karmic connection with a great being, even if the offering is as small as a cup of tea, its impact and result may be inexhaustible, because of the holiness of the person to whom you are making the offering.

10

Concluding Thoughts

DEATH IS A NEW BEGINNING. It is the doorway to a dawn of fresh opportunities for us to enjoy the fruits that we have cultivated, in accordance with the karmic law of cause and effect. While the cycle of karma is spinning all the time, its impact can be far more sweeping and direct after we die than it was during our life.

Why? As long as we are alive, our mind is programmed to operate within the structure of our physical body and daily routines. It is relatively hard to change these structures in a radical way. But once released from the body at death, the mind runs its own show. Then the only thing conditioning our perception will be the habits that we have sown in our mindstream.

We have all experienced how, when our minds are filled with joy, whatever we see, hear, or feel brings us joy. When our minds are enraged, everything irritates us. These reactions occur even more so after death, for then everything will manifest for us in accordance with our mental and emotional habitual tendencies alone. So, if we have given way to hatred, greed, and ignorance, we will be reborn in a place ravaged by hunger, stupidity, and hellish phenomena. If we have been kind, peaceful, and joyful, our world will manifest as one of peace and joy. If we have enjoyed the qualities of the Blissful Pure Land, we will be reborn there or in any pure land of peace and joy. And if we have realized the enlightened nature of the mind and perfected it, our minds will unite with the absolute universal true nature, the ultimate peace and joy, and our services to others will shine forth effortlessly, as the sun radiates naturally for all.

Some of us may be worried about what awaits us when we die. But this is not a time to be scared or sad. It is a time to recognize that we have a golden opportunity to get ready for our big day and turn our life in the right direction for now and forever, for ourselves and others.

Even if we are old, until our last breath it is not too late to change the course of our life. We don't need to do anything drastic. We just need to relax a little and enjoy the feeling of peace and joy that is innate in us, to whatever extent we can and according to whatever spiritual tradition we wish.

If we are young, it is best to rush to improve our future now, as we might not be able to later. All it takes to land at the doorstep of the next world is to exhale and be unable to inhale again. Youth cannot insure against that end.

All the prayers and meditations in this book are tools to cultivate spiritual qualities. Devotion is for sparking the energy of positive perceptions. Compassion is for opening our hearts to all with love. Prayers are for expressing positive thoughts and feelings. Pure perception is for seeing everything and everyone as a source and presence of peace and joy. Religious ceremonies are formulas for creating a positive culture in our lives. Visualizing buddhas and pure lands is for transforming our mental images and thoughts into positive, blessed perceptions. Experiencing the blessings of the blessed ones is for propelling us to peaceful and joyful rebirths. Receiving the prayers, meditations, and kindnesses offered by others is a great source of inspiration and merits.

In my native land of Tibet, many people would spend years in solitude and caves practicing for themselves and others. This kind of life and dedication is wonderful. But it is not a must. If we practice sincerely for just ten or twenty minutes a day, whether praying to the Buddha of Infinite Light or doing some other meditation, our practice will embody all the spiritual qualities mentioned above. Then, if we could remember what we felt during our practice session again and again throughout the day, its impact will gradually infuse our entire life. One day, we will find that our whole attitude has been transformed. We won't need to fabricate the feeling of peace, joy, and the presence of the blessed ones anymore. They will be what we have become. And death and rebirth will be a seamless flow of the wheel of peace and joy spun by the power of our own mind.

How could a few minutes of sincere meditation produce such great results? For the same reason that Shantideva says: "If you develop bodhichitta, from that time on, even if you fall asleep or get distracted, the force of the merits will increase without cessation, filling the extent of space." The important thing is the intensity of our practice more than its duration. If we push a wheel forcefully, it will keep spinning for a long time afterward. In the same way, if we start our meditation wholeheartedly, its spiritual force will remain alive continuously. That force grows even stronger every time we do the meditation.

I myself am not someone who says a lot of prayers or observes long meditation sessions. But somewhat by nature and upbringing I am a fervent believer in the ever-presence of sublime qualities in us and outside us. We could call them buddha-qualities. Most of the time, I live in awe of them, enjoying their presence. So when I reach the fork in the road at the other side of this life, I am pretty hopeful that some peaceful and joyful faces will caringly guide me to a happier land for my rebirth, a land of peace and joy.

I fervently wish that you, my dears, will enjoy the teachings of the Buddha and Buddhist masters that I have shared with you in this book, and that you will relish the benefits that I enjoyed or even better. How exciting to think of such a bright future for so many of us!

~~~~

Some Simple
Buddhist Death Rituals

It is important to practice liturgies of prayer and meditation on a buddha and buddha pure land before, during, and after a person's death. It might be a liturgy of any buddha, such as the Buddha of Infinite Light, Avalokiteshvara, Vajrasattva, the Hundred Peaceful and Wrathful Deities, Sarvavid Vairochana, or Vajrabhairava. Within the confines of this book I am not able to provide detailed traditional death rituals. Instead, I will provide some very simple but essential rituals that can be performed by a lama or by the helper for a dying or dead person.

The death rituals presented in appendixes A and B, which are among the most popular in Tibet, are based mainly on the prayers and meditation on the Buddha of Infinite Light. The particular texts that I use here are drawn from the works of great lamas of the Nyingma lineage.

If you undertake to perform any of these rituals, try to read the Tibetan words in boldface type if you can. If you prefer, you may read the English translations instead, but for the mantras and name-prayers you must read the Tibetan or Sanskrit lines that appear in boldface.

A few comments are in order about the pronunciation of Tibetan words that appear here in simplified phonetic spellings to enable readers to recite the prayers. Tibetan differentiates between some sounds that are not always heard as different by speakers of English. The predominant issue is that it may require some concentration for English speakers to differentiate between aspirated and unaspirated versions of certain consonants. So I wish to draw particular attention to the following sounds:

PH and TH: Tibetan aspirated P and T are written as PH and TH, respectively, as in words like *phowa* and *thamel*. These sounds are not pronounced like English *f* and *th* as in *fat* and *that*. Instead, they are much closer to English *p* and *t* taken alone. The contribution of aspiration can be heard in English in the *p* in "Put!" as opposed to the unaspirated *p* in *paper*, and the *t* in *butter* as opposed to the *unaspirated t* in *but*.

CH: It is important to note the difference between the Tibetan aspirated and unaspirated versions of the English CH sound. In these appendixes the aspirated Tibetan CH is followed by an apostrophe, as in the word *ch'o*. This is a more aspirated sound than *cho*. The aspirated CH' may be encountered in the English *cheese* as opposed to the softer *ch* in *chess*. The CH' or CH sound is never pronounced like the hard *ch* in English *chord*.

ZH is a cross between English *sh* and *z*, and is pronounced somewhat like the consonants in the name Zsa Zsa.

TS and its aspirant, TSH, are sounds rarely found in English at the beginning of a syllable, but can be heard in words like *its* and *heats*.

DZ is similar to TS, but with a *z* tone.

NG and NY are not always distinguished in English from *n*. However, their sounds can be heard respectively in *Long Island* (pronounced without a hard *g*) and in *canyon*.

~~~

Meditations on the Four Causes of Taking Rebirth in the Blissful Pure Land

T HE MEDITATIONS AND PRAYERS given in appendix A are from the common, or sutric, teachings of Buddhism (those based on the sutras, the words of the historical Buddha, Shakyamuni). If your mind is inspired by these practices, you are ready to learn and train in them.

They are the prayers and meditation trainings on the four causes of taking rebirth in the Blissful Pure Land. These trainings will pave the way for you to take rebirth in the pure land. They will also equip you to perform the death rituals for others.

According to the Buddhist sources,[1] numerous eons ago the Buddha of Infinite Light became a devotee of the bodhisattva path. His name was Dharmakara. Before a buddha named Lokeshvara, he started his spiritual journey by taking the bodhisattva vow. He vowed[2] to lead all who hear, remember and pray in his name with faith and devotion to his future pure land when he became a buddha:

All beings who hear my name
Will come to my pure land.[3]

If you have faith, trust in the buddha's vow, wisdom, and compassion, you are open to the effects of the power of the vow. Because of the power of the interdependent causation of the buddha's vow, if you pray in his name, joyous rebirth in his pure land—within you and outside you—will be assured. Master Shinran, the twelfth-century founder of the Jodo Shinshu, or True Pure Land School of Japan, said: "At the very moment when we are moved to utter the Nembutsu [mantra of the Buddha of Infinite Light] by a firm faith that our rebirth in the Pure Land is attained solely by virtue of the unfathomable working of Amida's [Amitabha's]

Figure 2. Amitabha, the Buddha of Infinite Light. Drawing by Robert Beer.

Original Vow, we are enabled to share in its benefits that embrace all and forsake none."[4]

If with total trust your mind is fully focused on the Buddha of Infinite Light, who is the body of compassion and wisdom, and on the power of his name-prayer, your whole life will become peaceful, pure and awakened. You will become a source of the same qualities for all around you. Negative concepts and afflicting emotions will have no place to harbor in you. Then you will have no need of any other means to attain liberation. Such a mind naturally embodies the qualities of all the six perfections: generosity, morality, patience, diligence, contemplation and wisdom.

If you enjoy trust in the buddha, you must apply it as the means of improving your death and rebirth through meditations such as the phowa. You must prepare long before your own death and also before performing death rituals for a dying person. If you have no meditative experience in advance, you may not be able to receive or offer much help through prayers or meditations. If you have no meditative connection with the Buddha of Infinite Light and his Blissful Pure Land, how can you take rebirth in the pure land or lead any other dying person there?

A dying person who has trained in this meditation in advance can meditate and pray alone and may not need to rely on others' support. Or, if an experienced dying person and a well-trained helper join together in the meditations and prayers, birth in the Pure Land could easily be assured.

So, it is essential to train in advance in the four causes, for success depends on your mental experience. You could train in the four causes as your daily meditation and prayers for months and years. You could keep repeating the name-prayers and mantras hundreds of thousands or millions of times.

If you have trained in the four causes, you will take rebirth in the pure land even if you have committed misdeeds, with the exception of two serious misdeeds.[5] One is the act of renouncing the Dharma. If you have renounced the Dharma, it will be impossible to have devotion to the Buddha of Infinite Light, for the root cause of rebirth in the pure land is trust in the Dharma. The second misdeed is the commission of any of the five immeasurable offenses: killing one's mother, killing one's father, killing a sage (Skt. *arhat*), causing schism in the spiritual community, and assaulting a buddha with malicious intention.

The main focus of the four causes is the prayers and meditation on the Buddha of Infinite Light and his Blissful Pure Land. The buddha is the embodiment of all the enlightened ones and the manifestation of the universal truth. The Blissful Pure Land is the appearance of the wisdom-light and wisdom-energies of the buddha as the pure land.

Even if you are not a devotee of the Buddha of Infinite Light, or even a Buddhist, practicing the four causes will generate enormous merit. Your mindstream and all your expressions in words and deeds will become peaceful and joyful, ensuring happy rebirths.

Figure 3. Sukhavati, the Blissful Pure Land of Amitabha Buddha. Collection of the Buddhayana Foundation.

Visualize the entire atmosphere before you now as the Blissful Pure Land as described in chapter 7: supremely bright and beautiful, prosperous and benevolent, joyful and peaceful, made of wisdom-light and wisdom-energies. In the center of it, visualize the majestic presence of the fully enlightened Buddha of Infinite Light, like a giant mountain of light.

Infinite wisdom-lights are emanating from his body, illuminating infinite universes and pure lands with great peace and joy. He is thinking of you and looking at you and at each being with omniscient wisdom, boundless power, and unconditional compassion, like that of a mother for her only child.

You can pray and meditate on the four causes for yourself, or someone else can do it for you, for your own rebirth in the Blissful Pure Land. You can do it for another person, whether they are dying or alive. Or you and others can perform it together for yourselves or for others. However, the following liturgy is phrased as if you are practicing for yourself and for the sake of all mother-beings.

With great trust, devotion, openness, and joy, concentrate on the buddha and meditate on the four causes. This liturgy has four aspects: the preliminary practice, the main practice on the four causes of taking rebirth in the Blissful Pure Land, the mantra and name-prayers, and the concluding practice.

PRELIMINARY PRACTICES

Going for Refuge

From the depth of your heart, take ultimate refuge in the Buddha of Infinite Light; in the Dharma, the teachings, the path of training, and the spiritual attainments; and in the Sangha, the spiritual community of bodhisattvas, arhats, and devotees.

Repeat three times:

Sang-gye ch'o-tang tshog-kyi ch'og-nam-la
To the excellent Buddha, Dharma, and Sangha

Chang-ch'ub par-tu dag-ni kyab-su-ch'i
I go for refuge until the attainment of enlightenment.

Dag-kee jin-sog gyee-pe sod-nam-kyee
By the merits of generosity and others,*

Dro-la phen-ch'ir sang-gye drub-par-shog
May I attain buddhahood for the sake of all beings.

---

* Generosity or giving is the first of the six perfections. The others are discipline, patience, diligence, contemplation, and wisdom.

Developing Enlightened Attitude (Bodhichitta)

Generate loving-kindness, compassion, sympathetic joy, and equanimity toward all beings as toward your own mother. Think that you are going to pray and meditate for the sake of all mother-beings to take rebirth in the Blissful Pure Land.

Repeat three times:

Sem-chen tham-ch'ed de-wa tang de-we gyu-tang den-par kyur-chig
May all beings enjoy happiness and the cause of happiness.

Duk-ngal tang dug-ngal kyi gyu-tang tral-war kyur-chig
May all be free from suffering and the cause of suffering.

Dug-ngal med-pe de-wa tam-pa tang mi-dral-war kyur-chig
May all never be disassociated from the supreme happiness, freedom from suffering.

Nye-ring ch'ag-dang nyee tang tral-we tang-nyom tshed-med-pa la ne-par kyur-chig
May all remain in boundless equanimity, free from both attachment to kin and hatred of foes.

THE FOUR CAUSES OF TAKING REBIRTH IN THE BLISSFUL PURE LAND

In order to take rebirth in any pure land, you must prepare yourself seriously. This includes purifying negative karmas and perfecting meritorious deeds with the formula of the four causes. The summary that follows is based on writings of the third Dodrupchen Rinpoche,[6] who, relying on the *Amitabhavyuha Sutra*,[7] describes the importance of the four (or at least three) causes for taking rebirth in the Blissful Pure Land of the Buddha of Infinite Light.

The First Cause: Remembering the Pure Land

The first cause is to think about and remember the amazingly beautiful structures, peaceful atmosphere, and joyful feelings of the Blissful Pure Land, again and again.

The Blissful Pure Land is an atmosphere that is supremely peaceful and joyful, radiant and beautiful, a prosperous and benevolent paradise where suffering is unknown. There is no concept or expression of afflicting emotions, such as greed, confusion, and hatred. All is made of wisdom-light and wisdom-energies of utmost peace and joy. It is a boundless paradise of mountains and fields of lights, rivers and lakes of light, gardens and flowers of light, trees and fruits of light, roads and mansions of light. It is filled with an infinite number of divine beings of radiant light in various forms, costumes, and activities. They fly and move through space in absolute peace and joy. They visit different manifested pure lands and receive teachings and blessings. Anything you wish will appear. The sounds of teaching and the music of Dharma fill the whole atmosphere. All who exist there are in the state of utmost peace and joy.

In the center, beneath a giant Tree of Enlightenment, is the Buddha of Infinite Light. His majestic and youthful body of reddish light is adorned with the signs of a supreme being. He is in the midst of an ocean of enlightened beings such as the eight bodhisattvas, who include Avalokiteshvara and Mahasthamaprapta. The whole atmosphere is filled with the light radiating from his body. His unconditional love, omniscient wisdom, and omnipresent power serve all without ceasing.

You must apply the four healing powers—positive images, words, feelings, and beliefs[8]—over and over again to strengthen your remembrance of the pure land:

1. Visualize the details of the Blissful Pure Land as given in chapter 7.
2. Think about the details of the pure land and their qualities with words and prayers.
3. Enjoy the feeling of their presence and blessings from the depth of your heart.
4. Believe that the Blissful Pure Land the Buddha of Infinite Light are in front of you, and believe in the power of the buddha's vow to lead you to rebirth in his pure land.

At the time of death, your mind will become free from the limitations imposed by your physical body and the culture of your environment. So, while you are alive, if you cultivate the habits of seeing and feeling the pure land in your mind, at the time of death your perceptions will spontaneously arise as the real pure land, and you will find yourself in it. Thus your rebirth in the Blissful Pure Land will be natural.

Not everyone will see the Buddha of Infinite Light and his Blissful Pure Land the same way. Our perceptions depend on our spiritual attainments. Some will see the pure land as it actually is; others will see it as a manifested pure land—though in reality the Blissful Pure Land is one.

If you are enlightened, you will see the Buddha of Infinite Light as the ever-present Buddha, the primordial wisdom. You will see his pure land as the ever-joyful pure land, the power and light of primordial wisdom itself. All forms and experiences are present naturally as nondual awareness. All appear as the true nature and pure quality, just as they are. Buddhist teachings call this pure land "the pure land of the enjoyment body" (sambhogakaya) of buddhahood. Taking rebirth in this pure land does not mean being reborn in a better world somewhere else. It is realizing the universal, omnipresent buddhahood with its inseparable pure land.

If you are an ordinary devotee, on the other hand, you will see the buddha and his pure land as a peaceful and joyful world filled with enlightened beings of unconditional love, omniscient wisdom, and boundless power—but you will perceive this world to be somewhere else, as if in another realm. You will also enjoy ineffable peace and joy—but you will still experience these things with a dualistic mind, using senses and emotions. Everything will be subject to change. The teachings call this state of pure land "the pure land of the manifestation body" (nirmanakaya). The extraordinary thing is that people like you and me—in fact, all mother-beings—can be reborn there. And once there, we will never regress but always progress in spiritual growth, so that one day we will realize the pure land of the enjoyment body of buddhahood.

To take birth in this manifested pure land, we must train in the four (or three) causes.

The Second Cause: Accumulation of Merits

You must make merits as the seeds of taking rebirth in the Blissful Pure Land. Positive karma or merits accumulated with total trust by positive mental and physical deeds are crucial for any peaceful and happy result, especially for taking rebirth in the Blissful Pure Land. It could be making offerings, giving gifts, serving others, saying prayers, purifying misdeeds, protecting lives, and being compassionate, caring, gentle, peaceful, devotional, mindful, and contemplative.

The Third Cause: Developing Enlightened Attitude

To develop enlightened attitude, or bodhichitta, you must vow or be determined to lead all mother-beings, without exception, to the Blissful Pure Land without any selfishness, and you must put that aspiration into practice through meditation and beneficial deeds.

However, quoting the sutra,[9] Dodrupchen points out that the development of bodhichitta is not an essential condition for taking rebirth in the Blissful Pure Land. Nonetheless, developing enlightened attitude will help you to ensure your rebirth in the pure land and will also make you be more effective once you are born there. Dodrupchen adds that making a promise or determination is more powerful than making an aspiration. He writes: "In order to accomplish any aspiration, it is important to develop a strong intention or pledge, such as thinking, 'In all my successive lives, I *will* train in the essence of compassion and emptiness, the path of Buddhism.' As you know, the thought 'I *will* wake up in the early morning' has a greater impact on your waking up on time than the thought 'May I wake up in the early morning.'"[10]

The Fourth Cause: Dedication and Aspiration

The fourth cause is to dedicate all your merits as the cause of taking rebirth in the Blissful Pure Land and to make aspirations for the same purpose. Even if you have the merits, you need to invest them for the particular purpose by dedicating them and making aspiration prayers again and again. Dedication and aspiration are not merely devices to invest the merits as seeds of rebirth in the pure land; they are also powerful means of making merits in themselves.

If you imagine that a buddha is before you, listening to and blessing your aspiration prayers, the results of your prayers will be even more powerful and effective.

In order to accomplish the prayers of aspiration, it is crucial to rely on a source of power. So it is very important to rely on a deity such as the Buddha of Infinite Light, the Buddha of Compassion, or Guru Padmasambhava. These sources of power must be someone for whom you have devotion and with whom you are already connected by prayers and meditation. You must see the source of power as the embodiment of all the Precious Ones. Pray to him or her for the accomplishment of all your aspirations.[11]

Teaching the four causes of taking rebirth in the Blissful Pure Land, Shakyamuni Buddha says:

> O Anand, there are people who [1] think of the details of the Buddha [of Infinite Light and his pure land] again and again. [2] They create many immeasurable merits. [3] They develop the mind of enlightenment. [4] And they dedicate the merits and make aspirations to take rebirth in the Blissful Pure Land. When they are about to die, before them the fully enlightened one, the Buddha of Infinite Light—thus gone, pacifier of the foes—will appear with a retinue of numerous ascetics, looking at them. Having seen the Buddha of Infinite Light, they will die with the mind of great clarity. Thereby they will take rebirth in the universe of the Blissful Pure Land.[12]

Or, as the same sutra teaches, you can also train yourself in the "three causes" (the first, second, and fourth cause, without the development of bodhichitta), and still take rebirth in the Blissful Pure Land. Think about the qualities of the pure land again and again, make as many merits as you can, and then dedicate the merits and make aspirations, saying, "May I take rebirth in the Blissful Pure Land."

The Liturgies of the Four Causes

Think about or visualize the presence of the Blissful Pure Land, a world of great joy and peace as described in chapter 7. In its center is the Buddha of Infinite Light, looking at you and thinking of you and all beings with wisdom, compassion, and power. This pure land is filled with an infinite number of enlightened beings in various forms, postures, and activities. With total devotion, pay homage:

Di-ne nub-kyi chog-rol teng-ki-cha
In the elevated land in the Western direction,

Sang-gye zhing-kham nam-tag de-wa-chen
There is the totally immaculate Blissful Pure Land of the Buddha

Mon-lam phun-tshog yong-trub gyal-we-chog
Accomplished by the power of his glorious aspirations, and there is the Supreme Buddha

Se-che sam-mi-khyab la chag-tshal-lo
And his disciples. All are inconceivably sublime. To you I pay
homage.[13]

Then, with a devotional heart and in a sweet melody, chant or sing the
following lines, and mindfully meditate on their meaning, again and
again:

Chom-den-de od-pag-med la ch'ag-tshal-lo
I pay homage to the Blessed One, the Infinite Light!

THINKING OF THE QUALITIES OF THE PURE LAND

Yang-yang tren-no zhing-kham de-wa-chen
I remember the Blissful Pure Land again and again.

Nying-ne tren-no dren-pa od-pag-med
I remember the Lord, the Infinite Light, from the depth of my
heart.

Tse-chig tren-no gyal-se gya-tshoo-khor
I remember the ocean of victorious disciples with one-pointed
mind.

Chin-kyee lob-shig kyab-med kyob-pe-tshog
The assembly, the protectors of those who have none—please
bless us.

SEVENFOLD ACCUMULATION OF MERITS

Thuk-jee dag-nyid gon-po khyed-nam-la
Compassionate Ones, Protectors, to you

Koo-pe ch'ag-tshal ch'od-trin gya-tshoo-ch'od
I prostrate myself with respect. I offer oceans of clouds
of offerings.

Dig-tung kun-shag ge-la jey-yi-rang
I confess all my misdeeds and faults. I rejoice over all the virtues.

Ch'o-khor kor-zhin mya-ngen mi-da-sol
Turning the wheel of Dharma, please remain without entering
nirvana.

Development of Enlightened Attitude

Dag-kee kha-nyam dro-we don-led-du
For the sake of all beings, boundless as the limits of space,

Yang-dag dzog-pe chang-ch'ub drub-che-ch'ir
To attain the fully enlightened state,

Sang-gye zhing-kham yong-su jong-wa-yi
The total accomplishment of the buddha pure land,

Nam-thar mon-lam gya-tsho dzog-kyur-chig
With oceans of enlightened aspirations and deeds—may
I be perfected.

Dedication and Aspirations

Dee-tshon ge-we dag-sog yid-chen-kun
By the power of merits, including this one, may all beings and I,

Ch'i-ma tag-pe zhing-kham de-wa-chen
In our next lives, in the Blissful Pure Land,

Med-chung ngo-tshar kod-pe rab-dzey-par
Beautified with an amazing array of wonders,

Kyey-ne theg-ch'og ga-ton nyong-war-shog
Take rebirth and enjoy the feasts of the Supreme Vehicle
[Mahayana].[14]

The Mantra and the Name-Prayers

The Mantra of the Buddha of Infinite Light

Om ami-tabha hri*
OM! Infinite Light. HRI!

The general meaning of the mantra is: "The body, speech, and mind of
the buddhas, the Infinite Light, please bestow your blessings upon us."

---

* In Chinese, NAMO OMITO-FO. In Japanese, NAMU AMIDA BUTSU.

The word-by-word meaning of the mantra in Sanskrit is as follows:

Oᴍ (a, o, m): Speech, body, and mind of the buddhas and the three doors of oneself. (Or: Oh!)

Aᴍɪ (Infinite): All-pervading, boundless

Tᴀʙʜᴀ (Light): Blessings, brightness, power

Hʀɪ: Heart seed syllable of the Buddha of Infinite Light. By saying ʜʀɪ, you are reaching toward or invoking the compassionate wisdom-heart of the buddha.

Repeat this mantra hundreds, thousands, and millions of times.

Name-Prayers to the Buddha and Bodhisattvas

Invoke the Buddha of Infinite Light (Skt. Amitabha; Tib. Opagme) by chanting his name-prayer in Tibetan or Sanskrit. Repeat it twenty-one, hundreds, and thousands of times.

Tɪʙᴇᴛᴀɴ

Chom-den-de de-zhin-sheg-pa dra-chom-pa yang-dag-par dzog-pe sang-gye gon-po od-pag-du-med-pa la ch'ag-tshal-lo ch'od-do kyab-su ch'i-o.

Sᴀɴsᴋʀɪᴛ

Namo bhagavate tathagataya-arhate samyak-sambuddhaya natha-amitabhaya pujayami sharanam gacchami.

Tʀᴀɴsʟᴀᴛɪᴏɴ

To the blessed one, "thus gone" one, worthy one, perfect, completely awakened protector, Infinite Light, I pay homage, make offerings, and go for refuge.

Invoke the Bodhisattva of Compassion (Skt. Avalokiteshvara; Tib. Chenrezig) by chanting his name-prayer in Tibetan or Sanskrit. Repeat the prayer seven or twenty times.

Tɪʙᴇᴛᴀɴ

Chang-ch'ub sem-pa sem-pa ch'en-po nying-je ch'en-po dang den-pa phag-pa chen-re-zig wang-ch'ug la ch'ag-tshal-lo ch'od-do kyab-su-ch'i-o.

Namo bodhisattva-mahasattva-mahakarunika arya-avalokiteshvaraya pujayami sharanam-gacchami.

TRANSLATION

To the bodhisattva *mahasattva* [great hero], great compassionate one, noble Avalokiteshvara, I pay homage, make offerings, and go for refuge.

Invoke the Bodhisattva of Power (Skt. Mahasthamaprapta; Tib. Thuchenthob) by chanting his name-prayer in Tibetan or Sanskrit. Repeat the prayer seven or twenty times.

TIBETAN

Chang-ch'ub sem-pa sem-pa-ch'en-po phag-pa thu-ch'en-thob la ch'ag-tshal-lo ch'od-do kyab-su-ch'i-o.

SANSKRIT

Namo bodhisattva-mahasatvaya arya-mahasthamapraptaya pujayami sharanam gacchami.

TRANSLATION

To the bodhisattva mahasattva, noble great powerful one, I pay homage, make offerings, and go for refuge.

CONCLUDING PRACTICE: DEDICATION AND ASPIRATION PRAYER

Jam pal pa woo chi tar khyen pa tang
As glorious Manjushri realizes,

Kun tu zang po te yang te zhin te
As well as Samantabhadra,

Te tag kun kyi jey su dag lob ch'ir
In order to train myself by following them,

Ge wa di tag tham ched rab tu ngo
I dedicate all my merits [to all mother-beings].

Too-sum sheg-pe gyal-wa tham-ched-kyee
All the buddhas of the three times

Ngo-wa kang-la chog-tu ngag-pe-tee
Highly praised the dedication [of merits to others].

Dag-ki ge-we tsa-wa di-kun-kyang
So all the virtuous deeds of mine

Zang-po chod-chir rab-tu ngo-war-gyi
I totally dedicate as the excellent deeds [for others].

Dag-ni ch'i-we too-ched kyur-pa-na
At the moment of my death,*

Drib-pa tham-ched tag-ni ch'ir-sal-te
May all my karmic obscurations be removed,

Ngon-sum nang-wa tha-ye te-thong-ne
May I see the Buddha of Infinite Light face to face,

De-wa chen-kyi zhing-ter rab-tu-dro
And may I go to the Blissful Pure Land.

Ter-song ne-ni mon-lam di-tag-kyang
Having arrived there, all the aspirations [of the excellent deeds]

Tham-ched ma-loo ngon-du gyur-war-shog
May I realize without any exception.

Te-tag ma-loo dag-kee yong-su-kang
By totally fulfilling all [aspirations] without exception

---

* In these lines, the personal pronouns "I" and "my" are used. If you are making aspirations for another person, such as a dying or dead person, you should use appropriate terms such as "he" and "his," "she" and "her," or "the deceased person," etc.

Jig-ten chi-srid sem-chen phen-par-gyi
May I serve all sentient beings as long as the universe remains.

Gyal-we kyil-khor zang-zhing ga-wa-ter
In the excellent and joyful assembly of the Victorious One

Ped-mo tam-pa shin-tu dzey-le-kyee
May I be born in a most exquisite sacred flower.

Nang-wa tha-ye gyal-we ngon-sum-tu
By the Buddha of Infinite Light, in person,

Lung-ten pa-yang dag-kee ter-thob-shog
May I be prophesied [to be enlightened].

Ter-ni dag-kee lung-ten rab-thob-ne
Having perfectly received the prophecy

Trul-ba mang-po che-wa thrag-gya-yee
With my hundreds of millions of manifestations

Lo-yi tob-kyee chog-chu nam-su-yang
And with my wisdom power in all the ten directions

Sem-chen nam-la phen-pa mang-po gyi.
May I provide a myriad benefits for the sentient beings.[15]

Sang-gye ku-sum nyee-pe chin-lab-tang
By the blessings of the buddha who is endowed with the three
    buddha-bodies,

Ch'o-nyid mi-gyur den-pe ch'in-lab-tang
By the blessings of the ultimate Dharma, the unchanging truth,

Ge-dun mi-ch'ed doo-pe ch'in-lab-kyee
By the blessings of the Sangha, the indivisible assembly,

Chi-tar ngo-wa mon-lam drup-par-shog
May all these dedications and aspirations be accomplished as I
    have intended them.

Explaining the benefits of remembering and repeating the name of the Buddha of Infinite Light, Shakyamuni Buddha says:

O Shariputra, if any son or daughter of good family, having heard the name of the Buddha of Infinite Life [Infinite Light], keeps his name in his or her mind undisturbed for one night, two nights, three nights, four nights, five nights, six nights, or seven nights—then when that son or daughter of good family dies, he or she will do so without upheaval. The Buddha of Infinite Light, accompanied by an assemblage of disciples and hosts of bodhisattvas, will appear in front of him or her. He or she will take rebirth in the Blissful Pure Land of the blessed one, thus gone, the Buddha of Infinite Light.[16]

~

Eight Esoteric Buddhist Rituals
for the Dying and the Dead

M OST OF THE MEDITATIONS and prayers given in this section are
tantric rituals, which are esoteric. This means that you need to
have been specially initiated and trained in them before you can practice
them. Those who are not trained in them should stick with the training
"The Four Causes of Taking Rebirth in the Blissful Pure Land" given in
appendix A.

INTRODUCTION TO THE EIGHT RITUALS

I have compiled here some of the most important prayers and meditations for performing death rituals. There are seven sections.

First, perform the preliminary practice of going for refuge in the
Three Jewels. Then develop the enlightened attitude of serving all beings
and especially the dying or dead person.

Second, visualize yourself as Avalokiteshvara, the Buddha of Compassion (known as Chenrezig in Tibetan), and contemplate him. Seeing
yourself as a buddha will make the ceremony more effective than performing these ceremonies in an ordinary state of mind.

Third, with meditative power, summon or invite the consciousness of
the dead (if they are dead) to the body or the effigy and give the teachings.
After death, the consciousness of the deceased wanders quickly like the
wind, with little ability to anchor itself, as the dead have only mental bodies. So you must draw the dead person's consciousness to the effigy and
hold it there through your meditative power and through the power of
the buddhas. Thereafter, you can teach the deceased and may be able to
liberate them.

Figure 4. Avalokiteshvara, the Buddha of Compassion. Drawing by Robert Beer.

Fourth, serve blessed sur offerings as food to the dead. There is an expression in Tibetan, "There is no one who does not desire food." The minds of the deceased may continue to strive for food. They can only enjoy the food that is dedicated to them, and the smell of food is easy to enjoy and is satisfying for them. If you don't have the materials to make a sur offering, you may skip this section. Or, if you don't have the facilities for burning the offered or burnable food, you could arrange some edible food and drink as the offering, and after the ceremony dispose of it in the woods or any clean and appropriate place.

Figure 5. The Effigy of the Deceased (art courtesy of Choten Gonpa, Gangtok, Sikkim, India). In death rites, the consciousness of the deceased is invited into the effigy and asked to settle there to receive teachings. The attractive image stands for the deceased's body; the name caption stands for his or her speech; the clear mirror for the mind; the clean dress for the clothing; the parasol for the dwelling; the white cushion for the seat; and the bamboo staff for something for the deceased to hold on to. The following name caption (with the blank replaced by the name of the deceased) would appear in the space below the image: "May the consciousness of the late ——— settle here. NRI DZA HUM BAM HO TISTANTU!"

Fifth, give instructions. You may speak out the instructions to the dying or dead with a compassionate mind, sweet and inspiring voice, and strength of confidence. However, if for any reason you feel it is not proper, you may omit this.

Sixth, pray and meditate on phowa. With strong devotional prayers and contemplation, transfer the consciousness of the deceased into the mind of the Buddha of Infinite Light. This meditation causes the deceased to take rebirth in the Blissful Pure Land (or even to attain enlightenment). This is the heart of the death ritual.

Seventh, if you are doing phowa as a meditation to train yourself rather than to help someone who is dying, afterward you may meditate on the Buddha of Infinite Life and say his mantra for longevity. This latter training, however, may also be omitted.

Eighth, finally, dedicate all your merits to all mother-beings and especially to the deceased, as the cause of taking rebirth in the pure land of the Buddha of Infinite Light, followed by strong aspiration prayers for their peace, happiness, and rebirth in the Blissful Pure Land.

The Performance of the Eight Rituals

If your main training is phowa, which is the main part of the eight rituals, for yourself or for a person who is alive, then you should start it with the preliminary practices (see page 252). Then go straight to the main phowa practice (starting on page 273) and conclude with the dedication and aspiration prayers (starting on page 278). You can train on this for weeks or months, or incorporate it into your daily practice.

For any meditation, especially phowa, it is very important to have some meditative experience before you perform it for yourself or a dying or dead person. It will be very helpful if the dying person has also trained in it in advance.

If you are performing it for a person who is dead, you may do all eight parts.

You might first do the preliminary practices. Then focus on the visualization and recitation of the Buddha of Compassion. Then conclude with the dedication and aspiration prayers. You can do this independently as your daily practice.

I have translated the following rituals as if one is performing them for a deceased person, unless the text clearly says otherwise. But anyway, since the subject and object in a Tibetan sentence are usually flexible, you may use the pronouns *we, us, our, she, he*, and so on, as appropriate.

PRELIMINARY PRACTICES

Going for Refuge

With strong devotion, take refuge in the Buddha of Infinite Light; in the Dharma, the teachings, the path of training and the spiritual attainments; and in the Sangha, the spiritual community of bodhisattvas and devotees.

Repeat three times:

Sang-gye ch'o-tang tshog-kyi ch'og-nam-la
To the excellent Buddha, Dharma, and Sangha,

Chang-ch'ub par-tu dag-ni kyab-su-ch'i
I go for refuge until the attainment of enlightenment

Dag-kee jin-sog gyee-pe sod-nam-kyee
By the merits of generosity, and other [virtues]

Dro-la phen-ch'ir sang-gye drub-par-shog
May I attain buddhahood for the sake of all beings.

Developing Enlightened Attitude (Bodhichitta)

Generate strong compassion for all, thinking that you are going to pray and meditate for the sake of all mother-beings, so that they may take rebirth in the Blissful Pure Land. Especially develop strong compassion for the deceased person. Without strong compassion, meditations such as phowa will not easily succeed.[1]

Repeat three times:

Sem-chen tham-ch'ed de-wa tang de-we gyu-tang den-par kyur-chig
May all beings enjoy happiness and the cause of happiness.

Dug-ngal tang dug-ngal kyi gyu-tang tral-war kyur-chig
May they be free from suffering and the cause of suffering.

Dug-ngal med-pe de-wa tam-pa tang mi-dral-war kyur-chig
May they never be disassociated from the supreme happiness, free from suffering.

Nye-ring ch'ag-dang nyee-tang tral-we tang-nyom tshed-med-pa la ne-par kyur-chig

May they remain in boundless equanimity free from both attachment to kin and hatred of foes.

VISUALIZATION AND CONTEMPLATION OF ONESELF AS THE BUDDHA OF COMPASSION

Hri! Rang-nyid ked-chig tren-pei ting-dzin-kyee

Hri! Through the contemplation that perfects oneself [as Avalokiteshvara Buddha] in instant recollection,

Tong-pe ngang-le pe-ma da-we-den

From the state of emptiness arise a lotus-and-moon seat.

Ped-kar hree-tshen yong-su kyur-pa-le

On them see a white lotus adorned with a HRI letter, which then transforms

Thug-jee nga-dag phag-ch'og chen-re-zig

Into the Lord of Compassion, Noble Avalokiteshvara.

Zhal-chig ch'ag-zhi ku-dog kar-la-tsher

His body is radiantly white, having one face and four arms.

Tang-poo chag-nyee thug-kar thal-mo-jar

The palms of his first two hands are joined at his heart.

Ch'ag-ye og-ma rin-ch'en shel-threng-nam

His right second hand holds a rosary of precious crystal.

Chag-yon ped-kar dab-trug yu-wa-dzin

His left second hand holds a white lotus by the stem.

Zhal-dzum chen-tang shang-kyi yib-tho-zhing

His face is smiling, his eyes are clear, and his nose is high and noble.

Wu-tra chang-lo thon-thing kyen-du-khyil

His dark blue hair is swirled up in a bun [at the top of his head].

Chi-tsug rig-dag nang-wa tha-ye-zhug
At the crown of his head is the Buddha of Infinite Light, Lord of
  the Lineage.

Rang-nyid te-tar sal-we thug-ka-ru
At the heart of one's visualized self,

Ped-ma kar-po dab-trug gye-pe-woo
Imagine a blossoming white lotus with six petals. At the center of it

Yi-ke hree-tshen dru-trug dab-teng-tu
Visualize a HRI syllable and on the six petals the Six Syllables
  [OM MANI PADME HUNG HRI].

Te-tar sal-we ku-le od-throo-pe
[Being touched by] rays of light projected from your body

Nang-wa tham-ched nang-tong lha-yi-ku
All the forms [of the universe] become the divine body, the union of
emptiness and appearances:

Phag-pe gyal-po thug-je ch'en-por-sal
The [body of] the Great Compassionate One, the king of the
  noble ones.

Ngag-le od-throo jung-we dra-la-sog
[Being filled by] rays of light projected from the mantra, the
  sounds of the elements and

Trag-pa tham-ched trag-tong ngag-kyi-dra
All sounds become the sound of mantra, the union of emptiness
  and sound.

Tren-tog kye-gag ne-sum tha-tral-ngang
My recollections and thoughts remain in the natural state, free
  from birth, abiding, and cessation,

Ma-sam jod-tral gong-pe ngang-la-zhag
The vision that transcends all concepts, expressions, and
  designations.

Te-tar sal-we rig-ngag dru-trug-po
Meditating in that manner, the Six Syllables, the esoteric mantra,

Tra-zur ma-nyam yi-ke trug-ma-da
I recite without diminishing the clarity of any part of it.

The Mantra of the Buddha of Compassion

Repeat the mantra hundreds, thousands, or more times:

OM MANI PADME HUNG (HRI).

HUNG (pronounced *hoong*) is the Tibetan pronunciation of the Sanskrit syllable HUM. HRI is omitted in some traditions.

General meaning of the mantra:

> The body, speech and mind of the buddhas with compassion (jewel) and wisdom (lotus), please bestow your blessings upon us.
> *Or:* O Buddha, who holds jewel and lotus, please heed us.
> *Or:* O the Buddha of wisdom and compassion, please heed us.

Word-by-word meaning of the mantra:

> OM (A, O, M): Body, speech, and mind of the buddhas and the three doors of oneself. (Or: Oh!)
> MANI (jewel): Skillful means, the fulfillment of wishes, compassion.
> PADME (lotus): Wisdom, undefiled purity.
> HUM/HUNG (union): Union of the skillful means and wisdom; *or* invoking the buddha for blessings.
> HRI (heart syllable): Heart seed of Avalokiteshvara (to reach or to invoke or unite with the compassionate heart of Avalokiteshvara. Many traditions don't use the HRI.)

Making Offerings to the Buddha of Compassion

Say the following mantra:

SANSKRIT

Om arya-avalokeshvara-mandala-saparivara vajra-argham pad-yam pushpe dhupe aloke gandhe naivedye shabda pratic-cha svaha.

TRANSLATION

O Noble Avalokiteshvara, your mandala and retinue, accept the indestructible drink, foot-bathing water, flowers, incense, lamps, perfume, food, and music. So be it.

Offering of Praise to the Buddha of Compassion

Hri! Chom-den thug-je chen-po ni
HRI! The Blessed and Compassionate One

Kyon-kyee ma-koo ku-dog-kar
Is white, as he is unstained by any faults.

Dzog-sang gye-kyee wu-la-gyen
His head is adorned by the fully enlightened buddha
    [Infinite Light].

Thug-jee chen-kyee dro-la zig
His compassionate eyes are watching beings.

Chen-re zig-la chag-tshal-tod.
Buddha of Compassion, to you I offer praise.

OM MA-NI PAD-ME HUNG HRI

Aspiration Prayer

Ge-wa di-yee nyur-du-dag
By the merits of this meditation

Chen-ri zig-wang drub-kyur-ne
May I realize the Buddha of Compassion.

Dro-wa chig-kyang ma-loo-pa
Without leaving a single mother-being behind.

De-yi sa-la khod-par-shog
May I be able to lead all into his buddhahood.

Summoning the Consciousness of the Deceased and Giving Teachings

Meditating on the seat and the form of the deceased, say the following mantra and prayers:

Om svabhava-shuddhah sarva-dharmah svabhava-shuddho-ham
Om! All phenomena are pure in nature; I am pure in nature.

Tong-pa nyid-tu kyur
All becomes emptiness.

Tong-pe ngang-le ped-ma tang da-we den kyi teng tu
From that emptiness sphere appears a lotus-and-moon seat.

Nri yong-su kyur-pa le
On it appears a NRI syllable.

Tshe-de kyi phung-po kham-tang kye-ch'ed tham-ched yong-su dzog-pa
Then the nri turns into the form of our deceased friend. His/her body is perfect with all faculties and senses

Son-too kyi ne-kab chi-ta-war kyur
As when he/she was alive [and well].

Repeating the following three times, summon the consciousness of the dead to the form (the body or effigy) through your meditative power:

Hri! Dag-nyid thug-je ch'en-poo kur-sal-we
Hri! I visualize myself in the form of the Buddha of Great Compassion.

Thug-ke hri-le od-zer rab-throo-pe
From the hri letter at my heart, rays of light are projected.

Tshe-de nam-shey jig-ten dun-poo-yul
They have brought the consciousness of our deceased friend, from
any of the seven world systems* in which he/she is.

Kang-na ne-kyang kug-te zug-la-tim
It has merged into the form [the body or effigy.]

Thus bring the consciousness of the deceased to the form through the
power of the Buddha of Compassion:

Na-mo! Ch'og-sum tsa-sum kun-doo thug-jee-lha
Homage! By the power of the truth of the compassionate deity,
who embodies the three jewels and three roots:

Dug-ngal rang-trol chen-re-zig wang-ki
Avalokiteshvara, the Natural Freedom from Suffering,

Den-pe tob-kyee tshe-de nam-shey-te
May the consciousness of the deceased

Nyur-wa nyid-tu tsham-chang di-la-khug
Be brought to this effigy immediately.†

**Om ma-ni pad-me hung hri. Tshe-de-kyi nam-par shey-pa
ang-gu-sha dza.**
OM MANI PADME HUNG HRI. May the consciousness of the deceased
be brought here.

Then, thinking that the departed is sitting before you, calmly and respectfully give the following teachings:

Hri! Di-nang le-thal tshe-de khyod-nyon-chig
HRI! O deceased, you who have gone beyond this life, please listen
to me.

---

* The six realms and the bardo.
† Instead of *tsham-chang* (effigy), one could say *phung-po* (body), if one is using the body
of the departed.

Rig-trug kar-kye dug-ngal dzin-three-ne
In the six realms, wherever you take rebirth, all are full of
suffering [as if living among] crocodiles.

Te-le don-ch'ir zug-ming yid-ch'ag-dze
In order to be liberated from them, at this effigy and name caption,
which are the materials to attract your mind and

Go-sum ten-dze di-la ten-par-zhug
The place to establish your three doors, please sit firmly.

Nri dza hung bam ho tee-thran-tu.
May your consciousness be brought to and stabilized with the
form!

Think that the deceased is firmly and calmly settled on the seat and
following the teachings.

The Sur Offering to the Deceased

This offering may be omitted if impractical.
Saying the following mantras, invoke the powerful Buddha of Purification, and empty all into ultimate openness:

Om vajra-krodha-hayagriva hum phat
OM! Indestructible, wrathful Hayagriva Hum Phat.

**Om svabhava-shuddhah sarva-dharmah svabhava-
shuddho-ham**
OM! All phenomena are pure in nature; I am pure in nature.

Tong-pa nyid-tu kyur
All becomes emptiness.

First, visualize the sur materials as pure, infinite wish-fulfilling objects:

**Tong-pe ngang-le, rin-po-ch'ee nod-kyi-nang-tu dod-yon kyi
ngoo-po zug-zang-wa dra-nyen-pa tri-zhim-pa ro-ngar-wa**

reg-cha-jam-pa tong-sum rab-jam nam-khey tha-tang-nyam-pa ch'en-po chig-tu kyur.

From that emptiness state, [appears] a [vast] vessel of precious materials filled with all the desirable materials of excellent forms, sweet sounds, [food of] delicious tastes, and [cloth] soft to the touch, which are as infinite as the extent of the space of the threefold world system.

Then, saying the three sacred syllables and the mantra, bless the sur materials to become pure, infinite wish-fulfilling objects:

OM AH HUM.
OM AH HUM.
OM AH HUM HO.

Om a-karo mukham sarva-dharmanam adyanutpannatvat om ah hum phat svaha.
OM! The syllable AH is the door, because of the primordial nonarising of all phenomena.

OM AH HUM PHAT SVAHA.

Seeing the sur objects as satisfying objects, chant:

Dun-tu rin-po ch'e-yi-nod
In front of you is the vessel of precious materials,

Yang-shing gya-ch'e trang-den-pe
Which are vast, spacious, and numerous.

Nang-tu lha-tang mi-sog-kyi
They are filled with the cuisines of gods and human beings:

Za-cha dag-zhib la-sok-ze
Foods to eat, chew, lick, and suck, and

Cha-ch'ang o-zho la-sog-kom
Drinks of tea, alcohol, milk, yogurt, and so forth.

Dzed-med yid-zhin ter-tu-kyur
May they become the inexhaustible wish-fulfilling treasures.

Repeating the following mantra three times, bless the sur materials so that they will become a means of satisfaction and a source of blessing:

Nama sarva-tathagatebhyoh vishva-mukhebhyah sarvatha kham udgate spharana imam gagana-kham svaha.

Homage to all the "thus gone" ones of all directions, who have appeared at all times as space, pervading this realm of space. So be it!

Then offer the sur materials to the deceased as follows:

Kha-ze ro-ch'og gya-den-pe
The cuisines with hundreds of excellent tastes:

Za-we ze-tang tung-we-kom
Food to eat and beverages to drink,

Go-we koo-tang yo-ched-dzey
Clothes to wear and the materials of necessities—

Mi-zed ter-tu chin-lab-ne
By blessing them as inexhaustible treasures,

Tshe-de khyod-la ngoo-pa-yee
I dedicate them to you, our deceased [friend].

Wang-po trug-dang rab-thun-pe
May they become suitable to your six senses,

So-soo long-chod phun-tshog-ter
Various treasures of enjoyable wealth.

Ngoo-pa chi-zhin thob-kyur-ne
May you receive them, as I am dedicating them to you.

Thral-tu ga-dee roo-tshim-zhing
For now, may you be satisfied with the taste of peace and joy.

Thar-thug nam-tag sar-chod-shog
Ultimately, may you attain the state of total purity [buddhahood].

Serve the food by burning it in a red amber flame and pour the drink around the fire. Then, as a brief sur offering, say the following lines:

Dod-yon nam-khey dzod-zhin-tu
May these desirable objects, be as [infinite as] the sky-treasures,

Long-chod ch'ed-pa med-par-shog
The inexhaustible wealth.

Tsod-pa med-ching tshe-med-par
May all [to whom we are offering] without struggles and violence

Rang-wang tu-ni chod-par-shog
Enjoy them freely.

Repeat the last four lines three, seven, or more times.

The heart of the sur offering prayer is the mantra of the Buddha of Compassion. So offer the sur by repeating the mantra many times with devotion to the buddha and compassion for the deceased.

Repeat hundreds or thousands of times:

OM MANI PADME HUNG (HRI).

At the end of the sur offering, chant the aspiration prayer:
Kye-ma! Jig-rung ne-su khyam-pe nar-we-dro
Alas! May the beings who are wandering in fearful places

Gyal-se thug-je chen-kyee kyob-pa-shog
Be protected by the compassionate Children of the Buddha.

Ye-shey nga-le sem-pey kur-trul-pa
By the power of the manifestations of the five primordial wisdoms as bodhisattvas—

Sa-nying nam-khe nying-po chen-re-zig
Kshitigarbha, Akashagarbha, Avalokiteshvara,

Ch'ag-dor drib-pa nam-sel thug-je-yee
Vajrapani, and Nivaranaviskambin—

Tshe-de wang-poo go-nge ned-sel-ne
May the defilements of the five senses of our deceased be dispelled.

Phun-tshog dod-yon nga-la long-chod-shog
May he/she enjoy the wealth of five desirable objects.*

Thog-med too-ne nyen-pe yi-tam-lha
The personal deities, whom we serve from beginningless time:

Dren-ch'og chang-sem nga-la kyab-su-ch'i
The five bodhisattvas, the supreme leaders, to you we go for refuge.

Thug-jee tshe-de chin-kyee lab-tu-sol
Please bestow blessings upon our deceased friend with your
    compassion.

Di-ne nub-kyi ch'og-rol-na
From here, in the direction of the west,

Od-pag med-pe zhing-kham-yod
There is the pure land of the Buddha of Infinite Light.

Su-zhig te-yi tshen-dzin-pa
Whoever remembers his name,

Zhing-ch'og te-ru kye-war-shog
May they be born in his supreme pure land.

Dharma Instructions to the Deceased

With a compassionate mind, the helper may give the following optional instructions to the deceased in a sweet voice that is inspiring, and
strong with confidence.[2] They may be omitted if felt to be improper for
any reason.

First, call the deceased by his or her name.

Then say three times, "The time of death has arrived for you."

---

* Enjoyable forms, sounds, smells, tastes, and objects of touch.

Then say, "Death has not come just for you. All who are born are subject to dying. From rich and powerful people to poor beggars, all are bound to die. There is no one who escapes death. So please don't feel sad. Please don't get attached to your loved ones or possessions, for no one will be able to come with you or help you. The Buddha has said:

If, when his time comes, even a king should die,
His wealth and his friends and relatives will not follow him.
Wherever people go, wherever they remain,
Karma like a shadow will follow them.

"If your mind is attached to loved ones or possessions, you may fall into unhappy realms. So, please, you must remember and rejoice that you have met the teachings of the Buddha. Even hearing the name of the Buddha makes your life meaningful. If you die with faith in the Buddha and a feeling of joy, you will be liberated from rebirth in inferior realms and will take rebirth in happy realms. So you must follow the Buddha, as your guide, with devotion. You must rely on Dharma, the teachings and the meditations, as your path. You must invoke the Sangha, the bodhisattvas, to support you.

"Especially, remember the Buddha of Infinite Light and his Blissful Pure Land. Remember the peaceful, joyful, and amazing qualities of the Blissful Pure Land, filled with an ocean of bodhisattvas and devotees such as the Bodhissattva of Compassion (Avalokiteshvara) and the Bodhisattva of Power (Mahasthamaprapta).

"The Buddha of Infinite Light has promised that if you remember his name and feel his presence and the qualities of his pure land, you will be protected from the frightening situations of the bardo. The causes of your taking rebirth in inferior realms will be purified. And he will guide you to take rebirth in his pure land.

"Now, in order to take rebirth in the Blissful Pure Land, please join with me in the special meditation of phowa.

Above you in space, with devotion, visualize—or, if you can't visualize, feel—the presence of the Buddha of Infinite Light and his Blissful Pure Land.

"Then visualize or think of your mind in the form of a HRI letter at your heart.[3] Now, remember that you have no gross body, only a mental body. When I say PHAT,[4] please think and believe that your mind in the form of a letter HRI shoots up from your body to the Blissful Pure Land. Focusing your mind one-pointedly, fly to the Blissful Pure Land without looking back."

Or if the deceased trained in the meditation in the past, the helper might instruct him or her by saying:

> With devotion, visualize above you in space the Buddha of Infinite Light and his Blissful Pure Land. Then visualize yourself as Vajrayogini. In the center of your body, visualize the central channel. The upper end of the central channel is open at your cranial aperture. Its lower end is sealed completely at the navel. At your heart level, in the central channel, visualize an energy sphere of a greenish color. In the center of that energy sphere, visualize your mind in the form of a red HRI syllable (or a small red ball). Then, above your head, visualize the Buddha of Infinite Light[5] in the middle of the amazing Blissful Pure Land.
>
> Next, please join me with strong devotion and joy in the prayer to the buddha and bodhisattvas. At the end of the prayer, when I say PHAT, please think and believe that your consciousness shoots up with the force of energy through your cranial aperture and merges into the mind of the Buddha of Infinite Light in the Blissful Pure Land.[6]

This instruction may be given before the rite of phowa.

For the words of instruction or introduction for highly accomplished masters, the helper should consult other texts.[7]

THE MEDITATION AND PRAYERS OF PHOWA: TRANSFERENCE OF CONSCIOUSNESS TO THE BLISSFUL PURE LAND

Phowa is a contemplative meditation with devotional prayers that transfers the consciousness of the deceased and unites it with the enlightened mind of the Buddha of Infinite Light. Through such meditation, a person may take rebirth in the Blissful Pure Land. It is very powerful and beneficial to practice phowa at any time, and especially to perform it for a person who is in the passage of dying or in the bardo. At the time of death, when your consciousness departs from your body, you will become unconscious. When you regain your consciousness, you will be out of your body and wandering in the bardo, solely in accordance with your mental habits, without knowing where you will end up. At that time, if you could meditate on phowa, it might lead you to the Blissful Pure Land, there to take joyful rebirth with little or no need to wander in the bardo.

You should therefore train in phowa when you are alive and healthy, so that your mind will be prepared while you are conscious and you will be ready when the actual time of transferring consciousness comes. Then, closer to death, you should focus more on the practice of phowa, either by yourself or by others practicing it for you. When your consciousness departs from your body, directing it to the familiar pure land will be ideal.

If you are dying, this training will not shorten your life, for the merits of meditation and the blessings of the buddha only lengthen your life and strengthen your peace and joy. Most important, this training will always help you to build your trust in the buddha and the buddha pure land and to prepare for a better death and rebirth, which can come to young or old, at any time.

If you are performing phowa for yourself, with the force of devotional energy to the Buddha of Infinite Light, shoot your mind into the heart of the buddha and merge together as one. Instantly, trusting that your mind and the wisdom-mind of the buddha have become one, totally relax in the state of awareness with no thoughts. Depending on your own meditative experience, that awareness could be the enlightened nature of the mind of Dzogchen, the union of great bliss and emptiness of tantra, or the freedom from concepts of the Madhyamaka path. The awakening of such realization could help you to attain buddhahood or take rebirth in the pure land.

Phowa performed by others for a person who is still alive is very beneficial for their establishing a real connection with the pure land. It could also be performed even weeks after a person's death, for the consciousness might very well be floating about directionless and without a body, and could be redirected to the pure land. At least it would create merits for the deceased even if they have taken rebirth.

According to some texts, if a helper is performing phowa for a dying person, there is one thing that the performer should be especially mindful about. If the dying person is young and hoping to survive, wait to perform phowa until their pulse has stopped. Many think that phowa is only for the dying or dead, so it might scare them or they might resent it. If the dying person is old and seriously ill, and if they are open to such a ceremony, then you could perform it even if the pulse has not yet stopped;[8] they are usually open to and appreciative of such rites. However, you should practice phowa at any time as a training and if the person is open to it, because it is good to perform it for anyone, including the young and healthy.

To perform phowa effectively for others, both Atisha and Milarepa agree[9] that the performer must have attained the "path of insight" (Skt. *darshanamarga*), which is the realization of the ultimate truth, the third of the "five paths" (accumulation of merits, joining, realization, meditation, and beyond training, which is buddhahood). Such attainment might be out of the question for most of us. Generally, however, meditators are thought to be qualified to perform it if they have devotion to the Buddha of Infinite Light, have compassion for the dying person, and are well trained in this meditation in advance.

Meditation

With a calm, one-pointed mind, enter into the meditation on phowa with total trust in the buddha. Meditate with pure perceptions or images, pure words or prayers, and pure feelings of strong devotion to the Buddha of Infinite Light, as well as strong compassion for all mother-beings, especially the deceased one.[10]

First, visualize the person for whom you are performing phowa in the divine form of Vajrayogini. That helps you to change from your usual perception of seeing and feeling others as impure, filthy, and confused. Vajrayogini is a wisdom-deity in female form who symbolizes openness. Her reddish complexion symbolizes her passionate force. Her standing posture demonstrates readiness to serve all, and her nakedness, indicating fearlessness, is ornamented with jewels representing richness and abundance. In her right hand, she raises high a curved blade, symbolizing primordial wisdom that cuts the grasping ego at its root. In her left hand, she holds a skull filled with nectar, symbolizing great bliss. With the energy of total devotion, her three eyes gaze up into the sky toward the Buddha of Infinite Light.

Visualize the central channel in the body of Vajrayogini. It is a straight, empty, clear, transparent, bluish channel of light. Its bottom end is closed at the level of her navel, and the upper end is wide open at the cranial aperture. All other openings of her body are totally closed. In the central channel at her heart level, her (that is, the dying person's) consciousness is in the form of a reddish HRI syllable. If you are not familiar with the HRI syllable, visualize it in the form of a small reddish ball of light. The HRI is encased within a greenish light ball of energy or air.

In some traditions one is also taught to see in meditation that nine out of the ten doors of the deceased's body are sealed by red HRI syllables. They are the openings of the anus, genitals, mouth, two nostrils, two ears, and two eyes. The door at the aperture at the top of the head is fully open, being the door out of which consciousness exits to merge with the mind of the buddha.

Also, the helper or performer of the ceremony should sit behind the head of the body of the dying or deceased. No religious objects should be placed around where the person's lower body or feet are pointing. From the beginning of the dissolution, no one should touch the dying person's lower body. No loved one should sit close to his or her feet or lower body. If they do, they might pull his or her attention downward and cause him or her to take the lower exits.

Visualize the world in which you are sitting as the very Blissful Pure Land. It is a beautiful world of fields, hills, flowers, gardens, streams, rivers, trees, and fruit, all made of light. Divine beings of radiant light are flying and moving through space in absolute peace and joy. Soothing sounds of teachings and the music of Dharma fill the air. All phenomena are in an atmosphere of utmost peace and joy. Visualize, think, and feel such qualities of the Blissful Pure Land, as if they are in front of you, again and again.

Then, above in the sky, in the midst of clouds of light, visualize the Buddha of Infinite Light. His reddish light-body is adorned with beautiful signs of perfection. Sitting in the meditative posture, he is wearing the simple, immaculate robes of an ascetic. With a contemplative gesture, his two hands hold a bowl filled with nectar. He illuminates and fills numerous worlds and pure lands with the light radiating from his body, providing peace and joy to everyone it touches. His youthful face blossoms with a smile of joy. His eyes gaze at you steadily with love and wisdom.

Develop devotional faith in the Buddha by thinking, that his unconditional love sees each of us with all the compassion that a mother feels for her only child. His omniscient wisdom sees all happenings simultaneously. His boundless and omnipresent power pacifies all the miseries of the world, providing peace and joy to all. He is the buddha who vowed to lead everyone who prays to him with trust to his pure land.

He is the embodiment of all the enlightened ones. He is the manifestation of the pure nature and enlightened qualities of the whole universe. He is the reflection of your own enlightened qualities, the buddha-nature that we all inherit as our true nature. By the mere touch of the rays of his body, he purifies all the fear, confusion, pain, sadness, and negative karmas of all.

Also visualize that the Buddha of Infinite Light is surrounded by the Bodhisattva of Compassion, the Bodhisattva of Power, and infinite hosts of other enlightened beings in various forms, costumes, postures, and activities. They are all looking at you with love, wisdom, and power.

Feel the warmth in the presence of these infinite enlightened ones, all of whom are looking at you and thinking of you with love. Feel that your rebirth in the Blissful Pure Land is absolutely assured by the power of the vow of the Buddha of Infinite Light and the blessings of all the enlightened ones. Feel that you are totally protected from any fear by the overwhelming power of the infinite enlightened ones. Know that you are totally secure in the presence of the enlightened ones. Experience the total fulfillment of all your needs by being in the presence of the buddha. Chagmed Rinpoche says, "At the juncture of dying, a feeling of happiness and confidence, instead of fear and confusion, is very important."[11]

If you can see the Buddha of Infinite Light with such qualities, your mind will open up and transform into the same qualities. That is the most important goal of such training.

You might also think and believe that the Buddha of Infinite Light is inseparable from your own Dharma teacher. Usually, teachers are the main instruments in our lives for awakening and strengthening our spiritual realization or experience. If that is the case for you, then that familiar positive memory will be an effective vehicle for reaching the pure land, whether it is an internal or external experience.

I wish to emphasize that in order to perform phowa for others, you must have good, solid experience in devotional meditation on the buddha. Generally, someone who has developed mental energy through concentration, even if they have little or no meditative experience of the pure land, can eject their own consciousness or that of the deceased, but they will not be able lead it to the pure land. But one who is connected to the Buddha of Infinite Light and the Blissful Pure Land through meditative experiences will be able to transfer the consciousness to the actual pure land. So it is essential to establish the meditative connection with the buddha and pure land by thinking about them, accumulating merits, and making aspirations with enlightened attitude, again and again, with a one-pointed mind and devotion.

Prayers

First, empty all the dualistic perception into openness by saying the following mantra in Sanskrit:

Om maha-shunyata-jnana-vajra svabhava-atmakon-ham
Oм! I myself have the indestructible nature of great emptiness and wisdom.

Then, chanting the following, visualize the dying or deceased in the form of the female deity Vajrayogini:

Ah! Rang-nang lhun-drub tag-pa rab-jam-zhing
Aн! All my perceptions spontaneously arise as the totally pure buddha land,

Kod-pa rab-dzog de-wa chen-kyi-woo
The fully arrayed Blissful Buddha Land. In the center of it

Tshe-de zhi-loo dor-je nal-jor-ma
The deceased is in the form of Vajrayogini,*

Zhal-chig ch'ag-nyee mar-sal tri-thod-dzin
With one head and two arms, transparently red, I hold a curved blade and a skull.

---

* If you are performing this chant for yourself, you should read this line as: *Rang nyid je tzun dor je nal jor ma* ("I am in the form of Vajrayogini"). If you are performing it for a person who is still alive, you should read the line as: *Mig yul zhi lu dor je nal jor ma* ("The person who is the object of my focus is in the form of Vajrayogini"). The pronouns in the following lines would similarly change, depending on whether you are doing phowa for yourself or another.

Zhab-nyee dor-tab chen-sum nam-khar-zig
I stand in the "advancing posture" [of compassion], and my three
eyes are looking upward into the sky.

De-yi khong-woo tsa-wu-ma
In the center [of my body] is the central channel,

Bom-tra da-nyuk tsam-pa-la
Of the thickness of a bamboo arrow shaft,

Tong-sang od-kyi bu-ku-chen
Empty, clear, hollow and luminous.

Yar-na tshang-bug ney-su-har
The upper end of the central channel is open at the cranial
aperture, and

Mar-na te-war zug-pa-yi
Its lower end reaches the navel.

Nying-khar tshig-kyee ched-pe-teng
On the knot at the heart

Lung-ki thig-le jang-kye-woo
In the center of a green sphere of air [energy]

Rig-pa hri-yig mar-por-sal
Is my awareness [mind] in the form of a red HRI syllable.[12]

Chi-wor tru-kang tsam-kyi-teng
At the length of a forearm [two feet] above my head

Sang-gye nang-wa tha-ye-ni
I visualize the Buddha of Infinite Light

Tshen-pe dzog-pe phung-por-al
Adorned with most excellent signs and marks.

Moo-koo trag-poo sol-wa-deb
I pray to him with strong devotion.

Chanting the Name-Prayers to the Buddha and Bodhisattva

Then, with the force of compassion toward all mother-beings and especially the deceased, and energy of total devotion to the Buddha of Infinite Light, chant the following name-prayer with sweetest melodies in either Tibetan or Sanskrit. Repeat it seven, twenty-one, or many times.

TIBETAN

Chom-den-de de-zhin-sheg-pa dra-chom-pa yang-dag-par dzog-pe sang-gye gon-po od-pag-du-med-pa la ch'ag-tshal-lo ch'od-do kyab-su ch'i-o.

SANSKRIT

Namo bhagavate tathagataya-arhate samyak-sambuddhaya natha-amitabhaya pujayami sharanam gacchami.

TRANSLATION

To the blessed one, "thus gone" one, worthy one, perfect, completely awakened protector Infinite Light, I pay homage, make offerings, and go for refuge.

Then chant the following name-prayer of the Bodhisattva of Compassion (Avalokiteshvara) in Tibetan or Sanskrit. Repeat it three, seven, or many times.

TIBETAN

Chang-ch'ub sem-pa sem-pa ch'en-po nying-je ch'en-po dang den-pa phag-pa chen-re-zig wang-ch'ug la ch'ag-tshal-lo ch'od-do kyab-su-ch'i-o.

SANSKRIT

Namo bodhisattva-mahasattva-mahakarunika arya-aval-okiteshvaraya pujayami sharanam gacchami.

TRANSLATION

To the bodhisattva mahasattva, great compassionate one, noble Avalokiteshvara, I pay homage, make offerings, and go for refuge.

Then chant the following name-prayer of the Bodhisattva of Power (Mahasthamaprapta) in Tibetan or Sanskrit. Repeat it three, seven, or many times.

TIBETAN

Chang-ch'ub sem-pa sem-pa-ch'en-po phag-pa thu-ch'en-thob la ch'ag-tshal-lo ch'od-do kyab-su-ch'i-o.

SANSKRIT

Namo bodhisattva-mahasattvaya arya-mahasthamapraptaya pujayami sharanam gacchami.

TRANSLATION

To the bodhisattva, mahasattva, noble great powerful one, I pay homage, make offerings, and go for refuge.

The Main Meditation of Phowa

In the following meditation, practiced with the force of devotion, you see the Buddha of Infinite Light as inseparable from your own root teacher, and you merge your mind with his enlightened mind. The enlightened mind of the buddha is the self-arisen state and the absolutely unexcelled pure land. It is also the supreme state of dharmakaya. If you are a highly accomplished meditator, you might attain buddhahood by merging with the enlightened mind of the buddha, the universal truth. If you are a simple meditator, you will not attain buddhahood, but by such devotional prayer and merging meditation, your rebirth in the Blissful Pure Land will be assured, or at least made possible by the power of the buddha and your devotion. This kind of meditation might also help you to merge your mind with the buddha briefly, by giving you flashes of realization during the death process (as mentioned in chapter 3, "The Ultimate Nature"), even if you might not be able to maintain it. Even a flash of experience of the buddha-mind—also called buddha-nature or the enlightened nature of the mind—will be a great source of merit and a powerful cause of taking rebirth in the Blissful Pure Land.

E-ma-ho! Ne rang-nang ton-kyi og-min na
Wonderful! In the self-arisen state, the absolutely unexcelled
    Buddha Pure Land,

Yid ted-gye ja-kur thrig-pe long
In the midst of a vast luminous aura of immense devotion,

Kyab kun-doo tsa-we la-ma ni
My root teacher, the embodiment of all the refuges,

Ku tha-mal ma-yin tang-me loo
Is present not in an ordinary body

Pal sang-gye nang-thei ngo-wor zhug
But as the pure body of the glorious Buddha of Infinite Light.

Yid moo-koo dung-we sol-wa deb
I pray to you with strong devotion.

Lam pho-wa jong-war ch'in-kyee lob
Please bless me to succeed in my meditation journey on the path
of phowa.

Ne og-min drod-par ch'in-kyee lob
Please bless me to reach the Unexcelled Pure Land.

Ying ch'o-koo gyal-sa zin-par shog
May I attain the supreme state of dharmakaya [the absolute
peace and openness].[13]

Repeat the nine lines three times or more. Finally, repeat the last line
three times.

After that, while concentrating on the consciousness of the deceased in
the form of the HRI syllable, as you have visualized earlier, whisper HRI
five times.

Then, with one-pointed concentration and devotion, shout PHAT! again
and again, five times.* As you are shouting PHAT! visualize, feel and believe that the mind of the deceased—which is in the form of a red HRI syllable in the sphere of a green energy ball—is shot upward by the power

---

* While shouting PHAT! you could meditate that the consciousness has merged into the
manifested body, the enjoyment body, the ultimate body, the changeless body, and the
fully enlightened body of the Buddha of Infinite Light. Some shout HIK! instead of PHAT!

of devotion and the force of the green energy sphere, through his or her central channel. It shoots out of the aperture of the deceased and merges into the center of the body of the Buddha of Infinite Light, the wisdom-mind, like water into water, again and again, five times. After the final one, feel and believe that the consciousness of the deceased has become totally one with the fully enlightened mind of the Buddha of Infinite Light. Remain one-pointedly in that experience for a while.

According to the teachings, if you are performing phowa for a dying person, the best time to do it is just when the person's breathing and pulse have stopped. Then their consciousness could be transported to the pure land by the support of the meditation, since their life-force has just been terminated but they haven't yet been trapped in any delusory net of the next life. Even if phowa did not cause rebirth in the pure land, and for the time being they are drawn into afflicting experiences, the meritorious effects of the meditations will certainly stay with them and will ripen when the opportunity arises.

You could also use the unification of your mind with the lama's mind as the phowa practice. At the time of death, visualize your mind in the form of a red HRI or white AH. Then, by the force of energy (air), your mind lifts up out of your body and merges into the heart of your root lama, who is sitting in the space above your head. Then the lama rises higher and higher and reaches the Blissful Pure Land. Finally, contemplate in the indivisible state of your mind and the lama's mind.

Tsele writes, "Recognize your own immaculate intrinsic awareness. Without falling into the path of delusions, strictly follow the teachings. Merge [your mind or the mind of the dead] into the ultimate sphere. That is called phowa."[14]

So, the way of phowa toward a better rebirth is not limited to one method.[15]

Prayer and Meditation on the Buddha of Infinite Life

If you are performing phowa as a training but not for an actual death ritual, at the end, as an optional practice, you can pray to and meditate on the Buddha of Infinite Life for your longevity.

First see that the Buddha of Infinite Light, on which you have been meditating, melts into a ball of light. It merges into you, and you instantly become the Buddha of Infinite Life. His complexion is bright red, and he sits in a meditative posture on a lotus-and-moon seat. He is in the form of the enjoyment body (sambhogakaya), adorned with crown, silk costume and jewel ornaments. His two hands, in the gesture of contemplation, hold a vase filled with the ambrosia of longevity.

De-tshe od-pag med-pe-ku
Then the image of the Infinite Light

Od-du zhu-ne rang-la-thim
Melts into light and merges into myself.

Kyen-tee ked-chig tren-dzog-su
Thereby I myself, instantly,

Rang-yang tshe-pag med-tu-kyur
Become the Buddha of Infinite Life.

Then, with devotional mind, saying the following mantra, pray to the Buddha of Infinite Life for his enlightened blessings and for longevity. Repeat twenty-one, one hundred, or more times.

MANTRA IN TIBETANIZED SANSKRIT

Om amarani dziwandaye soha

MANTRA IN SANSKRIT

Om amarani-jivantaye svaha

TRANSLATION

OM! Immortal life. So be it.

CREMATION OF THE EFFIGY

If you are performing phowa for a deceased person and using an effigy, you may cremate the effigy with the optional rite below. Remind yourself that you are the Buddha of Compassion, as you have meditated from the beginning. As you hold a torch and ignite the effigy, say the verses below. Remember that you, the Buddha of Compassion, are burning the effigy of the deceased with a flame, the power of the primordially pure and spontaneously present wisdom. Your meditative power purifies the physical, mental, emotional, and karmic deposits of the deceased into primordial purity, without leaving even a trace.

Hung! Ka-tag troo-tral me-thab-du
HUM! In the hearth of primordial purity free from concepts,

Rang-chung ye-shey me-bar-be
Igniting the spontaneously arisen [wisdom] flame,

Tshan-me nam-tok bud-shing-kun
All the conceptions of characteristics [body] as the fuel

Lhag-med dzod-chig dzo-la-ram
I burn with blazing fire without leaving any residue. RAM!

Nyon-mong ye-shey me-la-sreg
I burn the afflicting emotions with the flame of primordial wisdom.

Dag-nyee dag-med ying-su-sreg
I burn [the concept of] two selves [personhood and phenomena] into the sphere of no-self.

Kun-zhi ma-rig nyee-dang-che
The universal ground with two kinds of ignorance
    [innate and imputed]

Zhon-nu bum-ku'i long-du-sreg
I burn into the vast expanse of the youthful vase-body.

Khor-war dog-med gya-yee-dab
I stamp the seal [on the door of] samsara for his/her
    no-return.

Dod-ma'i trol-zhi ngon-kyur-ne
May you realize the primordially liberated basis

Tha-ye dro-don yong-drub-shog
And fully accomplish infinite services for all beings.

While burning the effigy, keep reciting and repeating OM MANI PADME HUNG, the Hundred-Syllable Mantra, and other purification mantras and prayers. At the end, sprinkle the ashes with blessed water and scatter blessed substances on them, if you have some. Finally, contemplate in the state free from concepts. Then dispose of the ashes of the effigy in a clean and pleasant place—on land or in a river or sea.

For the cremation of an actual body, it will be important to perform a detailed cremation rite. But if a detailed rite is not possible, this brief one will do, as long as you are initiated and trained in the esoteric trainings.

DEDICATION AND ASPIRATION PRAYER

Jam pal pa woo chi tar khyen pa tang
As glorious Manjushri realizes

Kun tu zang po te yang te zhin te
As well as Samantabhadra,

Te tag kun kyi jey su dag lob ch'ir
In order to train myself by following them

Ge wa di tag tham ched rab tu ngo
I dedicate all my merits [to all mother-beings].

Too-sum sheg-pe gyal-wa tham-ched-kyee
All the buddhas of the three times

Ngo-wa kang-la chog-tu ngag-pe-tee
Highly praised the dedication [of merits to others].

Dag-ki ge-we tsa-wa di-kun-kyang
So all the virtuous deeds of mine

Zang-po chod-ch'ir rab-tu ngo-war-gyi
I totally dedicate as the excellent deeds [for others].

Dag-ni ch'i-we too-ched kyur-pa-na
At the moment of my* death,

---

* If you are making aspirations for another person, alter the pronouns accordingly.

Drib-pa tham-ched tag-ni ch'ir-sal-te
May all my karmic obscurations be removed,

Ngon-sum nang-wa tha-ye te-thong-ne
May I see the Buddha of Infinite Light face to face

De-wa chen-kyi zhing-ter rab-tu-dro
And may I go to the Blissful Pure Land.

Ter-song ne-ni mon-lam di-tag-kyang
Having arrived there, all the aspirations [of the excellent deeds]

Tham-ched ma-loo nyon-du gyur-war-shog
May I realize without any exception.

Te-tag ma-loo dag-kee yong-su-kang
By totally fulfilling all [aspirations] without exception

Jig-ten chi-srid sem-chen phen-par-gyi
May I serve all sentient beings as long as the universe remains.

Gyal-we kyil-khor zang-zhing ga-wa-ter
In the excellent and joyful assembly of the Victorious One

Ped-mo tam-pa shin-tu dzey-le-kyee
May I be born in a most exquisite sacred flower.

Nang-wa tha-ye gyal-we ngon-sum-tu
By the Buddha of Infinite Light, in person,

Lung-ten pa-yang dag-kee ter-thob-shog
May I be prophesied [to be enlightened].

Ter-ni dag-kee lung-ten rab-thob-ne
Having perfectly received the prophecy

Trul-wa mang-po che-wa thrag-gya-yee
With my hundreds of millions of manifestations

Lo-yi tob-kyee chog-chu nam-su-yang
And with my wisdom-power in all the ten directions

Sem-chen nam-la phen-pa mang-po gyi.
May I provide a myriad benefits for sentient beings.[16]

Sang-gye ku-sum nyee-pe chin-lab-tang

By the blessings of the buddha who is endowed with the three buddha-bodies,

Ch'o-nyid mi-gyur den-pe chin-lab-tang

By the blessings of the ultimate Dharma, the unchanging truth,

Ge-dun mi-ched doo-pe chin-lab-kyee

By the blessings of the Sangha, the indivisible assembly,

Chi-tar ngo-ba mon-lam drup-par-shog

May all these dedications and aspirations be accomplished as I have intended them.

Notes

In these notes, the titles of works cited are indicated by abbreviations, the key to which can be found in the Bibliography. For instance, "TRD" stands for *Tshig Don Rin Po Ch'e'i mDzod.*

When traditional Tibetan paginations are cited, the abbreviated title is followed by the folio number; the front or back of the folio indicated by *a* or *b*, respectively; and the line number. An example is "TRD 186b/5."

INTRODUCTION

1. GRP 76/12.
2. See TRD 186b/5–227a/6.
3. DM 9a/6 makes clear that in other teachings "the arising of the luminosity of the basis" is included in the time of death, but in Dzogchen teachings it is in the bardo of ultimate nature.
4. See *The Tibetan Book of Living and Dying* (TBD) by Sogyal Rinpoche, p. 319.
5. See DDM 267b/4.
6. BP 32b/1.
7. "Dr. Kübler-Ross, Who Changed Perspectives on Death, Dies at 78," *New York Times*, August 25, 2004.

CHAPTER 1. HUMAN LIFE: OUR PRECIOUS DAYS

1. BP 2b/3.
2. GR 88a/2.
3. CT 209b/6.
4. CT 242a/2.
5. Ron French, "$325 Million: Big Win, Big Problems?" *Detroit News*, April 16, 2002.

6. BP 55a/2.
7. KBZ 82/3.
8. KBZ 85/7.
9. See *The Tibetan Book of Living and Dying* (TBD) by Sogyal Rinpoche, pp. 82–101.
10. *What the Buddha Taught* (WBT), p. 32.
11. KBZ 189/4 quotes these four lines from a sutra entitled *rGyal Po La gDams Pa* (Skt. *Rajavavadaka Sutra*, Sutra Taught to the King).
12. See TG 102/8.
13. See NK 58/13, 77/2.
14. KJ 242/5. "Sems kyis bsam zhing lus ngag gis 'jug pa'i phyir sems pa yid kyi las dang/ des bskyed pa ngag gi las gnyis su yang dbye-o/."
15. TG 275/15.
16. CND 31/16 (*mCh'an 'grel* 88b/2, 5): "What is the karma of intention (*Sems Pa*)? It is the intention that formulates the karma of the mind. It includes meritorious, unmeritorious, and neutral karmas. What is the karma of thought (*bSam pa*)? It is karmas of body, speech, and mind. They are virtuous and unvirtuous karmas."
17. KJ 258/3.
18. LC 519/14.
19. GRP 76/3.
20. GRP 76/4.
21. KJ 242/3.
22. SC, vol. I, 80a/1: "Where are the karmas based and where are they stored? . . . All the karmas both of samsara and enlightenment are based on the universal ground as the seed."
23. LS 203a/3.
24. LC 122b/6.
25. Tib. *chiwa, Byl Ba*, a rat or mouse.
26. LG, vol. Ha, 16a/3.
27. CT 237a/3 and LC 104a/5.
28. TG 87/4.
29. PK 62b/3.
30. CND 31/15.
31. *What the Buddha Taught* (WBT), 17.
32. See EJ 143.
33. GR 88a/2.
34. TZ 52/12.

35. KR 355/1.

36. See, e.g., DM 29a/1: "If you can maintain the realization of luminosity on occasions such as deep sleep, it will not be difficult to maintain the luminosity of the basis at this time [in the passage of ultimate nature]."

37. DM 41a/1.

38. GG 1a/6.

39. NM 590/2.

40. It could also be any other buddha and pure land, such as Tara and her pure land. See CP 1a/3.

CHAPTER 2. DYING: THE CRUCIAL HOUR OF LIFE

1. DM 7a/5.

2. This is the common interpretation, but according to TRD 224b/1, GG 1b/5, the dissolution is explained on many levels of the five elements (such as outer, inner, secret, and perfect qualities of each of the five elements), and also each dissolves into its own element, e.g., the energy (*nu pa, Nus-Pa*) of outer earth dissolves into inner earth, and so on. KBZ 579/5 and other sources describe them as dissolving the inner element (*kham, Khams*) of flesh into the outer element of earth, blood into water, heat into fire, and breathing into air. According to KZ 579/12, the upward-moving air, downward-moving air, fire-accompanying air, and pervasive air merge into the vitalizing or life-force air.

3. LC 158b/5.

4. PB 26a/1. But according to YB 59b/2: At the end of three short and long breathings, outer breathing will cease. Then air dissolves into your consciousness, and your intrinsic awareness becomes unconscious in your heart for a while. That is cessation of inner breathing. DM12b/3: Outer breathing ceases when consciousness dissolves into space.

5. PB 26a/2.

6. NS 389b/4, which is based on *Thal 'Gyur Tantra*: consciousness dissolves into space, and space into luminosity.

7. In DM 10b/6 and KZM 535/4, in the first and second experiences the order of the whiteness and redness visions is reversed. In some texts, the cessations of emotions, too, are interchanged.

8. DM 12b/2.

9. DM 18a/2.

10. CBS 46/4.

11. YB 59b/2.

12. KZM 536/1.

13. CH 66/16.

14. DM 15a/3.

15. DM 26b/4.

16. TRD 193a/3.

17. NM 590/2.

18. NS 388a/2.

19. BN 2/9.

20. This account is based on TC.

21. Based on GY.

22. Based on SM. Denma Sangye Senge was also known as Sho Thang 'Das Log and Trungchen mKha' sPyod Heruka.

23. Based on MRP. According to E. Gene Smith of the Tibetan Buddhist Resource Center in New York City, there were two Dagpo Trashi Namgyals. One was a Kagyupa from Daglha Gampo, and the other was a Sakyapa from Nalanda of Phanpo Valley. Smith thinks that it was the Sakyapa who was the delog. (Personal communication.)

24. Based on TT.

25. Based on RSM and PDN.

26. A *sadhana* (Skt.; Tib. *drubthab, sGrub Thabs*), or esoteric meditation practice and ritual, of the Longchen Nyingthig cycle of teachings.

27. Based on KB.

28. Based on TD.

29. Based on ND.

30. Based on SG.

31. Based on MNS.

Chapter 3. The Ultimate Nature

1. DM 9a/6. YB 60a/6 places the luminous nature of the basis in the period of dissolution of consciousness into the space of the ultimate sphere. TRD 201b/2 also places it as part of the transitional period of ultimate nature.

2. TRD 201a/6; DM 24a/6; NS 389a/4.

3. See TRD 201a/6; DM 13b/6 and 24b/4; and PB 26a/3.
4. See DM 13b/3, 6.
5. RC 256b/6.
6. BN 317/4.
7. GG 4a/2.
8. NM 590/6.
9. SR 10a/6. English translation: *The Practice of Dzogchen* (PD) by Longchen Rabjam, p. 333.
10. RC 257b/2.
11. RC 123a/2.
12. DM 39a/4.
13. Narrow path: Tib. *trang, 'Phrang.*

Chapter 4. The Bardo

1. According to SB and Tibetan delog accounts.
2. Based on NDK 216b/3; TCD, vol. Wam, 260b/4; and YB 73a/2.
3. SB 11b/5 and DM 38b/4 give white light for the god realm, red for the demigod realm, blue for the human realm, green for the animal realm, pale yellow for the hungry ghost realm, and smoky light for the hell realm. (For the hell realm, some texts say that since you will be going straight down to the hell realm, there will be no opportunity to see any light.) NN 4a/2 gives white light for the god realm, green for the demigod realm, yellow for the human realm, pale (*Mog Po*) for the animal realm, red for the hungry ghost realm, and dark maroon (*sMug Nag*) for the hell realm. RG f136b/3 gives white for the god and human realms, yellow for the demigod and animal realms, and dark for the hungry ghost and hell realms.
4. DM 38b/6.
5. NDK 217a/7; TCD, vol. Wam, 262b/3; and YB 73b/2. Other texts mention different images, as beings could have all kinds of visions of the realms. See DM 39b/2, SB 18b/6, NN 4a/2, and RG 136b/5.
6. LC 160b/3.
7. RC 253a/5.
8. *Liberation by Hearing* (Tib. *Thos Grol*) is the popular title of ZG. It is a series of texts in three volumes discovered as a ter (treasure text) by Karma Lingpa (1326–?). The *Tibetan Book of the Dead*

(*Bardo Thodrol, Bar do Thos Grol*) is one of its texts. See also DM
32b/6.

9. NM 591/3.

Chapter 5. Tales of the Bardo

1. KBZ 395/13.
2. Some pure lands are of the nirmanakaya; this might be referring to
   the sambhogakaya pure land.
3. Lha Yi Bu Mo (Divine Lady).
4. Based on PDN.
5. Based on KZ and GTD.

Chapter 6. Rebirth

1. See *Masters of Meditation and Miracles* (MMM) by Tulku Thondup,
   pp. 317–318.
2. NGR 8a/5, NL 4b/4, GRP 96/13, KM 48a/3, KBZ 176/2, among
   others.
3. BP 32b/1.
4. According to GRP 96/18, greed (Tib. *chag, Ch'ags;* Skt. *raga*)
   causes rebirth in the hungry ghost realm. In most texts, such as
   NLZ 5b/1 and 7b/2, miserliness (Tib. *serna, Ser sNa;* Skt. *matsarya*)
   is the cause of a hungry ghost birth, whereas desire/attachment
   (Tib. *dod chag, 'Dod Ch'ags;* also translated as Skt. *raga*) is the cause
   of human birth.
5. GRP 96/12.
6. TG 96/15.
7. KZZ 89/6.
8. Based on SB 2b/5. See also SR 2a/4.
9. Based on NDK 216b/3; TCD, vol. Wam, 260b/4; and YB 73a/2.
10. SB 12a/1 and 14a/6.
11. YB 75b/2.
12. Unless stated otherwise, this section is based on SB 18a/5, TRD
    225b/2, and NDK 217a/4, as well as NN 4a/1, RG f136, and DM
    40a/2.
13. YB 74a/4. These are not the signs that indicate your forthcoming
    birthplace, as some masters have thought. When you are seeing any
    of these, you have already been trapped in your birthplace. As writ-

ten in the *Nyida Khajor Tantra* (Union of the Sun and Moon Tantra):

> These are the signs that you have been admitted into the womb.
> Now, even if you wish to leave, you are trapped.
> Now you are bound.

14. NDK 216b/3; TCD, vol. Wam, 260b/4; and YB 73a/2. Again, different texts provide different kinds of signs for the six realms, as people may have different visions of the realms.

Chapter 7. The Buddha of Infinite Light and his Blissful Pure Land

1. DK 197b/2.
2. In ZGB 334/12, Je Tsongkhapa writes that there are descriptions of many manifested pure lands in the sutras, but the descriptions of the Blissful Pure Land were expounded by Shakyamuni Buddha in the greatest detail.
3. This chapter is mainly based on OK and DK (Tibetan translations of the Larger and Smaller *Sukhavati-vyuha*), and to some extent on PG by Jigme Tenpe Nyima. I also drew on other texts and commentaries: ZGB, RC 242a/2–245a/5, DD (the Tibetan translation of *Sukhavativyuha-nama-mahayana Sutra*), and DN.
4. OK 242b/6—248a/3. According to *Buddhist Mahayana Texts* (BMT), part 2, p. 73, forty-six vows are listed in the Sanskrit text and forty-eight in the Chinese translation.
5. OK 243a/3.
6. DK 196a/5.
7. OK 252b/6. Besides gold, silver, lapis, crystal, and red pearl, there are two other names in Tibetan: *sPug* and *rDo'i sNying Po*, which are unknown to me. According to BMT 33/19, the seven precious materials are gold, silver, beryl, crystal, coral, red pearl, and diamond. In BTA 202/32, they are gold, silver, beryl, crystal, coral, red pearl, and emerald.
8. DK 197a/4.
9. PG 25b/4 says, "According to *Don Zhags Kyi Ch'o Ga Zhib Mo* and other sources, the Buddha of Infinite Light also teaches in a palace made of precious jewels. It is not certain whether it is at the foot of the Tree of Enlightenment."
10. ZGB 349/10 and PG 25b/5: *rDul Med Ching rNam Par Dag Pa*.

11. See ZGB 343/10 and PG 6a/2.
12. PG 11a/2 and DN 381/7.
13. DD 139/1.
14. DD 138/5.
15. DN 390/2.
16. OK 258a/7.
17. PJT f308b/7.

CHAPTER 9. RITUAL SERVICES FOR THE DYING AND THE DEAD

1. ZP.
2. CM 114b/4.
3. ZP.
4. CM 113b/4.
5. Ibid.
6. CM 114a/5.
7. DM 27b/1.
8. On praying to the Buddha of Compassion as the source of blessings, see my book *The Healing Power of Mind* (HPM), pp. 182–186.
9. See TJ 150a/3.

APPENDIX A. MEDITATIONS ON THE FOUR CAUSES OF TAKING REBIRTH IN THE BLISSFUL PURE LAND

1. See OK 244a/5, DZM 219/7, and *Buddha of Infinite Light* (BIL) by
   D. T. Suzuki, pp. 29–32.
2. See the eighteenth and nineteenth of his fifty-one vows given in
   OK 244a/5.
3. OK 259b/7.
4. *Tannisho* (TS) by Yuien-bo, p. 5.
5. OK 244b/1 and DZM 219/6.
6. PG.
7. OK 258a/7.
8. See *Boundless Healing* (BH) by Tulku Thondup, pp. 33–36.
9. OK 258b/4.
10. CM 114a/6.
11. CM114b/2.
12. OK 258a/7.

13. DCM 151/4.
14. ZK 269/6.
15. ZP 361b/5.
16. DK 197b/7.

APPENDIX B. EIGHT ESOTERIC BUDDHIST RITUALS FOR THE DYING AND THE DEAD

1. PP 4a/4.
2. See *The Tibetan Book of Living and Dying* (TBD) by Sogyal Rinpoche, pp. 209–222. See also "Instructions for Buddhists and Those Open to Buddhism" in chap. 8 above, "How to Help the Dying and the Dead."
3. Some scriptures, such as CP 1a/2, say to visualize AH instead of HRI.
4. Some shout HIK instead of PHAT. The PHAT syllable is the union of *pha*, skillful means or compassion, and *t*, emptiness or wisdom.
5. It could also be another buddha, such as Manjushri, and his pure land. See CP 1a/3.
6. This instruction is mainly based on SN.
7. See YB, ZG, and RG.
8. PP 3a/4.
9. KBZ 384/13 and KBZ 569/14.
10. Most of the following prayers and the explanation of phowa are based on MS.
11. RC 247b/1.
12. Some scriptures say to visualize it as a white AH syllable.
13. MS 3/1.
14. DM 20a/1.
15. NLS 64/12. See also TB 190b/3–191b/1.
16. ZP 361b/5.

Glossary

Tibetan words in this glossary are first given in a phonetic spelling, followed by the transliteration.

Afflicting emotions (Tib. *nyonmong, Nyon Mong;* Skt. *klesha*): Harmful negative emotions. There are different systems of analyzing the afflicting emotions in Buddhism. In this book we are mainly concerned with the system of six afflicting emotions as the causes of birth in the six realms: ignorance (confusion, the unenlightened state), hatred (anger, aggression), arrogance (pride), greed, desire (craving), and jealousy. In another system, desire and greed are considered aspects of the same emotion, producing a fivefold scheme: ignorance, hatred, arrogance, greed (desire), and jealousy. Refining the system further, the root of all these negative emotions is the "three poisons": ignorance, hatred, and greed.

Amitabha: *See* Buddha of Infinite Light.

Amitayus: *See* Buddha of Infinite Life.

Arhat (Skt., destroyer of foes, worthy one; Tib. *dra chom pa, dGra bChom Pa*): Arhats are Buddhist adepts who have vanquished their enemies, the mental and emotional defilements. Although buddhas are also known as arhats, the term is mainly used for the adepts who have achieved the highest level of attainment through the trainings of common Buddhism (that is, sutric Buddhism as opposed to esoteric or Vajrayana Buddhism), the vehicles of the "hearers of the teachings" (Skt. *shravaka*) and the "solitary buddhas" (Skt. *pratyeka-buddha*).

Avalokiteshvara (Skt.; Tib. Chenrezig, sPyan Ras gZigs): Avalokiteshvara has two aspects. In reality he is the Buddha of Compassion. He serves beings in the form of the Bodhisattva of Compassion. In the Bliss-ful Pure Land, he is the highest-ranking bodhisattva.

Bardo (Tib. *Bar Do*; Skt. *antarabhava*): Transitional passage or interme-diate state. Many Tibetan esoteric (tantric) Buddhist writings designate different passages of life as bardo, transitional passage, saying that all are transitional periods between two stages. Many esoteric teachings classify bardo into four classes: (1) The natural bardo of birth, our present life. (2) The painful bardo of dying. (3) The bardo of ultimate nature, the lumi-nous basis. (4) The bardo of transitional passage (becoming), the karmic causation. Some teachings classify bardo into six by adding (5) the bardo of dream and (6) the bardo of absorption.

However, according to common (sutra) Buddhist teachings and also popular Tibetan culture, *bardo* is a term for the transitional passage be-tween death and rebirth. So in this book I am using the term *bardo* only for the period between death and rebirth (or between the ultimate nature and the rebirth). The other three passages of life are just termed "life," "dying," and "ultimate nature."

Blissful Pure Land (Skt. Sukhavati; Tib. Dewachen, bDe Ba Chan): A world or paradise of the buddhas. There are two kinds of pure lands. One is the ultimate pure land of the "enjoyment body" (*sambhogakaya*). The other is the relative pure land of the "manifested body" (*nirmanakaya*). Ac-cordingly, there are Blissful Pure Lands of the enjoyment body and also of the manifested body. (*See* Three Bodies.) The Blissful Pure Land dis-cussed in this book is a manifested body. It is manifested by the power of the vow of the Buddha of Infinite Light. All who have accumulated the "four causes" (or the "three causes") will take rebirth there because of the power of his vow.

Bodhichitta (Skt., mind of enlightenment, enlightened attitude): The bedrock teaching of Mahayana Buddhism, bodhichitta means taking on the responsibility of serving all mother-beings. Bodhichitta has two as-pects. The first is enlightened aspiration, which we plant in our minds by cultivating the four immeasurables: compassion, loving-kindness, sympa-thetic joy, and equanimity. The second aspect involves putting this aspi-ration into action by practicing the six perfections: generosity, discipline, patience, diligence, contemplation, and wisdom.

We can incorporate the practice on bodhichitta into our practice on the Blissful Pure Land. Before starting our Blissful Pure Land practice, we should think that we will practice for the sake of all beings. Then we should think that all beings are joining us in our meditation and prayers, and trust that all beings will take rebirth in the pure land. When we finish, we should dedicate all our merits to all beings as the cause of their rebirth in the pure land. This simple practice embodies both aspects of bodhichitta training.

Bodhisattva (Skt.): An aspirant to enlightenment who develops the mind of enlightenment (*bodhichitta*), the vow of bringing happiness and enlightenment to all mother-beings without any self-interest. Bodhisattvas are followers of the Mahayana path, which leads them to the attainment of buddhahood. The final goal of this path is the attainment of buddhahood, but one remains a bodhisattva until one reaches that goal. The bodhisattva must pass through ten stages on the way to becoming a buddha.

Buddha (Skt., awake; awakened one): A fully enlightened being. The enlightened state of all buddhas is one and undivided, yet there are limitless buddhas in manifestation, because the pure and universal buddha-nature (which we all possess) emanates in infinite forms and qualities or the benefit and service of dualistic and conceptual-minded beings. When capitalized, the name *Buddha* usually refers to the historical Buddha of this world age, Shakyamuni.

Buddha of Infinite Life (Skt. Amitayus; Tib. Tsepame, Tshe dPag Med): An aspect of Amitabha, the Buddha of Infinite Light. Amitabha appears in nirmanakaya form and leads devotees to his Blissful Pure Land at their death. As Amitayus, he manifests in sambhogakaya form and bestows longevity on his devotees. They are the same buddha, but with different names owing to different qualities and actions.

Buddha of Infinite Light (Skt. Amitabha; Tib. Opagme, A'od dPag Med): The buddha who presides over the Blissful Pure Land. His name in Sanskrit, Amitabha, has been translated as "Infinite Light" or "Boundless Light." *See also* Buddha of Infinite Life; Vow of the Buddha of Infinite Light.

Common Buddhism. Buddhist teachings based on the sutras, the words of the historical Buddha, Shakyamuni.

Daka (Skt.; Tib. *khadro, mKha' 'Gro*, sky-goer): 1. A class of buddhas in male form. 2. The masculine principle in esoteric Buddhism.

Dakini (Skt.; Tib. *khadroma, mKha' 'Gro Ma,* sky-goer): A term used in esoteric teachings, with several senses: 1. A buddha in female form. 2. The emptiness principle of the union of wisdom and emptiness, or wisdom of wisdom and skillful means, or emptiness of emptiness and compassion. 3. A highly accomplished female spirit-being who protect and guide the esoteric teachings and their followers. Dakinis can be in peaceful, wrathful, or semiwrathful form. 4. In Tibet, *Dakini* is also an honorific title for high female teachers and for the consorts of high lamas.

Dedication (Tib. *ngo wa, bsNgo Ba*): A practice in which we think and say prayers of giving away all our merits as the cause of happiness and enlightenment for all mother-beings.

Dependent origination (Tib. *tendrel, rTen 'Brel;* Skt. *pratitya-samutpada*): According to Buddhism, no mental state or physical phenomena develop or function either independently, by chance, or by the act of a high power, but through dependent origination of causes and conditions. The lives of beings develop and function through the chain of twelvefold dependent origination: ignorance (unenlightened state), formation, consciousness, name and form, the six sense faculties, contact, feeling, craving, clinging, becoming, birth, and old age and death. If we realize the ultimate nature, we will relinquish our ignorance and in so doing we will stop the wheel of twelvefold chain of dependent origination from spinning by reversing the links and finally attaining total freedom, enlightenment (buddhahood). The concept of what I am calling dependent origination has been translated variously as interdependent arising, dependent co-arising, co-dependent origination, and so on.

Dharma (Skt.): *See* Three Jewels.

Dharma King of the Lords of the Dead (Tib. Shinje Chogyal, gShin rJe Ch'os rGyal): The Dharma King, or King of the Law, presides over our judgment after we die. The Lords of Death are his lieutenants who oversee the implementation of the judgments. They are merely the reflections of our own mental habits, our karma.

Dharmakaya: *See* Three Bodies.

Delog (Tib. *'Das Log*): A "returner from death." In Tibet there have been many men and women who died for a number of days and then came back to life with many reports about what they had been through and the experiences they had in the passages of dying, the ultimate nature, and the bardo.

Dudtsi (Tib. *bDud rTsi;* Skt. *amrita,* nectar, ambrosia): Pills of medicinal herbs blessed as healing and liberating substances through many days of meditation ceremonies by a large congregation of many meditators.

Dzogchen or **Dzogpa Chenpo** (Tib. *rDzogs Ch'en* or *rDzogs Pa Ch'en Po;* Skt. Mahasandhi or Atiyoga): The highest level of the nine vehicles or stages of view, meditation, and attainment, according to the Nyingma school of Tibetan Buddhism.

Empowerment (Tib. *wang, dBang;* Skt. *abhishekha,* empowerment, initiation): An esoteric ceremony in which an accomplished master transmits his or her realized wisdom-power to disciples. The most important powers received in high esoteric ceremonies are the powers of body, speech, mind, and wisdom of the master, deity, or buddha. Meditators can also receive the empowerments through "self-empowerment," that is, in their own meditations, without the physical presence of the master.

Esoteric Buddhism: Vajrayana (the "Diamond Vehicle"), one of the major schools of Mahayana Buddhism. Vajrayana follows the esoteric teachings of tantra. Its trainings focus on pure perception: seeing, hearing, and feeling everything as buddha-forms, buddha-sounds, and buddha-wisdom. Its goal is to attain the three buddha-bodies (*see* Three Bodies), buddhahood, for the sake of all mother-beings.

Executioners (Tib. *le khen, Las mKhan*): The messengers of the Lords of the Dead or their agents, who carry out punishments.

Feast offering (Tib. *tsog khor, Tshogs 'Khor;* Skt. *ganachakra,* wheel of assembly): An important ceremony of esoteric practice consisting of three assemblies: the assembly of deities, to whom one makes the offerings; the assembly of food and drink, the materials of the feast; and the assembly of men and women who offer the feast.

Five buddha families: According to esoteric Buddhism, unenlightened beings experience their lives with the characteristics of five aggregates (consciousness, form, feeling, perception, and formation), five elements (earth, water, fire, and air, and space), and five afflicting emotions (ignorance, hatred, greed, arrogance, and jealousy). When you become enlightened, the presence of the five buddha families within you will awaken because you will have realized the five aggregates as the five male buddhas, the five elements as the five female buddhas, and the five afflicting emotions as the five wisdoms.

1. The Buddha (enlightenment) family is blue in color and pervades the center of the mandala that represents the enlightened cosmos. Presiding over it is the union (oneness) of the male buddha Vairochana, the purity of consciousness, and the female buddha Dhatvisvari, the pure quality of space. The wisdom of this buddha family is the wisdom of the ultimate sphere, which is the pure nature of ignorance.

2. The Vajra (adamantine) family is white in color and pervades the eastern part of the cosmic mandala. Presiding over it is the union of Akshobhya or Vajrasattva, the purity of form, and the female buddha Buddhalochana, the pure nature of water. Its wisdom is mirror-like wisdom, and it is the pure nature of hatred.

3. The Ratna (jewel) family is yellow and pervades the southern part of the mandala. Presiding over it is the union of the male buddha Ratnasambhava, the pure nature of feeling, and the female buddha Mamaki, the pure nature of earth. Its wisdom is that of equanimity, the pure nature of arrogance.

4. The Padma (lotus) family is red and pervades the western part of the mandala. Presiding over it is the union of the male buddha Amitabha, the pure nature of perception, and female buddha Pandaravasini, the pure nature of fire. Its wisdom is omniscient wisdom, the pure nature of greed.

5. The Karma (action) family is green and pervades the northern part of the mandala. Presiding over it is the union of the male buddha Amogasiddhi, the pure nature of formation, and the female buddha Samayatara, the pure nature of air. Its wisdom is the wisdom of accomplishing, the pure nature of jealousy.

Five immeasurable offenses (Tib. *tsham med pa nga, mTshams Med Pa lNga;* Skt. *panchanantarya*): Killing one's mother, killing one's father, killing a sage (*arhat*), assaulting a buddha with malicious intention, and causing dissension in the spiritual community (*sangha*). Committing any of these offenses means facing the worst karmic consequences, such as rebirth in the hell realms.

Four causes: There are four causes for taking rebirth in the Blissful Pure Land. They are (1) remembering the qualities of the Blissful Pure Land along with the Buddha of Infinite Light, again and again, (2) the accumulation of merits, (3) the development of bodhichitta, or enlightened attitude, and (4) dedicating merits as the cause of taking rebirth in the Blissful Pure Land and making aspirations for rebirth there. One can also train in the "three causes" (the first, second, and fourth causes), without the development of bodhichitta, for taking rebirth in the Blissful Pure Land.

Grasping at "self" (Tib. *dag dzin, bDag 'Dzin*; Skt. *atmagraha*): Grasping at "self" is the root of our mental illusions, afflicting emotions, and physical sicknesses. It is the mind's tightness that comes from grasping at oneself as "I," "my," and "me," and grasping at others as "this," "that," "he," "she," and so on. To the extent that the grip of grasping becomes tighter, pain and confusion becomes more stressful and severe. To the extent that the grip of grasping is loosened, we will be peaceful and feel at ease. Total release of grasping is total liberation.

Guru. *See* Lama.

Guru Padmasambhava (Skt., Lotus-Born): One of the greatest adepts and teachers of esoteric Buddhism, known popularly in Tibet as Guru Rinpoche, Precious Teacher. From India, he traveled to Tibet in the eighth century and founded Tibetan Buddhism, tamed human and non-human forces opposing the Dharma, transmitted Vajrayana (esoteric) teachings, and through his mystical power concealed teachings and religious objects for future followers to find. Those concealed teachings and treasures (Tib. *terma, gTer Ma*) are still being discovered in Tibet. See *Masters of Meditation and Miracles* (MMM), pp. 74–92, and *Hidden Teachings of Tibet* (HTT).

Guru Rinpoche: *See* Guru Padmasambhava.

Guru Yoga (Skt.): A practice in which one accepts a spiritual master or religious teacher, such as Guru Padmasambhava, as the object and source of spiritual inspiration, blessing, and awakening.

Helper: Monks, nuns or laypeople with meditation and ritual training for serving the dying and the dead. They are termed either lamas or helpers in this book. Caregivers, survivors, and family members of the dying or dead could also be helpers, if they are trained in prayers and meditations.

To offer real spiritual guidance and blessings, the helper should be well trained in meditations and rites. However, if helpers have devotion to the "source of blessings" and/or compassion for the dying or dead, then even if they are not well trained, any positive thought, prayer, or service that they offer will be a great source of benefit.

Karma (Skt.): A habitual pattern sown in our mindstream by our thoughts, words, and deeds. Our karmic patterns determine the kind of life experiences we will have, now and in the future. The term also sometimes means simply a "deed" or "action."

Knowledge-holder (Tib. *rigdzin, Rig 'Dzin;* Skt. *vidyadhara*): A title for esoteric masters or those who have reached high stages of attainment through Buddhist trainings.

Lama (Skt. *guru*): A Tibetan term for both male and female senior Buddhist teachers. A lama must be a highly learned and/or accomplished master. Lamas preside over or lead ceremonies such as the death rituals.

Lords of the Dead (Tib. *shin-je, gShin rJe*) The deputies of the Dharma King. *See* Dharma King of the Lords of the Dead.

Luminosity (Tib. *osel, A'od gSal;* Skt. *prabhasvara*). In esoteric teachings we meditate on the union of emptiness and luminosity, also referred to as the clear light, and realize the perfection of the union of emptiness and luminosity, which is the true nature of the mind—the ultimate goal.

Mahasthamaprapta (Skt.; Tib. Thuchenthob, mThu Ch'en Thob): The name of a bodhisattva who symbolizes power or strength. In the Blissful Pure Land, he is the second highest-ranking bodhisattva, after Avalokiteshvara.

Mandala (Skt; Tib. *kyil khor, dKyil 'Khor*): 1. An assembly of many deities. 2. A circle of deities. 3. An altar for esoteric rites. 4. A symbol or diagram of the buddha pure land. 5. A heap of wealth or treasure.

Merit making (Tib. *tshog sag, Tshogs bSags*): The accumulation of positive effects caused by virtuous thoughts and deeds such as generosity, moral discipline, tolerance, diligence, patience, and contemplation.

Mother-beings: All sentient beings. Every being, even the smallest insect, has in one lifetime or another been our mother, and we are therefore taught to regard all "mother-beings" with loving compassion.

References

SOURCES CITED AND KEY TO ABBREVIATIONS

When traditional Tibetan paginations are cited in these references, the title abbreviation is followed by the folio number; the front or back of the folio indicated by *a* or *b*, respectively; and the line number. An example is "TRD 186b/5."

Those texts designated as being from the collection of "Kajur" are teachings of the historical Buddha (sutras) translated mostly from Sanskrit into Tibetan in ancient times and preserved among the Kajur collection of about 108 volumes. The texts designated with the word "Tenjur" were written by ancient Buddhist scholars of India, translated into Tibetan, and preserved among the collection of Tenjur of about 225 volumes.

BH   *Boundless Healing: Meditation Exercises to Enlighten the Mind and Heal the Body* by Tulku Thondup. Boston: Shambhala Publications, 2000.

BIL   *Buddha of Infinite Light* by D. T. Suzuki. Boston: Shambhala Publications, 1997.

BMT   *Buddhist Mahayana Texts*, edited by E. B. Cowell et al. New York: Dover Publications, 1969.

BN   *Bar Do'i sMon Lam rNam gSum* by Karma Lingpa. In ZG, vol. 3, pp. 315–318. New Delhi: Collection of Dudjom Rinpoche.

BP   *Byang Ch'ub Sems dPa'i sPyod Pa La 'Jug Pa* by Shantideva. Wood block print, Dodrupchen Monastery.

BTA   *Buddhist Texts Through the Ages*, edited by Edward Conze et al. New York: Harper Torch Books, 1964.

CBS   *Ch'os Nyid Bar Do'i gSal 'Debs Thos Grol Ch'en Mo* by Karma Lingpa. In ZG, vol. 3, pp. 41–114. New Delhi: Collection of Dudjom Rinpoche.

CH   *Counsels from My Heart* by Dudjom Rinpoche, pp. 59–75. Translated by the Padmakara Translation Group. Boston: Shambhala Publications, 2001.

CM   *Ch'i Kha Ma'i Man Ngag* by Jigme Tenpe Nyima. *Tam-Tshog*, vol. Kha, pp. 424–427. *Dodrupchen Sungbum.* Gangtok, Sikkim: Choten Gonpa.

CND   *Ch'os mNgon Pa mDzod Kyi Tshig Leur Byas Pa* by Vasubandhu. Chendu, China: Sichuan Mirig Publishing.

CP   *Chig Ch'ar 'Pho Ba'i gDams Pa* by Jampal Gyepe Dorje [Mipham]. Single folio.

CT   *Ch'ed Du bJod Pa'i Tshoms. Dode,* vol. Sa, f209a/1–253a/6. Dege Edition

DB   *'Dod sByin (gSur)* by Jigme Lingpa. *Nyingthig Doncha,* vol. 1, pp. 395. Gangtok, Sikkim: Choten Gonpa.

DCM   *bDe Ba Chan Kyi sMon Lam* by Nagarjuna. In DP, vol. 2, pp. 151–155.

DD   *bDe Ch'en Zhing bKod Zhes Bya Ba Theg Pa Ch'en Po'i mDo bsDus Pa.* In DP, vol. 1, pp. 138–139. Chendu, China: Sichuan Mirig Publishing, 1994. Tibetan translation of the Sanskrit *Sukhavati-vyuha-nama-mahayana Sutra.*

DDM   *'Phags Pa De bZhin gShegs Pa bDun Gyi sNgon Gyi sMon Lam Gyi Khyad Par rGyas Pa. Gyud-bum,* vol. Da, f2481/1–273b/7. Dege Edition.

DE   *Destructive Emotions: How Can We Overcome Them? A Scientific Dialogue with the Dalai Lama,* narrated by Daniel Goleman. New York: Bantam, 2003.

DK   *'Phags Pa bDe Ba Chan Gyi bKod Pa Zhes Bya Ba Theg Pa Ch'en Po'i mDo,* vol. Ja, f195b/4–200a/2. *Dode,* Kajur. Dege Edition. This is the Smaller *Sukhavati-vyuha Sutra.* An English translation is found in *Buddhist Mahayana Texts* (BMT), part 2, pp. 90–103.

DM   *Bar Do sPhyi'i Don Thams Chad rNam Par gSal Bar Byed Pa Dran Pa'i Me Long* by Tsele Natshog Rangtrol. Neuthang, Tibet: Wood block print. English edition: *The Mirror of Mindfulness,* by Tsele Natsok Rangdrol, translated by Erik Pema Kunsang (Boston: Shambhala Publications, 1989).

DN   *bDe Ba Chan Gyi Zhing sByong Ba'i Dad Pa gSal Bar Byed Pa Drang Srong Lung Gi Nyi Ma* by Mipham Jamyang Namgyal. In DP, vol. 2, pp. 366–391. Chendu, China: Sichuan Mirig Publishing, 1994.

DP   *bDe sMon Phyogs bsGrigs,* vols. 1 & 2. Chendu, China: Sichuan Mirig Publishing, 1994.

DR   *Klong Ch'en sNying Gi Thig Le Las gSang sGrub Thugs rJe Ch'en Po sDug bsNgal Rang Grol* by Jigme Lingpa. *Tsapod,* vol. Ah. New Delhi: Dilgo Khyentse.

DRC   *Rdzogs Pa Rang Byung Ch'en Po'i rGryud. Nying-gyud,* vol. Ta. New Delhi: Dilgo Khyentse Rinpoche.

DZG   *dPal Ngan Song sByong Ba'i sDig sByong sGo dGu'i rNam bShad gZhan Phan mDzes rGyan* by Kun-ga Palden. Gantok, Sikkim: Sangor Düde.

DZM   *rNam Dag bDe Ch'en Zhing Gi sMon Lam* by Khedrup Ragasya. In DP, vol. 2, pp. 217–232. China: Sichuan Mirig Publishing, 1994.

EJ   *Enlightened Journey* by Tulku Thondup. Boston: Shambhala Publications, 2001.

GG   *Bar Do'i sMon Lam dGongs gChig rGya mTsho* by Jigme Lingpa. New Delhi: Dilgo Khyentse.

GL   "'Gro mGon Bla Ma rJe'i gSang gSum rNam Thar rGya mTsho Las Thun Mong Phyi'i mNgon rTogs rGyal Sras Lam bZang." Autobiography of Jigme Gyalwe Nyugu. Manuscript, collection of Tulku Pema Wangyal.

GR   *'Phags Pa rGya Ch'er Rol Ba Zhes Bya Ba Theg Pa Ch'en Po'i mDo. Dode,* vol. Kha. Kajur. Dege Edition.

GRP   *rGyal Po La gTam Bya Ba Rin Po Ch'e'i Phreng Ba* by Nagarjuna, pp. 74–124. Taipei: TCBBEF.

GTD   "mKhyen brTse Heruka'i gSang Ba'i rNam Thar Grub rTags sTon Tshul 'Thor bsDus" by Rigpe Raldri et al. Manuscript, collection of Zenkar Rinpoche.

GTT   *sGra Thal 'Gyur Ch'en Po rTsa Ba'i rGyud. Nying-gyud,* vol. Tha. New Delhi: Dilgo Khyentse Rinpoche.

GY   *Ye Shes mKha' 'Gro Gling Za Ch'os sKyid Kyi 'Das Log sGrung Yig.* Darjeeling: Konchog Lhadripa.

HPM   *The Healing Power of Mind: Simple Meditation Exercises for Health, Well-Being, and Enlightenment* by Tulku Thondup. Boston: Shambhala Publications, 1996.

HTT   *Hidden Teachings of Tibet* by Tulku Thondup. London: Wisdom Publications, 1986.

KB   *Khri Ch'en rGyal Ba gYung Drung bsTan 'Dzin Gyi Bar Do'i rNam Thar* by Gyalwa Yungtrung Tenzin. New Delhi: Bonpo Foundation, Solan.

KBZ   *Klong Ch'en sNying Thig Gi sNgon 'Gro'i Khrid Yig Kun bZang Bla Ma'i Zhal Lung* by Ogyen Jigme Chokyi Wangpo. Chendu, China: Sichuan Mirig Publishing.

KJ   *mKhas Pa'i Tshul La 'Jug Pa'i sGo* by Mipham Jamyang Namgyal Gytsho. Chendu, China: Sichuan Mirig Publishing, 1990.

KM   *dGongs Pa Zang Thal Gyi rGyud Chen Las sMon Lam bTabs Pa Tsam Gtis Sangs rGya Ba'i rGyud* by Rigdzin Goddem. *Gongpa Zangthal,* vol. Hri. Kham, Tibet: Adzom Edition.

KR   *rMi Lam Bar Do'i Krid Yig Khrul Pa Rang Grol* by Karma Lingpa. In ZG, vol. 2, pp. 341–361. New Delhi: Collection of Dudjom Rinpoche.

KZ   *sNgags 'Ch'ang 'Ja' Lus rDo rJe'i rNam Thar mKda' 'Gro'i Zhal Lung.* New Delhi: Lama Sangye.

KZM   *sKu gSum Zhing Khams sByong Ba'i gSol 'Debs sMon Lam by Khyentse'i Odzer.* Nyingthig Doncha, pp. 527–532. Gangtok, Sikkim: Choten Gonpa.

KZZ   *sNying Thig sNgon 'Gro'i Khrid Yig Kun bZang Bla Ma'i Zhal Lung Gi Zin Bris* by Ngagwang Palzang. Chendu, China: Sichuan Mirig Publishing 1992.

LC   *Byang Ch'ub Lam Rim Ch'e Ba* by Nyammed Tsongkhapa Chenpo. Kalimpong, India: Bumed Tshogpa.

LG   *Las brGya Thams Pa. Dode,* vols. Ha & Ah. Kajur. Dege Edition.

LS   *'Phags Pa Lang Kar gShegs Pa Rin Po Ch'e'i mDo. Dode,* vol. Cha. Kajur. Dege Edition.

MMM   *Masters of Meditation and Miracles: Lives of the Great Buddhist Masters of India and Tibet,* by Tulku Thondup. Boston: Shambhala Publications, 1999.

MN   *Bar Do'i sMon Lam Ngo sProd* by Longchen Rabjam. Single folio.

MNS   *'Das Log Byang Ch'ubs Seng-Ge'i dMyal sNang Shar Ba Las dGe sDig Gi gShan 'Byed Dang gShin rJe Ch'os Kyi rGyal Po'i Phrin Yig rGyas Pa.* Bhutan: Dgon-pa Dkar-po, 1976. Collection of Tibetan Buddhist Resource Center.

MRP   "dMyal Ba'i bsKal [dKar?] Ch'ags Rin Ch'en Phreng Ba" by Shar Dagpo Trashi Namgyal (1513–1587). Manuscript, collection of TBCR.

MS   *Klong Ch'en sNying Gi Thig Le Las 'Pho Ba Ma bsGom Sangs rGyas* by Jigme Lingpa. *Tsapod,* vol. Hum. New Delhi: Dilgo Khyentse Rinpoche.

ND   *Lo Ch'en Rig 'Dzin Ch'os Nyid bZang Mo'i rNam Par Thar Pa rNam mKhyen bDe sTer.* Autobiography of Shugseb Lochen. New Delhi: Sonam Kazi.

NDK   *Nyi Ma Dang Zla Ba Kha sByor Ba Ch'en Po gSang Ba'i rGyud. Nying-Gyud,* vol. Ta, f193b/–218a. New Delhi: Dilgo Khyentse Rinpoche.

NGR   *Tshe 'Das gNas 'Dren 'Gro Drug Rang Grol* by Karma Lingpa. In ZG, vol. 2, pp. 1–52. New Delhi: Collection of Dudjom Rinpoche.

NK   *Shes Rab Lu'i Tshig Don Go Sla Bar rNam Par bShad Pa Nor Bu Ketaka* by Mipham Jamyang Nampar Gyalwa. Varanasi, India: Tarthang Tulku, 1966.

NL   *Nam mKhyen Lam bZang* by Jigme Lingpa. Compiled by Jigme Thrinle Ozer. Gangtok, Sikkim: Choten Gonpa.

NLS   *rNam mKhyen Lam bZang gSal Byed* by Khyentse'i Wangpo. Gangtok, Sikkim: Choten Gonpa.

NLZ   *Thugs rJe Ch'en Po sDug bsNgal Rang Grol Gyi gNas Dren rNam Grol Lam bZang* by Jigme Thrinle Ozer. *Tsapod,* vol. Hri, pp. 291–308. New Delhi: Dilgo Khyentse.

NM   *Bar Do'i gDams Pa Tshangs sPrugs Su gDab Pa gNad Kyi Man Ngag* by Drimed Ozer   (Longchen Rabjam). *Sung Thorbu,* vol. 2, pp. 590–592. New Delhi: Sanji Dorje.

NN   *Dam Ch'os rDzogs Pa Ch'en Po Ngo sProd Kyi sKor Las/ rNam Shes 'Byung 'Jug gNas gSum Ngo sProd* by Namgyal Zangpo. In ZG, vol. 2, pp. 443– 467. New Delhi: Collection of Dudjom Rinpoche.

NP   *(Bar Do'i) Ngo sProd* by Longchen Rabjam. Single folio.

NS   *Yon Tan Rin Po Ch'e'ei mDzod Kyi 'Grel Ba rNam mKhyen Shing rTa* by Jigme Lingpa. New Delhi: Sonam Kazi.

OK   *'Phags Pa Od dPag Med Kyi bKod Pa Zhes Bya Ba Theg Pa Ch'en Po'i mDo. Kontseg,* vol. Ka, f237b/1–270a/3. Kajur. Dege Edition. Tibetan translation of the Sanskrit *Amitabhavyuha-nama-mahayana Sutra,* known as the Larger *Sukhavati-vyuha Sutra.*

PB   "Bar Do'i gDams Pa Ngo sProd dBang Gi Man Ngag Pra Khrid Srog gZer Gyi sBas Ch'os" by Ratna Lingpa. Manuscript, collection of Gyatul Rinpoche.

PD   *The Practice of Dzogchen* by Longchen Rabjam. Introduced, translated, and annotated by Tulku Thondup. Edited by Harold Talbott. Ithaca, N.Y.: Snow Lion, 1996.

PDN   "dPal Ri'i Dag sNang" by Dawa Drolma. Manuscript, collection of Chagdud Rinpoche.

PG   *bDe Ba Chan Gyi Zhing Las brTsams Pa'i gTam dGe Ba'i Lo Tog sPel Byed dByar sKyes sPrin Ch'en Glal Ba'i sGra dByangs [rGyu bZhi]* by Jigme Tenpe Nyima. *Dodrupchen Sungbum,* vol. Nga. Gangtok, Sikkim: Choten Gonpa.

PJT　　*'Phags Pa 'Jam dPal Gyi rTsa Ba'i Gyud.* Vol. Na f88–end. *Gyudbum,* Kajur. Dege Edition.

PK　　　*'Phags Pa sNying rJe Ch'en Po'i Padma dKar Po. Dode,* vol. Ch'a, f56a/1–128b/7. Dege Edition.

PP　　　"'Pho 'Debs Thugs rJe'i lChangs Kyu Songs 'Pho Lung" by Ragaasi. Manuscript, Nālandā Translation Committee, Halifax, Nova Scotia.

RC　　　*Ri Ch'os mTshams Kyi Zhal gDams* by Karma Chagmed. U.P., India: Tashijong, 1970.

RG　　　*Kun bZang dGongs Pa Zang Thal Gyi Khrid Yig Rig 'Dzin dGongs rGyan* by Tshulthrim Zangpo. Wood block print. Golok Province, Tibet: Do Shugchung Gon.

RP　　　*bsNgo Ba Rin Po Ch'i Phreng Ba* by Tshul Khrims Blo Gros (Longchen Rabjam). *Sung Thorbu,* vol. 2, pp. 596–607. New Delhi: Sanji Dorje.

RR　　　*Rig Pa Rang Shar Ch'en Po. Nying-Gyud,* vol. Tha, pp. 1–166. New Delhi: Dilgo Khyentse.

RSM　　"Rig Drug Gi mThong sNang Shel dKar Me Long" by Dawa Drolma. Manuscript, collection of Chagdud Rinpoche.

SB　　　*Srid Pa bar do'i Ngo sProd gSal 'Debs thos grol ch'en mo* by Karma Lingpa. In ZG, vol. 3, pp. 115–162. New Delhi: Collection of Dudjom Rinpoche.

SC　　　*Sems Nyid Ngal gSo'i 'Grel Ba Shing rTa Ch'en Mo* by Longchen Rabjam. Kham, Tibet: Adzom Edition.

SG　　　*'Das Log dKar Ch'ag Thar Pa'i Lam sTon gSal Ba'i sGron Me* by Tagla Konchog Gyaltsen. Wood block print. Kham, Tibet: Dzogchen Monastery.

SGG　　*gSang sNgags Nang Gi Lam Rim rGya Ch'er 'Grel Pa Sang rGyas gNyis Pa'i dGongs rGyan* by Gyurmed Tshewang Chogtrub. Leh, Ladakh: Padma-Chos-'lDan, 1972.

SM　　　*'Dan Ma Sangs rGyas Seng Ge'i dMyal sNang Rang Grol gZigs Pa'i dMyal Ba'i dKar Ch'ag Nyung bsDus gSal Ba'i Me Long.* New Delhi: Sherab Gyaltsen Lama.

SN　　　*gShin 'Pho Ngo sProd* by Rangchung Dorje. *Tsapod,* vol. Hum, pp. 7–11. New Delhi: Dilgo Khyentse Rinpoche.

SR　　　*Srid Pa Bar Do'i Khrid Yig Srid Pa Rang Grol* by Karma Lingpa.

In ZG, vol. 2, pp. 419–432. New Delhi: Collection of Dudjom Rinpoche.

TB *rJe Tham Chad mKhyen Pa Tsong Kha Pa Ch'en Po'i bKa' 'Bum Thor Bu* by Je Tsongkhapa. *Je'i Sung-Bum*, vol. Kha. Wood block print. Privately printed, India.

TBD *The Tibetan Book of Living and Dying* by Sogyal Rinpoche. New York: HarperCollins, 1992.

TC *'Das Log Karma dBang 'Dzin Gyi rNam Thar Thar Pa'i lChag Kyu* by Khrag 'Thung rDo rJe. Bhutan: Mani Dorje, 1981. Collection of Tibetan Buddhist Resource Center.

TCD *Theg mCh'og Rin Po Ch'e'i mDzod* by Longchen Rabjam, vols. E and Wam. India: Choten Gonpa.

TD *Grub Ch'en Khro Zur rGyal Sras rDo rJe dDud 'Dul Rin Po Ch'e'i 'Das Log mThong Ba Don lDan* by Ugyen Wangchug Rabten. Wood block print. Collection of Zenkar Rinpoche.

TG *Thar Ba Rin Po Ch'e'i rGyan* by Lhaje Sodnam Rinchen [Gampopa]. Chendu, China: Sichuan Mirig Publishing, 1989.

TGC *CCh'os Nyid Bar Do'i gSal 'Debs Thos Grol Ch'en Mo* by Karma Lingpa. In ZG, vol. 3, pp. 41–114. India: Collection of Dudjom Rinpoche.

TJ *Tshe 'Pho Ba Ji lTar 'Gyur Ba'i mDo. Dode*, vol. Sa, f145b/4 –155a/1. Kajur. Dege Edition. Tibetan translation of Sanskrit *Ayushpatti-yathakara-paripriccha Sutra* (Sutra on What Happens at Death).

TRD *Tshig Don Rin Po Ch'e'i mDzod* by Longchen Rabjam. Kham, Tibet: Adzom Edition.

TS *Tannisho: Passages Deploring Deviations of Faith* by Yuien-bo. Translated by Bando Shojun and Harold Stewart. Japan: Otani University, 1980.

TT "mTho Ris Thar Pa'i Them sKas Nyid Kyi mThong Tshul 'Ga' Zhig" by Tsunma Samten Chotsho." Manuscript, collection of Zenkar Rinpoche.

TZ *rTsod Pa bZlog Pa'i Tshig Leur Byas Pa* by Nagarjuna. Taipei: CBBEF 2000.

WBT *What the Buddha Taught* by Walpola Rahula. New York: Grove Press, 1974.

YB *Klong Ch'en sNying Gi Thig Le Las Khrid Yig Ye Shes Bla Ma* by Jigme Lingpa. New Delhi: Dilgo Khyentse Rinpoche.

ZD *dPal Kun Rig Gi Ch'o Ga gZhan Phan mTha' Yas Las Nag'Gros bKlags Ch'og Mar bKod Pa gZhan Phan bDud rTsi* by Palden Lodro Tenpe Gyaltsen. Dehra Dun, India: Sakya Gonpa.

ZG   *Zi khro dgongs pa ran grol gyi chos skor,* discovered by Karma Lingpa, vols. 1, 2, and 3. New Delhi: Collection of Dudjom Rinpoche.

ZGB   *bDe Ba Chan Du sKye Ba'i sMon Lam Zhing mCh'og sGo 'Byed* (with autocommentary) by Je Tsongkhapa. In DP, vol. 2, pp. 334–365. Chendu, China: Sichuan Mirig Publishing, 1990.

ZK   *Zhing Ch'og sKor* by Jigme Tenpe Nyima. *Dodrupchen Sungbum,* vol. Ka, pp. 239–272. Gangtok: Choten Gonpa.

ZN   *Zas bsNgo. Nyingthig Doncha,* 397–399. Gangtok, Sikkim: Choten Gonpa.

ZP   *bZang Po sPyod Pa'i sMon Lam Gyi rGyal Po. Phal Po Ch'e,* vol. Ah, f358b/7–362a/4. Kajur. Dege Edition. Tibetan translation of the Sanskrit *Bhadracharya-pranidhanaraja Sutra* (Sutra of the King of Aspiration of Excellent Deeds).

Index

and clarity, union of, 62, 71
prayer, prayers, 71–72, 77–78,
    109–110
rebirth and, 173
See also under emptiness
Owl-Headed Guard of the North, 80n
Ox-Headed Awa (Lord of the Dead),
    65, 131–132, 136, 138, 139, 150

pain, 4
    See also suffering
passages of life, four, 5, 8, 9, 292
    See also bardo (transitional pas-
        sage); dying, passage of; human
        life; ultimate nature, passage of
peace
    attitude of around the dying, 197,
        200–201, 210, 219
    bardo manifestation of, 95
    in Blissful Pure Land, 191
    causes of, 173
    cultivating, 41, 95
    effects of, 3, 8–9
    ultimate, realization of, 207
peaceful deities, 72, 75
Pema Dechen Zangpo, 64, 133–134
Pema Ozer, 84
Pema Sheltrag of Nyag-rong (her-
    mitage), 62
perceptions
    in the bardo, 99, 118, 137–138
    of buddhas and pure lands, 238
    delusory, 59
    in the passage of ultimate nature,
        71, 76–77, 83
    See also pure perception
Perfection of Wisdom *(Prajna-
    paramita)*, 15
perfections, six (Skt. *paramita*), 43, 292
personhood, self of, 30
phenomenal existents, 8, 30
phowa *('Pho Ba*, Tib.; transference of
    consciousness), 43–44, 223, 299
    for accomplished meditators, 273
    accounts of, 58, 98–99, 137, 142
    benefits of, 216, 265–266

best time for, 50, 275
effigy, use of, 276–278
general instructions, 251, 265–267
for the living, 266–267
main meditation, 273–275
meditation on, 267–270
for ordinary people, 66
prayers and mantras, 270–273
preliminary practices, 252–265
training in, 161, 275–276
who should perform, 267,
    269–270
Pig-Headed Guard of the South,
    80n
Pig-Headed Lord of the Dead, 123
Pig-Headed Rakshasa, 139
Ponlob Jetrung Rinpoche, 128
positive emotions, 93, 173
Potala (pure land of Avalokiteshvara),
    152
Prajnaparamita. See Perfection of
    Wisdom
prana (Skt.). *See* airs
prayer(s), 227
    for accomplished meditators, 81
    in the bardo, 93, 94, 133
    benefit of, 84, 139, 140–141, 179
    for the dead and dying, 198–200,
        201, 205–206
    dedication and aspiration, 199,
        244–246, 278–280, 294
    language of, 188
    longevity, 275–276
    for non-Buddhists, 200–201
    pure land, leading to, 211
    purification, 212, 214
    rebirth, as aid to, 182
    as source of blessings, 11
    See also aspiration, prayers of;
        mantras; name-prayers
precious materials, seven, 189, 190,
    287n7
pride, 176
primordial wisdoms, five, 71–73,
    75–76, 296

in Blissful Pure Land, 152, 190
in the passage of ultimate nature,
71
source of blessings, 239
in the bardo, 92
death ceremonies, role in, 13, 201,
205
definitions, 11, 300–301
as focus for survivors, 198
space
body and, 46
death, at time of, 49, 50
ultimate nature of, 18
spheres (Tib. *thig-le, Thig Le*), 47, 129
spirits, effect on the living, 145
spiritual development
conditions for, 23
cultivating, 199–200, 215, 227
spiritual masters and teachers
ceremonies for others, performing,
214–215
death rituals, performing, 212
deaths of, 12, 14–16
mind, uniting with, 53, 62, 220,
275
passage of dying, account of, 63–65
in the pure land, 152–153, 157,
165
rebirth of, 169, 178
recollection of, 202, 218–219
remains of, 224
as source of blessing, 198
visualizing, 269
spiritual practice, 41
benefits of, 227
death, at time of, 51–53
duration and intensity of, 227–228
motivation for, 21, 28
See also meditation
Stevenson, Ian, 169
stupas
corpse appearing as, 137
miniature (Tib. *tsatsa, Tsa-tsha*),
223–224
subject-object duality, 4, 18, 59

suffering, 4
in the bardo, 120, 176
of hell realm, 107, 134–135,
160–161, 174, 176
liberation at arising, 162
liberation from, 142
noble truth of, 36–40
of the six realms, 176
Sukhavati (Skt.), 184
See also Blissful Pure Land
Sukhavati-vyuha Sutra, 185, 186
sur (*gSur*, Tib.; burnt food offering),
88, 99, 100, 222–223, 249,
259–263
Sutra (tradition), 138
symbols
of authority, 7–8
of birthplaces, 181, 286n13
cultural attributes of, 96
pebbles, 102, 103, 136, 150
of rebirth, 90

Tagla Konchong Gyaltsen (delog)
bardo, account of, 133–137
passage of dying, account of,
63–65
Tara, 184
See also White Tara
ten endowments. *See* endowments,
ten
Tendzin Dargye, 136
terma (*gTer Ma*, Tib., hidden mystical
teaching), 165, 297
thig-le (Tib.). *See* essences; spheres
Thondup, Tulku
aspirations of, 228
recognition of, 14–15
training of, 13
thought
in the bardo, 87, 88, 95, 137–139
importance of, 42
three bodies. *See* buddha-bodies
three doors. *See* doors, three (mind,
speech, and body)
Three Jewels, 53, 146, 182, 301